In Private Hands: 200 Years of American Painting

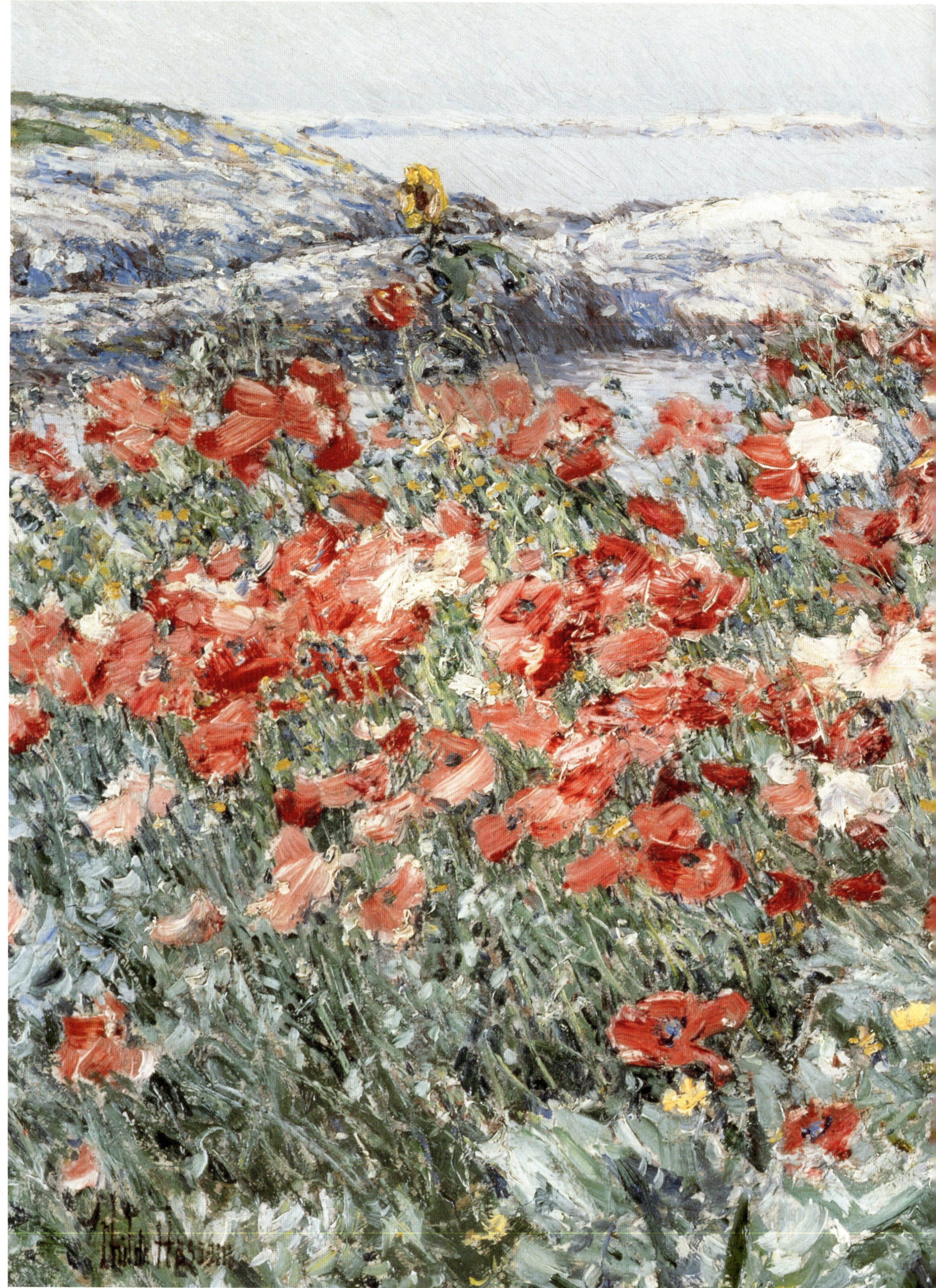

In Private Hands: 200 Years of American Painting

Contributors

Lynn Marsden-Atlass

Nicolai Cikovsky, Jr.

Robert Rosenblum


Editorial Supervisor

Kim Sajet

This publication has been generously supported
by the Connelly Foundation.

Published on the occasion of the exhibition organized by the
Pennsylvania Academy of the Fine Arts celebrating its 200th anniversary.

October 1, 2005–January 8, 2006.



Edited by Mary Christian
Designed by Phillip Unetic, 3r1 Group.com
Printed by Butler and Tanner, Ltd., Frome, England

ISBN 0-943836-27-1

Library of Congress Control Number:  2005905791

Cover:
Charles Demuth (1883–1935)
Detail of plate 41, *Jazz (Jass)*, 1921
Oil on canvas, 20 x 16 inches
Private Collection

Frontispiece:
Childe Hassam (1859–1935)
Detail of plate 26, *Poppies*, ca. 1890–94
Oil on canvas, 18 x 25¼ inches
Private Collection, Washington, D.C.

# Contents

John Vanderlyn (1775–1852)
*Ariadne Asleep on the Island of Naxos*, 1809–1814
Oil on canvas, 68½ x 87 inches
Pennsylvania Academy of the Fine Arts,
Gift of Mrs. Sarah Harrison (The Joseph Harrison Jr.
Collection), 1878.1.11

The preparatory oil study for the painting, *Sleeping
Ariadne–Torso Study* (plate 1), executed from life, is
publicly exhibited for the first time in this exhibition.

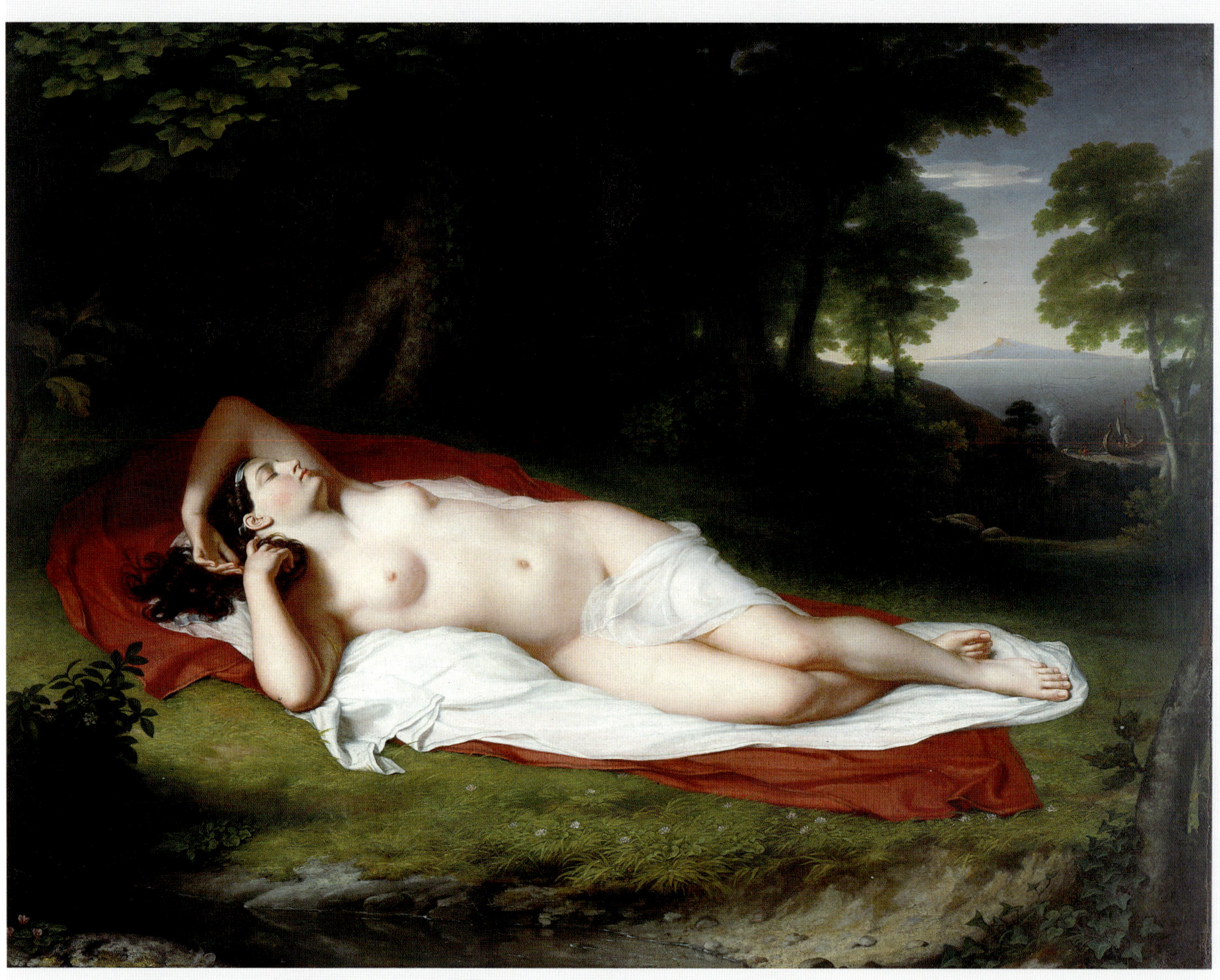

# Chairman's Message

*Donald R. Caldwell*
Chairman of the Board of Trustees

*In Private Hands: 200 Years of American Painting* represents one of the most ambitious exhibitions that the Pennsylvania Academy of the Fine Arts has undertaken. It is clearly a fitting celebration of our 200th anniversary year. The year 2005 marks an incredible moment in our history: the beginning of a third century of excellence in collecting, exhibiting, and teaching.

As a nationally renowned institution, the Academy has a responsibility not only to its own illustrious past but also to the future of American art. We are deeply linked with a celebrated roster of painters, sculptors, and printmakers, going back two hundred years, yet for most of this time we have also been willing to show the present state of American art.

*In Private Hands* links the earliest paintings with the most recent works of art, the East and the West Coasts, and the representational with the abstract in ways that show the magnificent outcome of the Academy's original quest to encourage the arts of this nation. We have focused on painting to create a manageable and coherent exhibition, and we are thrilled at the response we have had from great collectors across the United States.

I want to acknowledge the role in this exceptional project of the late Vivian Potamkin, former vice-chair of the Board of Trustees and great Academy benefactor, who, together with her husband, Pat, taught me so much about American art. She in turn brought the exhibition co-chair Max N. Berry, Esq. to the board. Max with his wise counsel and his deep experience both on major museum boards and as a collector with his wife, Heidi, has been quite invaluable in putting this show together. The same is true of co-chair Luther W. Brady, M.D., who is celebrated for his own wonderful collection as well as for his generosity to organizations in Philadelphia and across the nation.

I certainly hope that *In Private Hands* will encourage our many new friends across the country to visit us often, to urge us on to yet greater achievements, and to support our crucial dedication to teaching and showing each new generation of American artists. Our task in the years ahead will be to ensure that the Academy matches the perspicacity of major private collectors in looking for the best, the most interesting, and the highest quality works of art. A hundred such works are shown here. I truly hope you enjoy them.

John Marin (1870–1953)
*Sun, Sea, Land–Maine*, 1921
Watercolor and charcoal on off-white wove paper,
16½ x 19½ inches
Pennsylvania Academy of the Fine Arts,
Acquired from the Philadelphia Museum of Art
(Samuel S. White 3rd and Vera White Collection)
in partial exchange for the John S. Phillips Collection
of European Drawings, 1985.21

This modernist watercolor by John Marin relates closely
to *Deer Isles, Islets, Maine* (plate 42) that is included in
this exhibition.

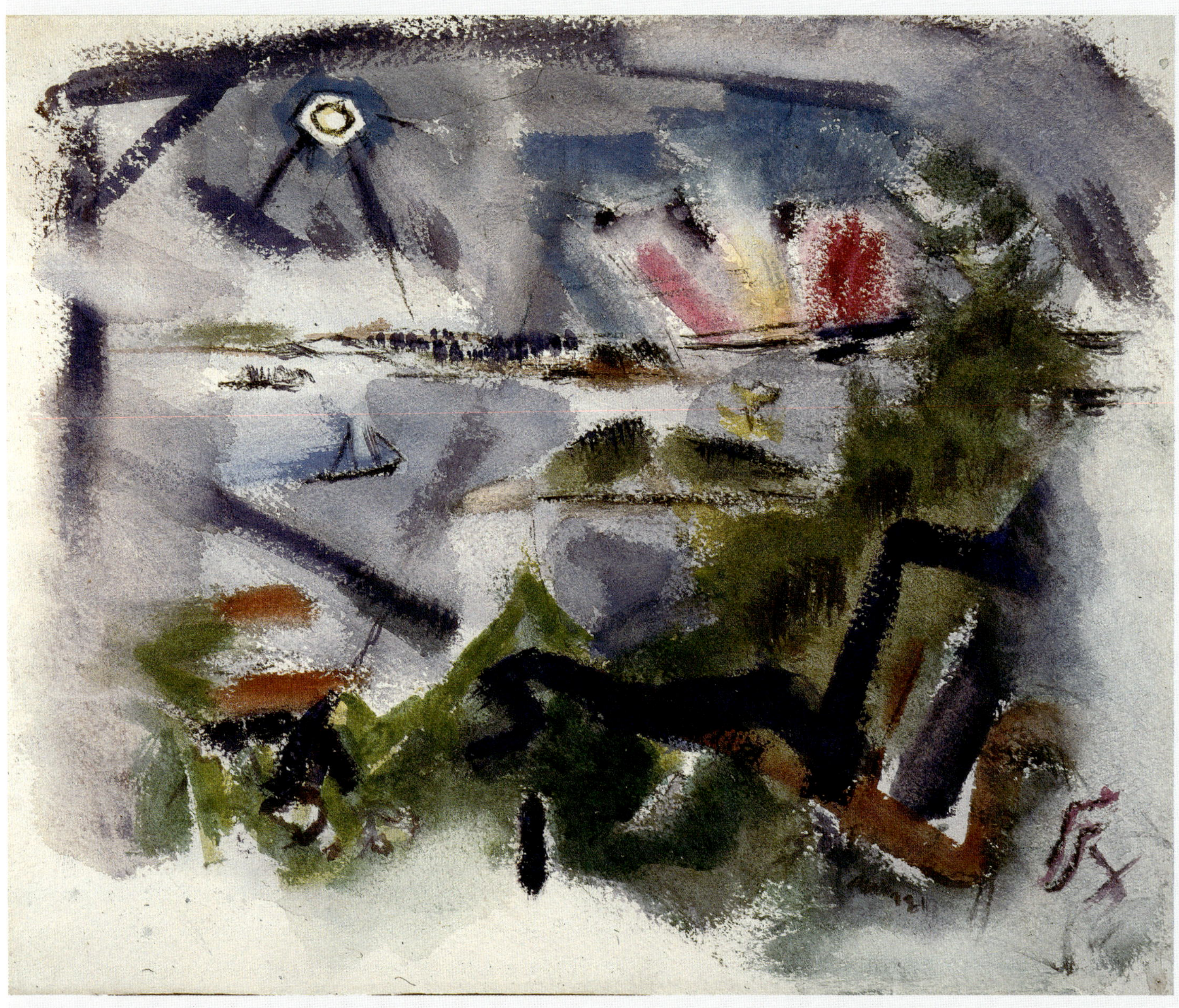

   IN PRIVATE HANDS: 200 YEARS OF AMERICAN PAINTING

# Foreword

*Derek A. Gillman*
President and the Edna S. Tuttleman Director

The making of *In Private Hands* has been an extraordinary journey, which began several years ago in the apartment of the late Vivian and Pat Potamkin, with Vivian and Academy chair Don Caldwell giving voice to the need for the Academy to retake its place at the center of the American art world. We saw a wonderful opportunity in our 200th anniversary year to make a very special request to existing and new friends of the Academy to allow us to borrow for a period of three months some of their most spectacular masterpieces of American art.

Unlike museums, which can usually substitute even major paintings in their galleries, private collectors of extraordinary works naturally want to enjoy them in their homes. We knew that for many people this was a considerable sacrifice. I was personally thrilled at the exceptional generosity of so many people, who willingly, often enthusiastically, volunteered their most precious paintings to support a unique artistic and educational project.

As the first arts institution in the United States and one of the oldest in the world, we knew that it was very important to mark the occasion of our bicentennial with spectacular one-time events. The opportunity, therefore, to bring together a major exhibition spanning the scope of American art over those two centuries seemed too good to pass up. On the one hand, it represents many of the greatest achievements of painting in the United States, and on the other, it points to the central role that the Academy has always played in educating and exhibiting the work of American painters.

I would like to extend my sincere thanks to all the lenders to *In Private Hands*; they have shown their confidence in the Academy's past, present, and future. Some have been particularly helpful in another way, by persuading other major collectors of the importance of this institution and this exhibition, thereby securing further loans. It is the lenders who have made this a stellar exhibition.

In addition, I am deeply grateful to the show's co-chairs, trustee Max N. Berry, Esq. of Washington, D.C., and Luther W. Brady, M.D. of Philadelphia, for their support, personal generosity, and determination that this should be a landmark event. Guest curator Nicolai Cikovsky, Jr., brought his immaculate connoisseurship and helped to connect us to many of the great collectors represented here. He and Professor Robert Rosenblum have contributed insightful essays on the nineteenth and twentieth centuries. I am especially grateful to Academy senior curator Lynn Marsden-Atlass, who has spent the past two years diligently crossing the United States, researching collections, talking to collectors, and bringing the exhibition to its present highly successful state. Her essay on the Academy's place in forming our understanding of American art also makes an important contribution to this volume.

Many members of the Academy's staff have been involved in this massive project, managed by senior vice-president and deputy director Kim Sajet, who has again served the Academy so well both by overseeing the complex logistics of the show and by acting as the editorial supervisor for the catalogue. Although the Academy staff are identified by name in Lynn Marsden-Atlass's Acknowledgements, I would like to extend my own appreciation for all their hard work and expertise.

An exhibition as impressive as this also calls for practical financial support, and I extend my profound thanks to Josephine C. Mandeville, chair of the Connelly Foundation, and her board for their enthusiastic help in funding this publication.

No exhibition, not even of a hundred works, can truly do justice to the triumph of American painting over the last two centuries nor represent all the major artists—if we could ever reach agreement on a definition of "major." But I hope that our visitors will find *In Private Hands* a truly satisfying experience, enjoy some of the greatest American paintings in existence, forgive the omissions, and take heart in the commitment and support that this venerable Academy continues to have toward the vitality of American art.

Horace Pippin (1888–1946)
*John Brown Going to His Hanging*, 1942
Oil on canvas, 24⅛ x 30¼ inches
Pennsylvania Academy of the Fine Arts,
John Lambert Fund, 1943.11

*John Brown Reading His Bible* (plate 52)
reveals Brown's quiet contemplation preceeding
the dramatic action of the Academy's painting
illustrated below.

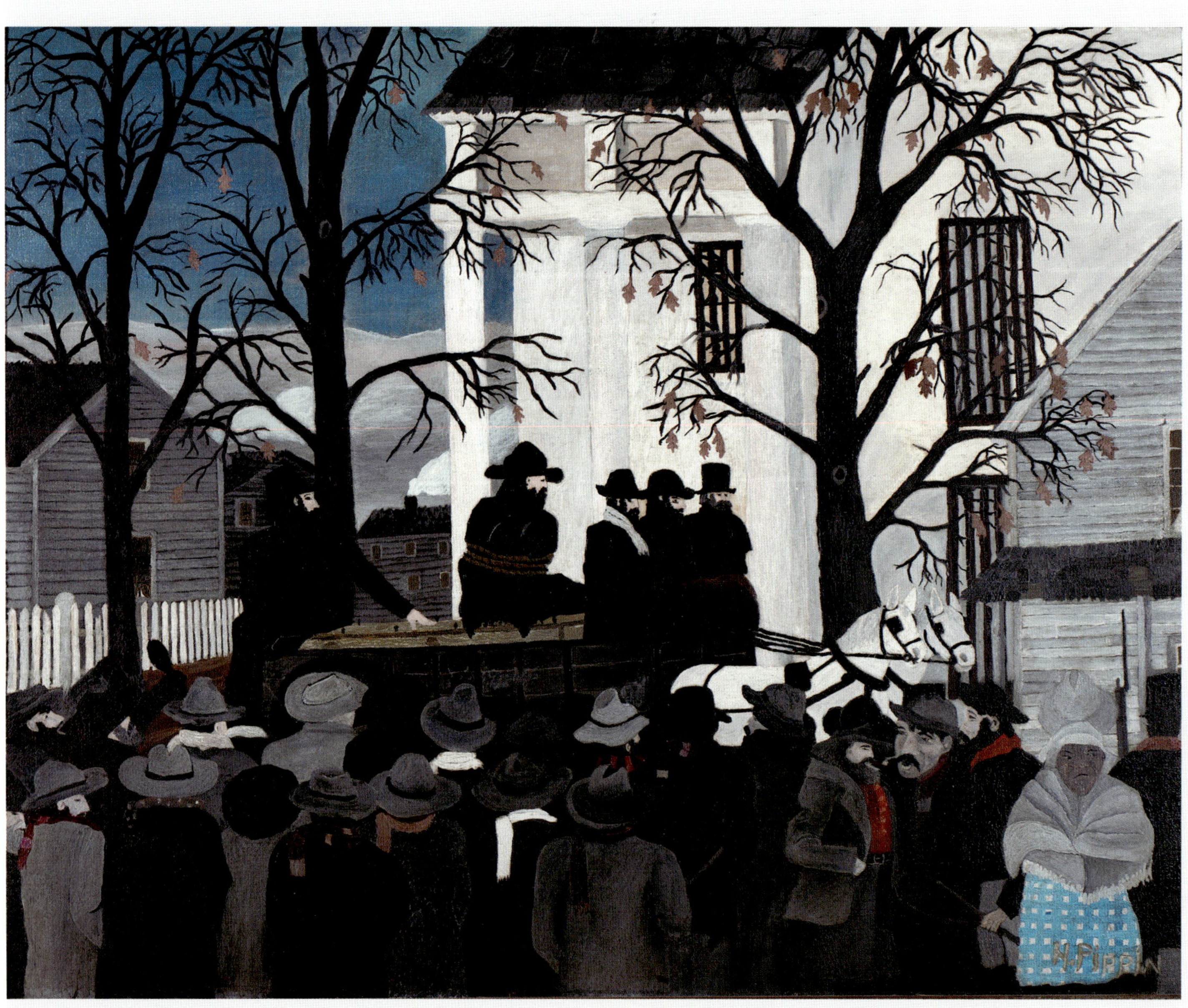

# Acknowledgments

*Lynn Marsden-Atlass*
Senior Curator

When I arrived at the Pennsylvania Academy of the Fine Arts in December 2003, little did I realize what a wonderful adventure organizing *In Private Hands: 200 Years of American Painting* would be. In celebration of the Academy's 200th Anniversary, *In Private Hands*, with one hundred paintings representing two hundred years of American art, has taken shape over the past three years.

All of us at the Pennsylvania Academy are deeply grateful to the fifty-four private collectors who have so generously lent paintings to this landmark exhibition. You, the lenders, champion American art, its past, present, and future. We are honored to share your treasures with a wider audience, and we thank you for your continued confidence in the Pennsylvania Academy.

There are so many people who have lent vision and warmly supported this project. First, I would like to thank Donald R. Caldwell, chair of the Academy's Board of Trustees, and Derek A. Gillman, president and the Edna S. Tuttleman Director, for their ongoing encouragement and commitment to this project.

I also want to extend my sincerest thanks to the exhibition co-chairs, trustee Max N. Berry, Esq. and Luther W. Brady, M.D. for their guidance, support, and personal generosity. Several board and committee members have been especially helpful: James C. Biddle, Robert L. Byers, Sr., Jonathan L. Cohen, Kevin F. Donohoe, Mary P. Graham, Barbara L. Greenfield, Mary Louise Krumrine, Ph.D., Marguerite Lenfest, Thomas N. Pappas, Herbert S. Riband, Jr., Esq., Linda Richardson, William H. Schorling, Esq., Samuel J. Savitz, Edna S. Tuttleman, and Debora A. Zug. Museum Committee members Connie Kay, Gabriele Lee, Charles Mather, III, and Perry Ottenberg, M.D. have also been helpful in our research and deserve special thanks.

Guest curator Nicolai Cikovsky, Jr., has been an inspiring and generous colleague. His scholarship and expertise are exemplary. I have learned a great deal from his example and extend my sincerest thanks for his involvement. Robert Rosenblum's inspired and insightful essay on twentieth-century painting contributes important scholarship to the exhibition. His many suggestions for the exhibition have been invaluable.

Over the course of the past two years, this ambitious project has involved almost all of the Academy's staff. I especially want to thank Kim Sajet, senior vice-president of museum and public programs and deputy director. She has set the exhibition on its course, has been the editorial supervisor for the catalogue, and has weathered all the exhibition's challenges. Within the museum, special thanks go to Cheryl Leibold, archivist (with special recognition of her invaluable and extensive research on Academy exhibitions); Robert Harman, associate registrar; Barbara Katus, manager of rights and reproductions; Aella Diamantopoulos, chief conservator; and Joan Hendrix, assistant to the deputy director for their helpful involvement in this project. To my curatorial colleagues Alex Baker, curator of contemporary art, Robert Cozzolino, associate curator, and Brooke Fitzpatrick, curatorial intern, my thanks for their good-natured support and assistance.

Additional thanks to Judy Ringold, director of public education, and her staff; Gale Rawson, registrar; Anthony D'Antonio, volunteer; Judith Thomas, registrar assistant; Nora Lambert, intern; Brian Murray, chief preparator; Mark Knobelsdorf, assistant preparator; and Paul Carroll, director of operations and safety for their hands-on involvement and superb installation.

John Hewett, senior vice president of development and marketing and his staff; Audrey Schneider, director of the 200th Anniversary Celebration; Gene Castellano, director of marketing, and his staff; Mark DeLelys, director of retail sales, and his staff; John Knox, senior vice president of finance, and his staff; Leslie Moody, senior vice president of human resources and administration and her staff; Bill Woytovitch, director of security and the security staff; and Sheryl Kessler, assistant to the president, all deserve recognition and thanks for their participation in support of this exhibition.

I would like to thank Mary Christian, editor, Maine Proofreading Services, Phillip Unetic and Fred Cohen, 3r1 Group for the design and production of this beautiful catalogue. I would also like to thank Jim Armbruster, consultant for the exhibition design.

Many professional colleagues have generously offered their time and assistance over the course of our research, and I gratefully thank them: Susan Austin, Jonathan Boos, Tara Cederholm, William Gerdts, Charles Hillburn, Erica Hirshler, Franklin Kelly, Mary Landa, Sara Miller, Milo Naeve (with special recognition), Judith O'Toole, Meg Perlman, and Theodore E. Stebbins, Jr. Several colleagues in the art galleries and auction houses have provided enthusiastic assistance to this project and deserve our thanks as well: Douglas Baxter, James Berry-Hill, Thomas Colville, Stuart Feld, Ann Freedman, Jan and Ron Greenberg, David Hill, Bridget Moore, Washburn Oberwager, David Robinson, Paul Thiebaud, Terry Vose, Douglas Walla, Meredith Ward, Joan Washburn, Eric Widing, and Daria Winter.

I would like to extend my heartfelt thanks to the nearly one hundred and fifty private collectors whom we have contacted and visited over the past two years. Visiting your personal collections has been an extraordinary privilege. Without your kindness and generosity, this exhibition could not have been realized.

We offer our deepest thanks to the Connelly Foundation, who made this publication possible.

Richard Diebenkorn (1922–1993)
*Interior with Doorway*, 1962
Oil on canvas, 70 ⁵⁄₁₆ x 60 inches
Pennsylvania Academy of the Fine Arts,
Henry D. Gilpin Fund, 1964.3

Diebenkorn's *Interior with Doorway*
closely relates to the pure abstraction of
his later *Untitled* (*Ocean Park Series*)
(plate 79) in this exhibition.

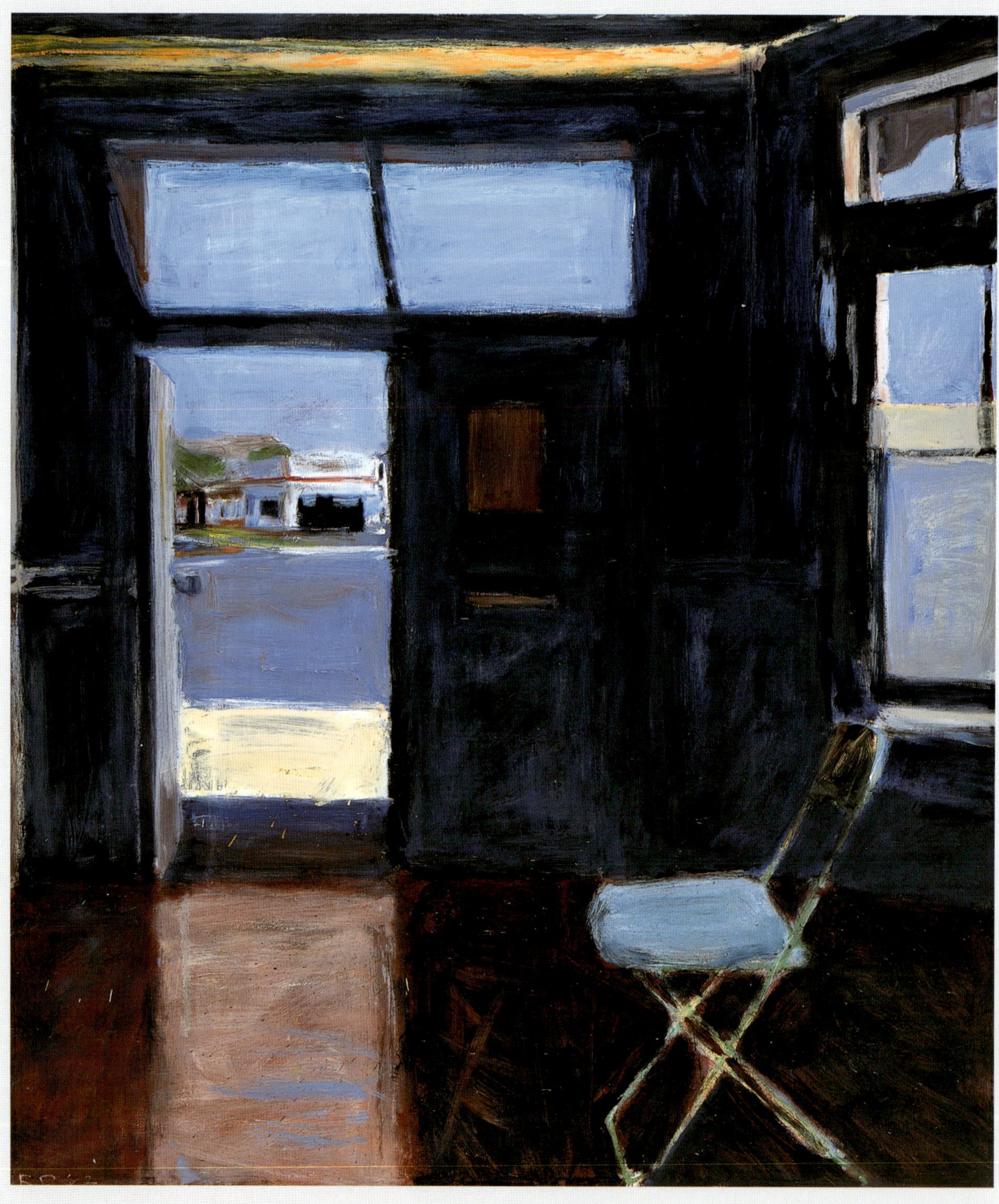

# Lenders to the Exhibition

Gisela and Dennis Alter

The Andalusia Foundation

The Anschutz Collection

Luther W. Brady

The Broad Art Foundation

Mr. and Mrs. Allan E. Bulley, Jr.

Jonathan L. Cohen

David and Thelma Driskell

Estate of Herbert Ferber

The Gund Art Foundation

Marie and Hugh Halff

The Hevrdejs Collection

Samuel and Ronnie Heyman

The Margaret and Raymond
Horowitz Collection

Robert J. Hurst

Linda Lichtenberg Kaplan

Mrs. George M. Kaufman

Karen A. and Kevin W. Kennedy

Jane and Leonard Korman

William H. Lane Collection

Mrs. Robert S. Lee

Aimee and Robert Lehrman

Marguerite and Gerry Lenfest

The Manoogian Collection

Jan and Frederick Mayer

James and Barbara Palmer

Marsha and Jeffrey Perelman

Private Collection (7)

Private Collection, courtesy of
Thomas Colville Fine Art

Private Collection, courtesy of
Meredith Ward Fine Art, New York

Private Collection, Minneapolis,
Minnesota

Private Collection, New York (2)

Private Collection, Tuscaloosa,
Alabama

Private Collection, Washington, D.C. (3)

Eileen Rosenau

Mari and Peter Shaw

Rachel Skolnick and Joshua Skolnick

Eugene V. Thaw

A Virginia Collector

Harriet and Larry Weiss

Mr. and Mrs. Andrew Wyeth

Anonymous Loan (4)

*Lynn Marsden-Atlass*

# Good Grain and So Little Chaff:
# The Pennsylvania Academy's Role in Forging a National Art

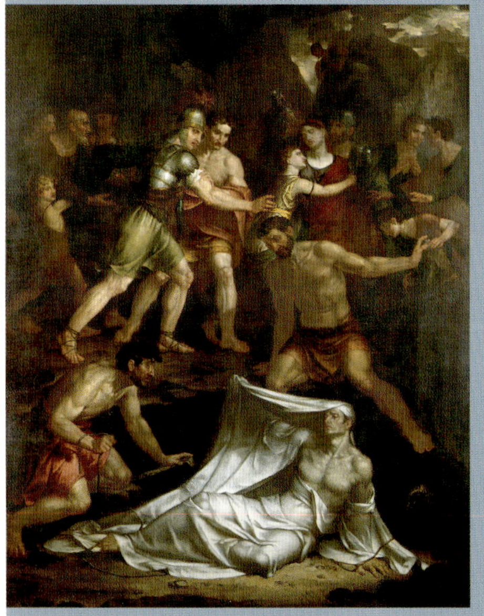

FIG. 1 (opposite)
Cover of the Pennsylvania Academy Exhibition:
*Exhibition of Paintings by American Artists at Home and in Europe*, November 7 [sic]—December 26, 1881

FIG. 2
Washington Allston (1779–1843)
*The Dead Man Restored to Life by Touching the Bones of the Prophet Elisha*, 1811–13
Oil on canvas, 156 x 122 inches
Pennsylvania Academy Purchase, by subscription, 1816.1

"Does American art represent the ideals of the American people? Is it national; is it modern; is it living? Has it any connection with what we are all doing and thinking and hoping? Does it have any lesson, inspiration or influence?"[1] These insistent questions were posed by a critic of the New York *Independent* in the winter of 1907–8. Nearly one hundred years later, critics and scholars continue to question the nature of American art.

As the oldest museum and art school in the country, the Pennsylvania Academy of the Fine Arts has been the venerable torchbearer of American art for the past two hundred years. The Academy's history is inexorably linked to the development of artists and exhibitions in America. The Academy's threefold mission of art education, annual exhibitions, and special exhibitions fostered the fledgling nation's artists and their patrons. Remarkably, the Academy has mounted over one thousand exhibitions in the past two hundred years. While its annuals have chronicled the growth and identity of a national art, the Academy's special exhibitions have been more international in scope. As an integral feature of the Academy's program since 1811, the annuals increasingly became a source of acquisitions for the permanent collection. By the mid-nineteenth century the annuals were a nationally anticipated event.

In the early nineteenth century, American artists had struggled to determine what would be a national art. Artists of means studied abroad, several under the tutelage of Benjamin West in England. Trained in the "grand manner" tradition, their paintings reflected the intellectual and morally uplifting historical, mythological, and religious subjects that won favor with the Royal Academy in London.

Early benefactors to the Academy also favored paintings of the European style, as exemplified in the Academy's first major purchase in 1816. Washington Allston's large canvas *The Dead Man Restored to Life by Touching the Bones of the Prophet Elisha* is an excellent example of the grand manner tradition (fig. 2). Despite the support of forty-six stockholders, the Academy was forced to mortgage its building to cover the cost of this acquisition. In May 1816 Allston's renowned canvas was featured at the *Exhibition at the Pennsylvania Academy of the Fine Arts of Mr. Allston's Celebrated Pictures*, The Dead Man Restored to Life by Touching the Bones of the Prophet Elisha *and* Donna Mencia in the Robber's Cave *together with Many Valuable Paintings in Addition to the Stationary Paintings of the Academy*. It was the fourth special exhibition ever held, and the first to include a printed catalogue with explanatory texts about contemporary works of art.

In 1836, to acquire Benjamin West's heroic and monumental *Death on the Pale Horse* (fig. 3) from the artist's son Raphael, the Academy stockholders mortgaged the building yet a second time. Such a move would have been daring at any moment in an institution's history, but it was a visionary act of faith by those founding fathers in support of contemporary American art.

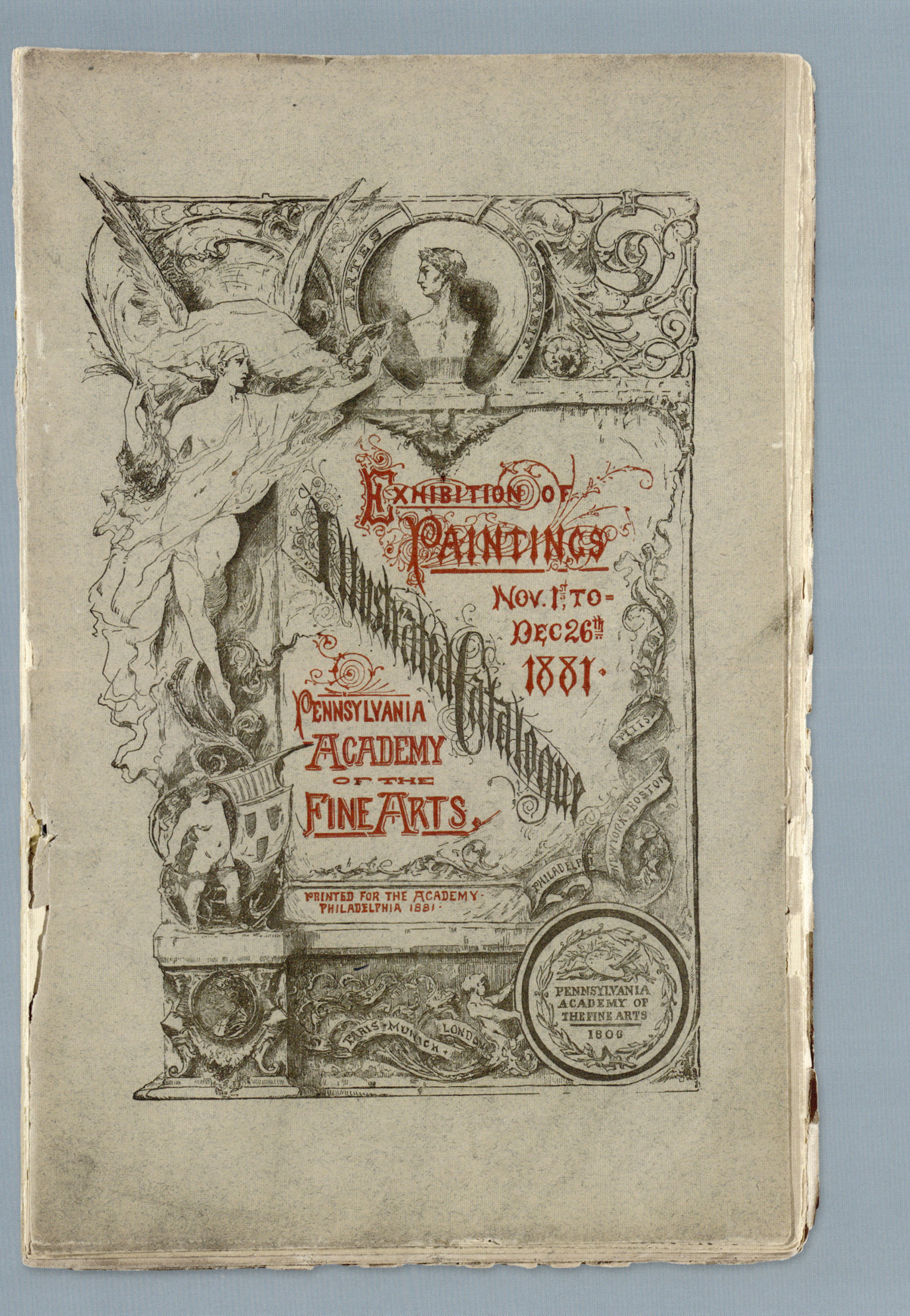
ARTES
HONORAT
EXHIBITION OF
PAINTINGS
NOV. 1st TO
DEC 26th
1881
Illustrated Catalogue
PENNSYLVANIA
ACADEMY
OF THE
FINE ARTS
PRINTED FOR THE ACADEMY
PHILADELPHIA 1881
NEW YORK · BOSTON
PARIS · MUNICH · LONDON
PENNSYLVANIA
ACADEMY OF
THE FINE ARTS
1805

By necessity, the Academy's special exhibition program varied widely until the late 1880s. Prior to that, nearly half of the exhibitions featured European art. One such example in 1833 was the *Celebrated Gallery of Paintings from England. Catalogue of Paintings by the Great Masters* that traveled to the Academy from its venue at the Atheneum [sic] Gallery, Boston.

Thomas Cole's panoramic cycle of paintings *Voyage of Life* was exhibited in conjunction with the Academy's annual exhibition in May 1844. Renowned leader of the Hudson River School, Cole intended his Voyage of Life (fig. 4) for a popular audience, who had already enjoyed his earlier five-part series, the *Course of Empire* (1836). While Samuel Ward's heirs denied Cole the opportunity to exhibit the original version of *Voyage of Life*, the artist painted a second version of the series in Rome during the winter of 1841–42 that he exhibited in New York, in Boston, and subsequently in Philadelphia at the Academy. Its popularity was immediate, and in 1848 the *Voyage of Life* attracted perhaps as many as 500,000 people to the American Art-Union's memorial exhibition of Cole's work. Revered by a broad audience, *Voyage of Life* was reproduced in printed editions that were hung in many an American home over the next thirty years.[2]

Hiram Powers's statue *The Greek Slave* was exhibited at the Pennsylvania Academy in 1848 (fig. 5). As the catalogue's introduction states: "The exhibition of a statue by a native artist, which has successfully passed the ordeal of European criticism, and achieved an established renown before reaching our shores, is an event comparatively so rare, and in itself so worthy of consideration, that a natural curiosity is excited to learn the circumstances attending its production, the history of the sculptor, and the true design of the work."[3]

Powers was among the first generation of American sculptors to reside in Florence, Italy, and his presentation of *The Greek Slave* was the first example of American-made nude sculpture on this continent. It was a resounding artistic and financial success at the Academy, and indeed wherever it was exhibited. According to the artist, his sensual idealized nude was inspired by accounts of the atrocities committed by the Turks on the Greeks during the Greek



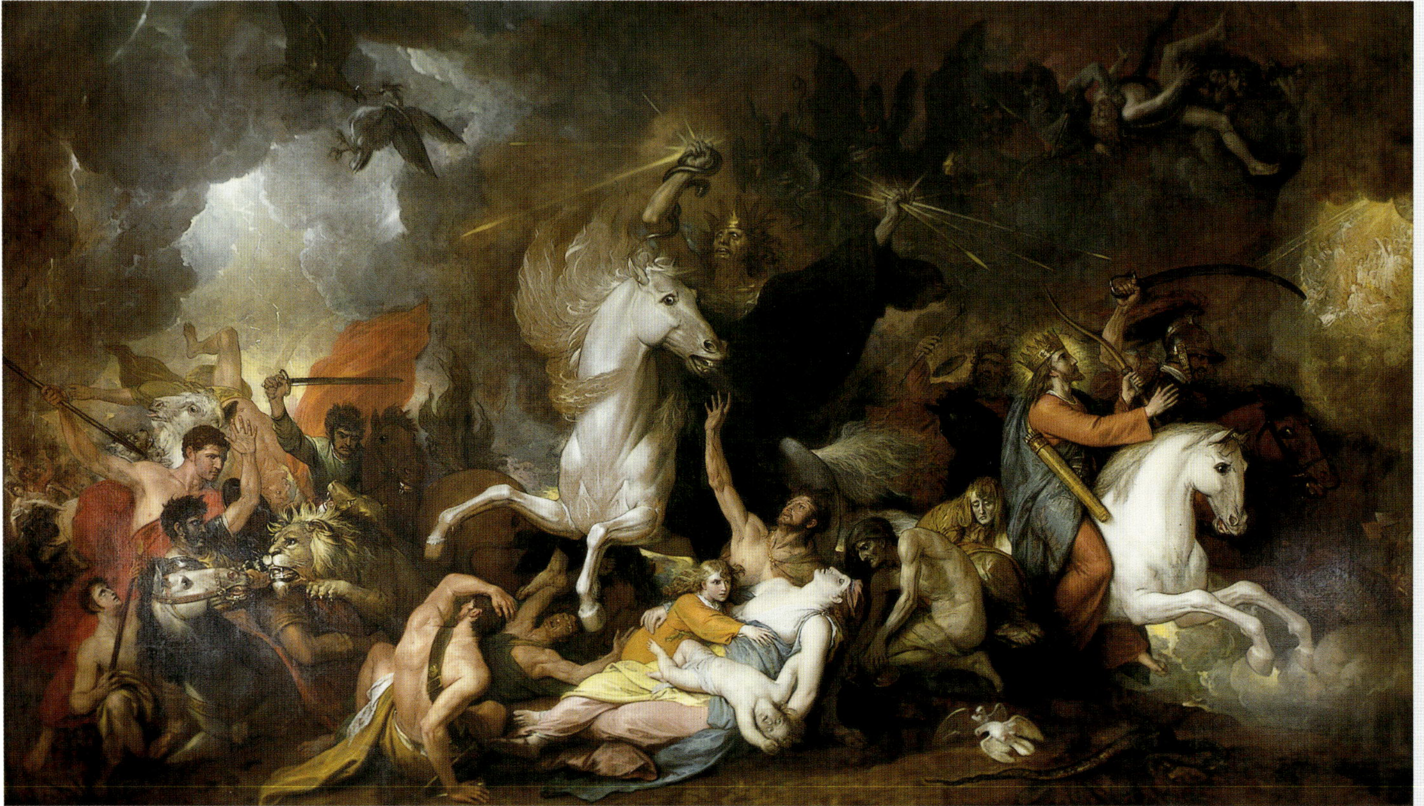

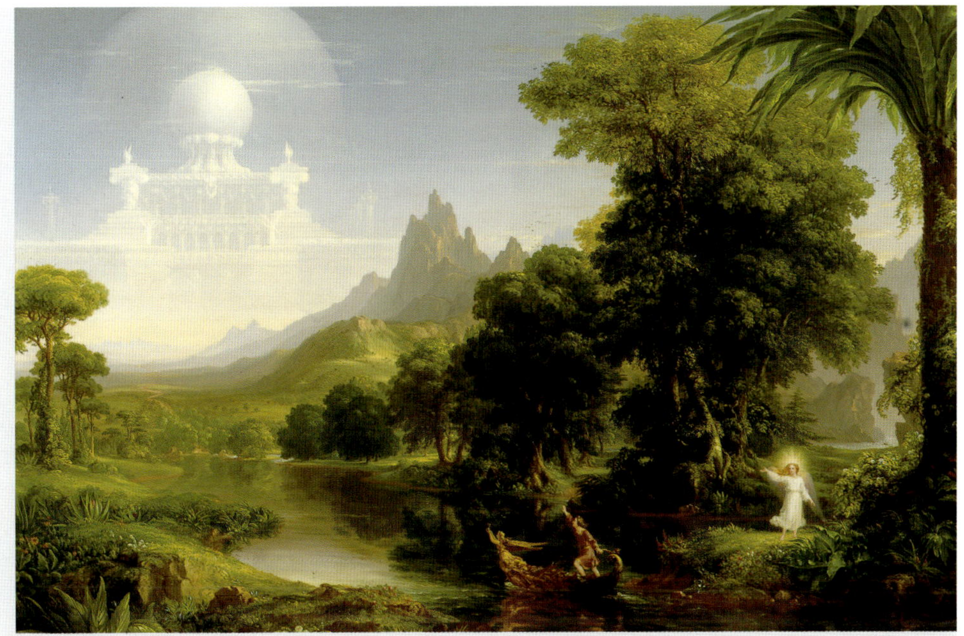

revolution. He described *The Greek Slave* as the beautiful girl who was sold in the slave markets of Turkey and Egypt. "These were Christian women, and it is not difficult to imagine the distress and even despair of the sufferers while exposed to be sold to the highest bidder," Powers said.[4] Scholar Lynda Hyman has posited that contemporary critics, "by attributing to the young woman a lofty purity, a saintly spirituality, and a heart of gold, and then by endowing her with a certain air of haughty pride, they were able, in a sense to bypass her nakedness and see beyond her purity."[5]

From 1850 to 1870 the Academy's board minutes record three important exhibitions, each featuring a single renowned painting: *Heart of the Andes* by Frederic Edwin Church (February–April 1860), *Christ Rejected* by Benjamin West (1862), and *Domes of the Yosemite* by Albert Bierstadt (June–July 1867). Landscape painting dominated and defined American art at midcentury. Church's exotic flora and fauna of South America and Bierstadt's depictions of indigenous people and the vast wilderness of the American West were seen as prime expressions of Manifest Destiny as well as the opportunities and abundance of America's expansionism. These widely exhibited paintings were popular as dioramas and brought the artists considerable revenue. Naturally these paintings furthered public interest in travel, which greatly increased with the completion of the transcontinental railroad in 1869.

In 1876, when the Pennsylvania Academy moved into its grand High Victorian building (designed by Frank Furness and George Hewitt) at Broad and Cherry Streets, the new galleries provided a great deal more exhibition space (fig. 6). As a result, special exhibitions were held with much greater variety and frequency, and the Academy's influence reached its peak. Renowned for its faculty (that included Cecilia Beaux, William Merritt Chase, Thomas Eakins), its students, and its defining annual exhibitions, the Academy flourished. In addition to exhibiting its permanent collection, numerous landmark exhibitions were held in the new galleries during the late nineteenth century, among them the Philadelphia Photographic Salons (1898–1901), and the English Pre-Raphaelites (1858, 1892), as well as Japanese (1890, 1894) and Chinese art (1895). In fact the 1895–1896 special exhibition season represented one of the most international and culturally diverse in the Academy's history. It included illustrations from *Century Magazine*; caricatures (under the auspices of the students of the Academy); Chinese Buddhist paintings; works of contemporary Swedish artists; an art poster show; pictures of the Glasgow School; burnt wood panels by J. William Fosdick; competitive designs for the decoration of the Common Council Chamber, City Hall, Philadelphia; pastels by Edwin Austin Abbey; the annual architectural exhibition; paintings by Theodore Robinson; and two solo exhibitions.

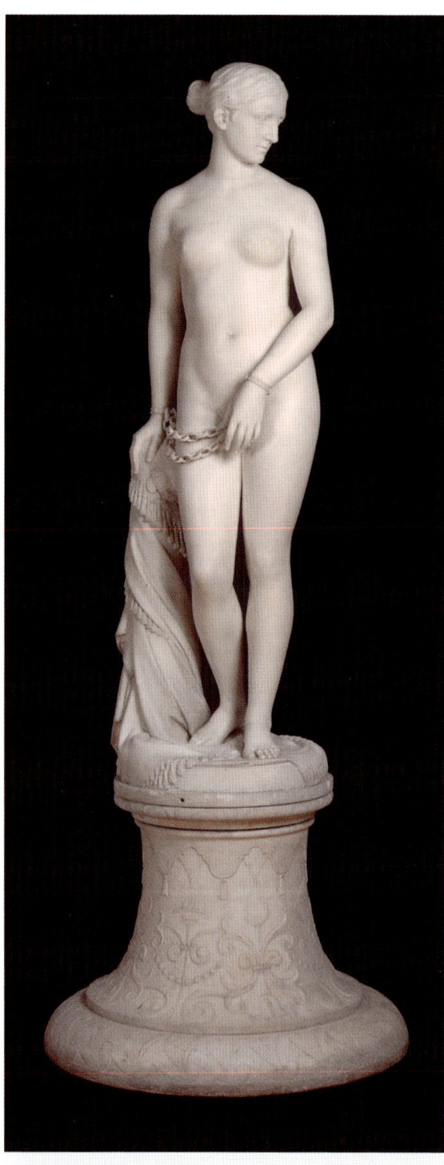



One of the most ambitious exhibitions ever held at the Academy was the *Special Exhibition of Paintings by American Artists at Home and in Europe*, (fig.1) which opened on November 7 and continued to December 26, 1881. Art critic J. Eugene Reed extolled the event: "The beautiful galleries of the Pennsylvania Academy of the Fine Arts are now lined with a collection of pictures by American painters that is, perhaps, the best ever assembled in this country. . . . Certainly we have never examined a similar collection of pictures in which there was so large a proportion of good grain and so little chaff. There are 425 paintings in all, including 136 contributions from American artists, temporarily abroad for study, some of whom are represented for the first time in a strictly national exhibit."[6]

Three international committees of artists were appointed by the Academy's board to select representative paintings from Paris, London, and Munich. In actuality, the lion's share of the 136 contributions came from Paris. The final exhibition catalogue had 430 entries, including last-minute additions. While monumental in breadth, the exhibition featured several entries that today are considered masterpieces. Perhaps the most controversial painting in the exhibition was entry 191, James Abbott McNeill Whistler's *Arrangement in grey and black, portrait of the artist's mother* [sic] (fig. 7). The *Evening Telegraph* critic was not impressed. "Mr. Whistler is a famous man, but the average person may not at once perceive in this picture the reasons for his fame. It is a portrait of his mother, an ordinary looking old lady, in a black gown, sitting in an aggressively un-picturesque attitude, in profile against a white wall. . . . The severity of this picture is . . . but a laboriously studied and artful simplicity, and the apparent feebleness of the painting has been produced by most elaborate work."[7]

Other paintings of note were Thomas Eakins's *William Rush Carving His Allegorical Figure of the Schuylkill* (priced at $1000) and *Mending the Net* (priced at $600). An article in *Harper's Weekly* reveals contemporary opinion of the former: "Mr. Eakins is an artist who is apt to astonish and to irritate by his assertion of a very unique individual, but even he pleases rather than excites antipathies by his chief contribution to this collection. It is true that he shows his 'William Rush,' which was the subject of considerable dispute when it was exhibited in New York some seasons ago. Then, however, it was an aggravation among aggravations, while in the present Philadelphia collection it appears to fall into place naturally with its surroundings, and instead of commanding consideration at all hazards, it has to be sought for. Mr. Eakins's other canvas represents some fishermen spreading . . . their net on a gentle acclivity by a river-side. It is undoubtedly the most pleasing work that this able but eccentric artist has thus far executed."[8]

Three paintings received lavish praise from critics. Charles Sprague Pearce's *The Decapitation of St. John the Baptist* (listed "For Sale" in the catalogue), *An Interesting Game, Cairo Café*, by F. A. Bridgman (priced at $300), and *Waiting for Father*, by F. C. Penfold (priced at $217). All three artists studied in Paris and their works reflect the vogue for Orientalism, "grand manner," and Barbizon landscape painting. By today's standards these paintings appear overly dramatic and sentimental; however, they well represent high Victorian morals and taste.

In October and November 1891 the Pennsylvania Academy mounted an exhibition of the *Thomas B. Clarke Collection of American Pictures*. It was exceptional for two reasons. The first was for the quality and breadth of the collection. Secondly, Mr. Clarke authored the exhibition catalogue, writing biographical profiles on each of the 119 artists and lengthy descriptions of the 207 paintings in the exhibition. He was one of the first collectors to become a scholar of American art. As Charles Henry Hart, the chairman of the Committee on Exhibitions at the Academy, noted: "The manuscript for the present catalogue has been furnished by the generous owner of the collection. . . . The Academy takes this occasion to testify its high appreciation of the good work done in the true interest of American art and artists by Mr. Clarke, and to acknowledge its indebtedness to him for the privilege of holding the present exhibition of his unrivaled collection of the best works of our artists."[9]

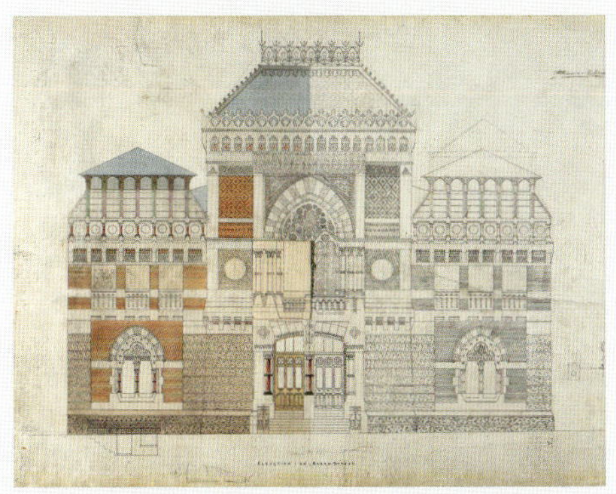



**FIG. 6**
Furness & Hewitt Architects (1871–1875)
Frank Furness (1839–1912) and George W. Hewitt
(1841–1916)
*The Pennsylvania Academy of Fine Arts, Design of
Broad Street Elevation*, 1873
Black ink, watercolor wash, and pencil on white paper
mount, 25½ x 34½ inches
Pennsylvania Academy of the Fine Arts,
Gift of the architect (Frank Furness), 1876.6.8

**FIG. 7**
James Abbott McNeill Whistler (1834–1903)
*Arrangement in Grey and Black No. 1:
Portrait of the Artist's Mother*, 1871
Oil on canvas, 56¾ x 64 inches
Musée d'Orsay, Paris, France

Many of the artists, such as Winslow Homer and George Inness, are included in most museum collections today, but others, such as Dennis Bunker and Thomas Waterman Wood, have been brought to light only in recent scholarship and auctions. One critic who reviewed the exhibition on October 15 noted its unique character: "Mr. Clarke's collection, as now displayed in the Academy, fills the main room with 207 numbers, no one of which is too large to find wall space in a roomy house, and more than half of which are small cabinet pieces. This circumstance alone gives the collection a character of its own, because it involves a complete absence of the gigantic canvases, dear to artists and the despairing Hanging Committees, which appear in every exhibition and salon. . . . The collection puts to the fore the two most original of American artists, Winslow Homer and George Inness."[10] Twelve works each by Homer and Inness were included in the exhibition, the largest display to date of these artists' work at one time in Philadelphia (fig. 8).

In 1892 Harrison S. Morris (1856–1948), the nation's first professional arts administrator, was appointed to the Academy. During his tenure acquisitions and special exhibitions transformed the institution. Morris's knowledge of modern American art and his friendships with contemporary artists brought many daring special exhibitions that attracted national recognition.

From the late 1880s through the first decade of the twentieth century, American Impressionism was the leading contemporary art trend. This new wave of American artists painted their landscapes *en plein air*, outdoors, directly after nature. Seizing the fugitive effects of light and color, their subject matter was found in daily life. Women at leisure, summer resorts, friends and family were often captured by these artists in a transitory moment. Impressionism, an art movement that began in France in 1874, was championed at home by a group known as the Ten American Painters. In the spring of 1898 these ten men simultaneously resigned from the Society of American Artists and subsequently held annual exhibitions together for the next twenty years. The artists were Frank Benson, Joseph DeCamp, Thomas Dewing, Childe Hassam, Willard Metcalf, Robert Reid, Edward Simmons, Edmund Tarbell, John Twachtman, and J. Alden Weir. After Twachtman's untimely death in 1902, William Merritt Chase joined the group.

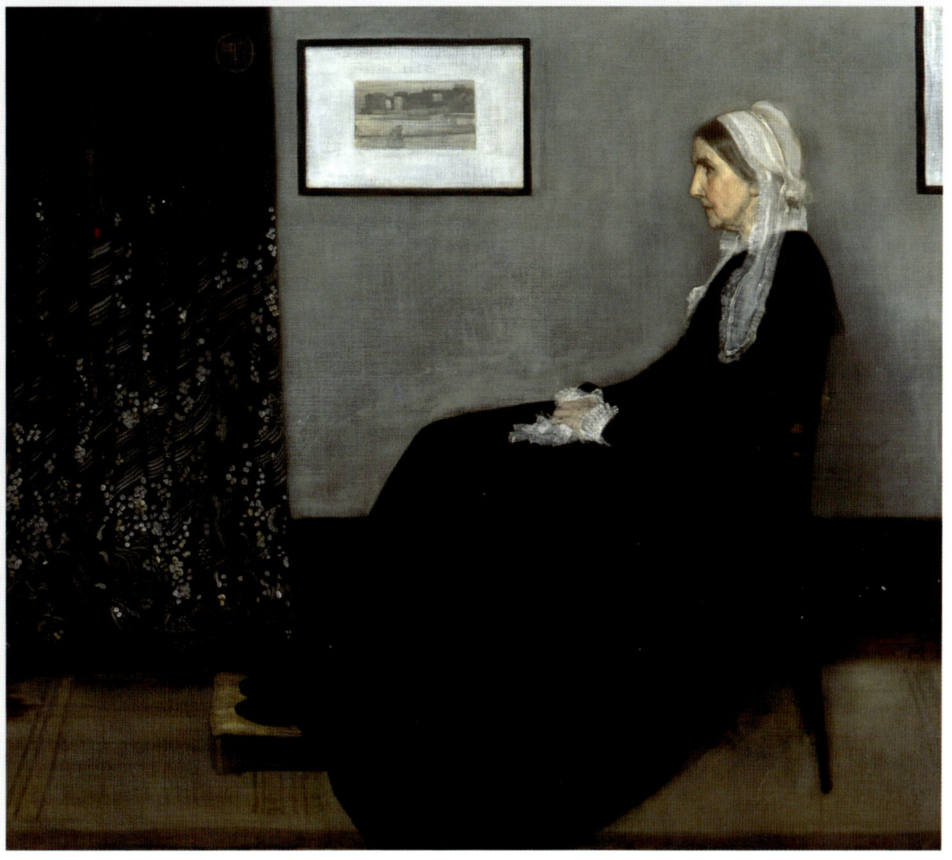

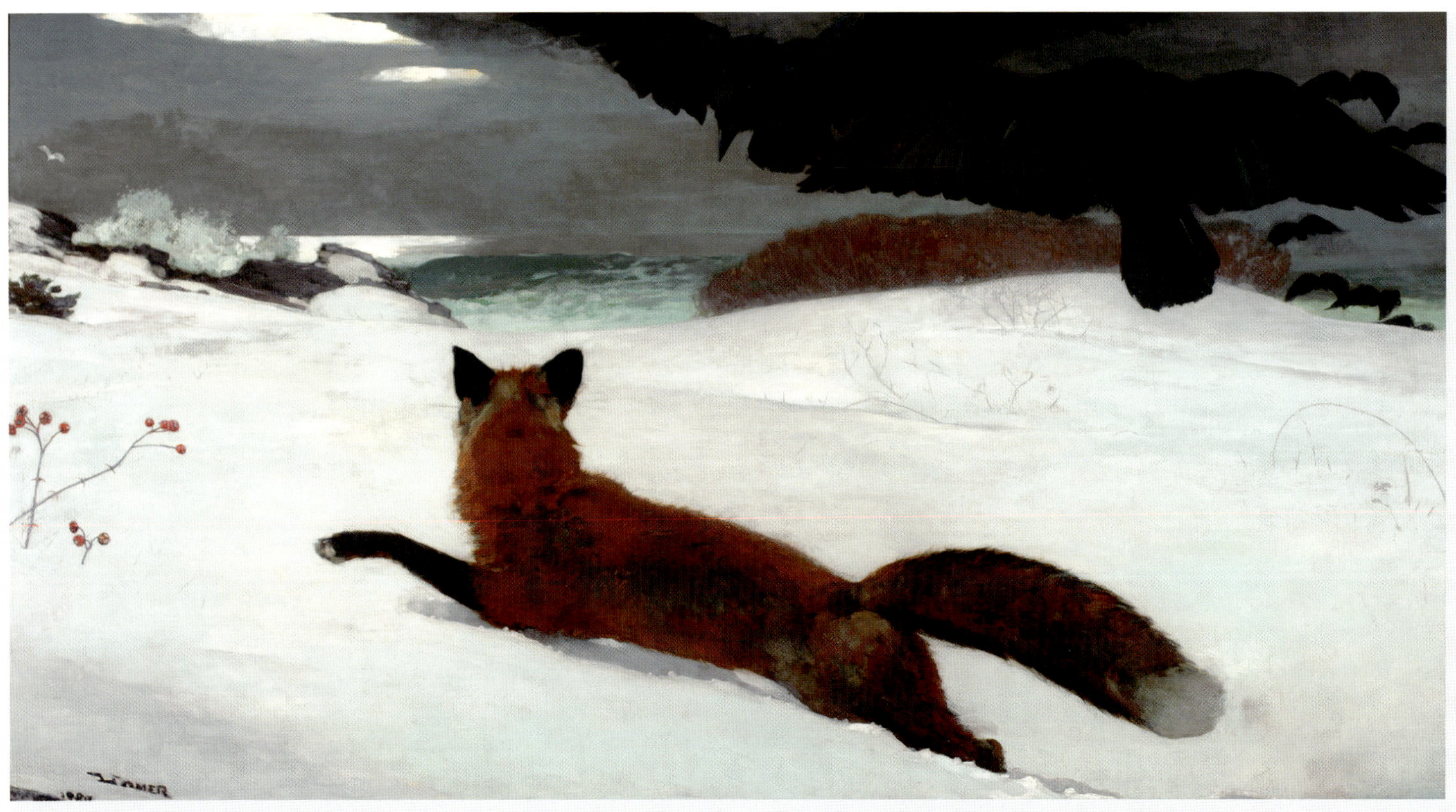



FIG. 8
Winslow Homer (1836–1910)
*Fox Hunt*, 1893
Oil on canvas, 38 x 68½ inches
Pennsylvania Academy of the Fine Arts,
Joseph E. Temple Fund, 1894.4

In 1908 the tenth anniversary exhibition of The Ten was held at the Pennsylvania Academy. "Bound together only by ties of mutual respect and of ability, they have held a showing of current work; and now on their tenth anniversary have organized this exhibition, which presents for the first time such a collection of their works as will give opportunity for a fuller study of their aims and accomplishments."[11] Each artist was free to present ten canvases representing their best work. Fifteen private collectors, among them Andrew Carnegie and Charles L. Freer, lent to the exhibition. Only one painting was loaned by a museum—the portrait of *Edward Robinson* by Edmund Tarbell—lent by the Museum of Fine Arts, Boston, while Edward Simmons's *Mother and Child* was lent by the City of St. Louis. Some of the paintings on view were *Eleanor* by Frank Benson, *Ring Toss* by William Merritt Chase (plate 30), Childe Hassam's *The Room of Flowers*, and J. Alden Weir's *The Red Bridge*. Chase's *The Ring Toss* was heralded by one critic as one of his best descriptions of childhood. In memory of John Twachtman, *Sailing in the Mist* (ca. 1895) was added to the exhibition. The Pennsylvania Academy had purchased this painting in 1906, four years after the artist's death (fig. 9). Strongly influenced by French Impressionism, the American Impressionists adopted their style and technique while painting subject matter wholly relevant to the American scene.

Critic William Howe Downes, special correspondent for the *Boston Evening Transcript*, began his review by stating, "The exhibition of paintings by the Ten American Painters in the galleries of the Pennsylvania Academy of the Fine Arts may be set down as the best exhibition of American paintings ever held. . . . Report has it that there has been some talk of an invasion of London by the Ten. Such an exhibition . . . would certainly make London sit up and take notice, if good painting has not been too long obsolete there. For . . . I am not boasting about American art when I say that it would not be possible to get together in any other country such a collection of ninety-four paintings by contemporary artists."[12]

While The Ten represented a well-established movement of contemporary painting in 1908, yet another avant-garde group burst on the scene in 1908 with an exhibition at the Macbeth Galleries in New York. These "men of rebellion," quickly known as The Eight, were Arthur Davies, William Glackens, Robert Henri, Ernest Lawson, George Luks, Maurice Prendergast, Everett Shinn, and John Sloan.

The head of this group was Robert Henri, caustically referred to as "the leader of an expedition to an artistic Promised Land by a group of painters who admire his style."[13] (Five of The Eight began their careers as students at the Pennsylvania Academy: Henri, Glackens, Luks, Shinn, and Sloan). The works of Thomas Eakins and Thomas Anshutz, with their aesthetics of intense realism, made lasting impressions on these students. Their Academy years, and their work as illustrators for various Philadelphia newspapers formed the basis of their training that led to accurate depictions of gritty New York subject matter.

Greatly mystified by what he saw at the Macbeth Galleries, critic James Townsend derided the paintings of The Eight, especially the studies of Prendergast, as incomprehensible. "To Maurice B. Prendergast must be given the palm for handing out to the art public of New York, so-called pictures that can only be the product of the cider much drunk at St. Malo in Brittany, where his crazy quilt sketches were conceived and executed. Blotches of paint on canvas without harmony of color or tone—these are all that can be made out of these curious performances."[14]

Not all of the critics attacked the startling new work by this band of realists. Giles Edgerton (*nom de plume* for Mary Fenton Roberts) in *The Craftsman* paid warm tribute to The Eight, concluding the review with the following thoughts: "Art to every man must be his personal confession of life as he feels it and knows it. The lack of human quality in painting or sculpture means the lack of that vitality which makes for permanence. . . . And so it seems that the basis of future American art lies in our artists' appreciation of the value of the human quality all about them, which is nothing more or less than seeing the truth, and then expressing it according to their individual understanding. The exhibition of the eight American artists seems to us to have acquired this very quality."[15] The press declared the initial exhibition at the Macbeth Galleries very successful. Seven paintings were sold and the attendance was equal to that at an Academy show.


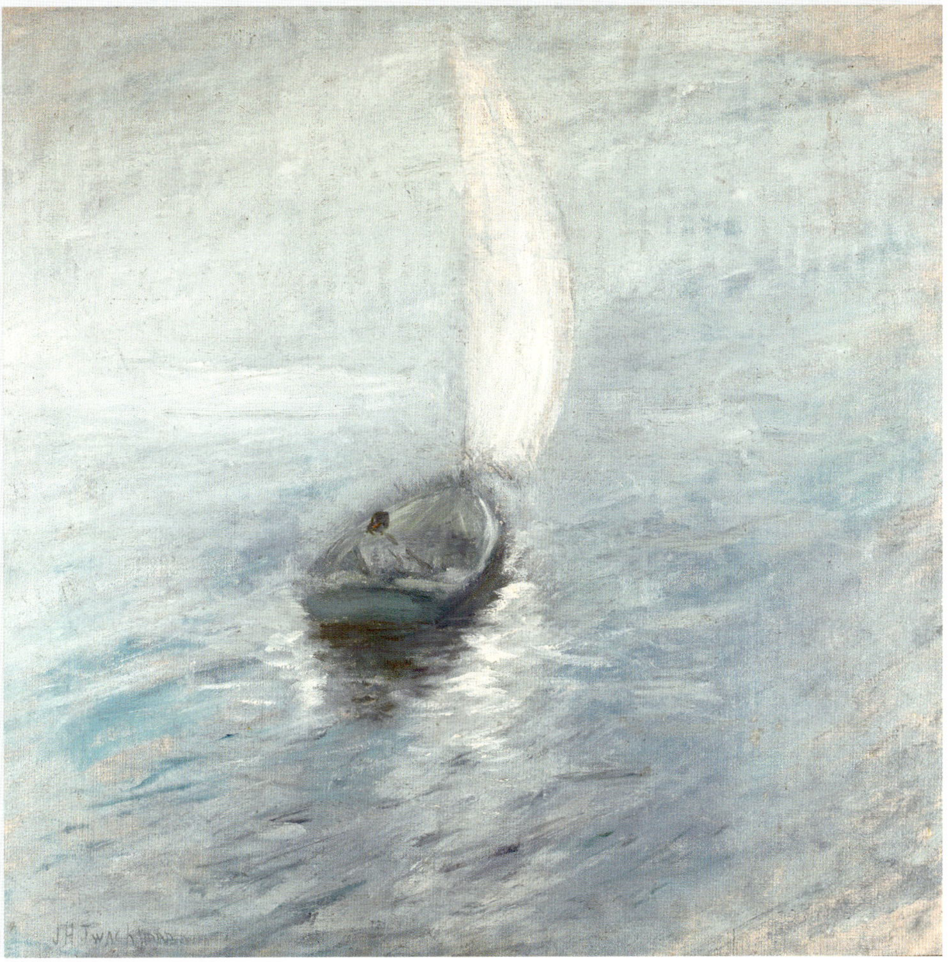



FIG. 9
John Twachtman (1853–1902)
*Sailing in the Mist*, 1890s
Oil on canvas, 30 3/16 x 30 1/8 inches
Pennsylvania Academy of the Fine Arts,
Joseph E. Temple Fund, 1906.1

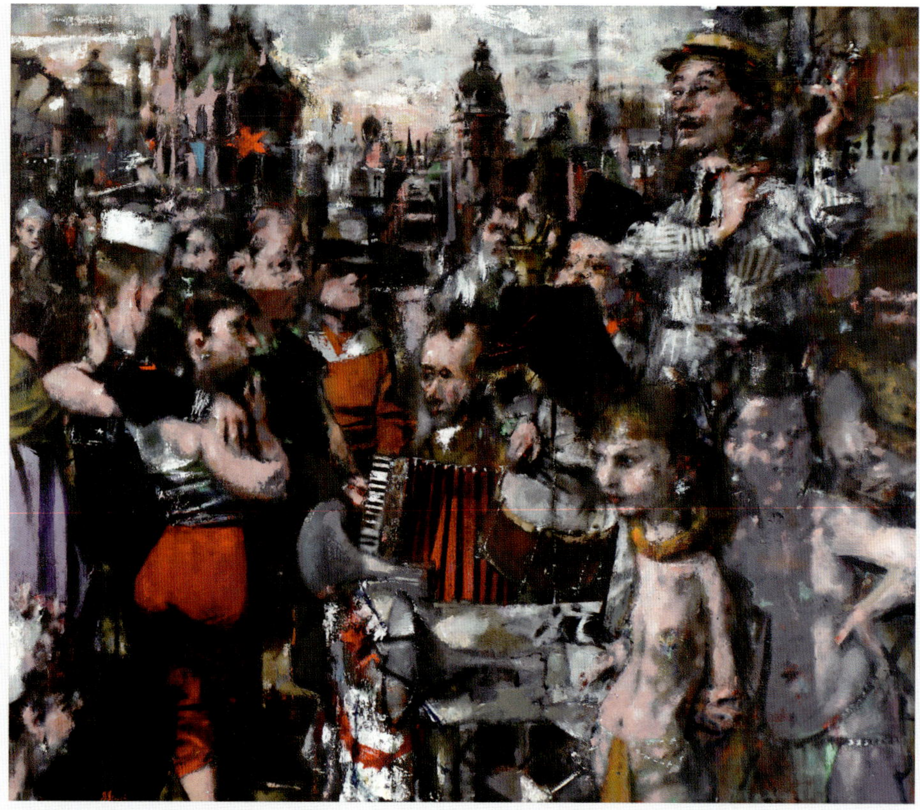

Immediately on the heels of their New York success, the Pennsylvania Academy opened an exhibition of The Eight on March 7, 1908. While the Macbeth Galleries featured five paintings by each artist, the Academy presented a much larger exhibition of sixty-four paintings. Lawson and Luks displayed five paintings each, Davies included six, Glackens and Sloan had seven, Henri and Shinn exhibited nine, and Prendergast presented sixteen works, eight of which were studies of St. Malo, France. The exhibition catalogue notes that the pictures were for sale at studio prices. These prices varied widely; ranging from Robert Henri's painting *Spain* listed for sale at $100, to William Glackens's *The Shoppers* and Arthur B. Davies's *Girdle of Ares*, both priced at $3,000.

Although many Academy students worked in conservative representational styles in the early twentieth century, early American modernists Stuart Davis, Charles Demuth, John Marin, Morton Schaumberg, and Charles Sheeler all were students at the Pennsylvania Academy. The Academy's role as a leader in promoting avant-garde art was at its peak when three modernist exhibitions were held in 1920, 1921, and 1923. Deeply influenced by the 1913 New York Armory Show, Academy instructors Hugh Breckenridge, Henry McCarter, and Arthur B. Carles were pivotal in the organization of the exhibition *Paintings and Drawings by Representative Modern Masters* in 1920. While most of its 254 works were painted by artists of the European avant-garde (such as Braque, Matisse, Picasso, and older masters Cézanne, Degas, Gauguin, and Manet), American expatriate painters Mary Cassatt, Stanton MacDonald-Wright, and James Abbott McNeill Whistler were also included in the exhibition.

A year later, in 1921, the Academy held its *Exhibition of Paintings and Drawings Showing the Later Tendencies in Art.* Hailed as the "first comprehensive display of American modernist works in an American museum," the exhibition included 280 paintings and works on paper by 88 American artists. The selection committee included such diverse personalities as Thomas Hart Benton, Arthur B. Carles, Joseph Stella, and Alfred Stieglitz. Bold and at times shocking, the show caused a great stir, drew a large audience, and attracted favorable reviews from the critics.

Emboldened by those recent successes, the Pennsylvania Academy mounted a third modernist exhibition of the collection of Albert C. Barnes, entitled *Contemporary European Paintings and Sculpture*, in 1923. With the help of his friend William Glackens, Dr. Barnes had assembled an

  IN PRIVATE HANDS: 200 YEARS OF AMERICAN PAINTING

extraordinary collection of paintings, drawings, and sculptures of the European and American avant-garde. The exhibition (organized primarily by Carles and McCarter) featured Barnes's most daring and latest acquisitions of the European modernists. Seventy-five works were exhibited in the Academy's galleries, including works by Lipchitz, Modigliani, Soutine, Derain, Picasso, and Matisse, among others. Dr. Barnes's five-page introductory essay sought to provide the public with an explanation of modernist tendencies. His efforts were in vain. Outraged critics derided these works, especially those by Soutine, and as a result the exhibit failed to attract acclaim. Affronted, Barnes withdrew to suburban Merion, determined never again to share his collection with the Philadelphia arts establishment.[16]

Perhaps in reaction to the vitriolic criticism of the Barnes exhibition, the Academy did an about-face from modernism, turning inward and adopting a conservative stance during the late twenties. With the turmoil of the Depression and World War II, the Academy's exhibition program refocused on Philadelphia artists and the annuals. This focus continued until the 1960s. There were several war-related exhibitions during the 1940s; among them were *Soldiers of Productions: Eight American Artists Appointed to Record Activities in Defense Areas* (1942), *Sketches by Former Academy Students Serving in the Armed Forces* (1942), *War Posters* (1943), and *Sixteen Pictures on Wartime Transportation* by Thornton Oakley (1944). In September 1944 the Academy celebrated with *Star Presentation: Works from the Permanent Collection Returned after Wartime Storage*, an exhibition featuring the gems of the collection.

While Abstract Expressionism took New York by storm in the 1950s, Philadelphia and the Academy continued to focus on figurative art, considering abstraction as a passing fad; however, many abstract painters did exhibit at the annuals during the 1950s. The Academy missed an extraordinary opportunity to purchase from the 1956 annual Jackson Pollock's *Convergence*, priced at $ 6,000. Instead they acquired Jack Levine's *Medicine Show* (fig. 10) and Rico Lebrun's *Buchenwald Cart*.[17]

Important exhibitions of the 1950s included an exhibition of *N. C. Wyeth Drawings* (1950), the *Arthur B. Carles Memorial Exhibition* (1953), and the *One Hundred Fiftieth Anniversary Exhibition* (1955).

The next decade saw a national trend to transform museum exhibitions into blockbusters. The Academy was no exception. It attained national fame with the retrospective of the largest

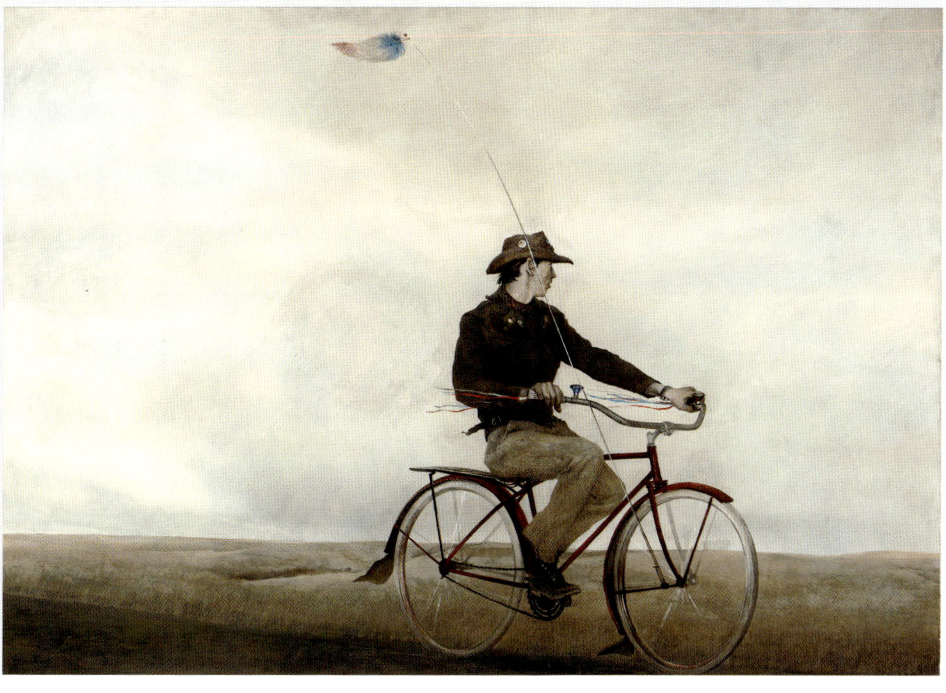

collection of Andrew Wyeth paintings ever assembled (fig. 11). The exhibition opened to the public on October 8, 1966, and to the astonishment of the staff and board of the Academy, it became an overnight success. When the Academy's doors closed on November 27, more than 173,000 visitors had seen *Andrew Wyeth* in seven weeks. Amusingly, the press was quick to note the economic ripple effect of a blockbuster on Philadelphia: "Andrew Wyeth left Philadelphia Sunday night, and a lot of soft-pretzel vendors are unhappy. Wyeth was great for the soft-pretzel business. One of the all-time greats in Philadelphia's history in fact."[18]

*Today's Art* noted, "The Pennsylvania Academy of the Fine Arts, in Philadelphia, has gathered 222 of Wyeth's works: tempera, watercolor, dry brush paintings and drawings. About 80% of the works come from private collections, the rest from museums in New York; Chicago; San Francisco; Houston; Dallas; Wilmington, Del.; and Oslo, Norway."[19] The article began, "Andrew Wyeth has become a kind of American hero in the Art world. Defying the endless 'isms' which push each other across the scene, Wyeth has retained his faith in, and his dedication to, painting persons, objects, and views exactly as an artist with keen eyes, and a desire for absolute truth would." Among the works in the large retrospective was the deeply introspective watercolor *The Drifter*, also included in this exhibition (plate 69).

In 1975 the Academy's first full-time professional curator, Frank H. Goodyear, Jr., joined the staff and began mounting important exhibitions and documenting the collection. The Academy closed its building from May 1974 to April 1976 for a major restoration. During this time, part of the permanent collection toured to several museums.

For the April 22, 1976 reopening of the Historic Landmark Building, Goodyear organized a stunning special bicentennial exhibition, *In This Academy: The Pennsylvania Academy of the Fine Arts, 1805–1976* which featured 341 paintings, sculptures, and works on paper from museums, private collections, and the Academy's permanent collection. The accompanying exhibition catalogue continues to serve as a resource on Academy history, exhibitions, and the collection.

Nine years later one contemporary exhibition, *Red Grooms: A Retrospective, 1956–1984*, took Philadelphia by storm. Grooms's sprawling exhibition of 170 objects showed painting, sculpture, prints, and drawings opened on June 21, 1985, organized  by Academy curator Judith Stein. His witty cartoon-character depictions of American life, exemplified in his "sculpto-pictoramas" of *The City of Chicago, Ruckus Manhattan*, and *Philadelphia Cornucopia* (a piece that had resided at the city's Visitors Bureau since 1983), won the hearts of visitors. Grooms's comic and satirical pieces rewrote history, like his 1967 reinterpretation *William Penn Shaking Hands with the Indians* that spoofs the Academy's *Penn's Treaty with the Indians* (1771) by Benjamin West. He satirized art history too, as is evidenced in *A Room in Connecticut*, where Marcel Duchamp is seated in the living room of his avant-garde patron Katherine Dreier (fig. 12). Master of high and low art, Grooms combined his references from the raunchiest of New York street scenes to the most sublime *Madonna and Child* from the Italian Renaissance.

In broadening audiences with Grooms and other blockbuster shows, the Academy dispelled its stereotyped image of artistic elitism. As the oldest art school and galleries in the nation, the Pennsylvania Academy was hallowed ground for academic figurative art. Breaking public perception of this premise brought renewed vitality to the Academy's galleries and outreach programs.

Another traveling retrospective organized by the Academy, *I Tell My Heart: The Art of Horace Pippin*, brought national recognition for a self-taught African-American artist from West Chester, Pennsylvania, when it opened on January 21, 1994. The exhibition included 100 of Pippin's 137 known works and was the result of five years of research by curator Judith Stein. While the Academy acquired *John Brown Going to His Hanging* (page 10) from the 1943 annual

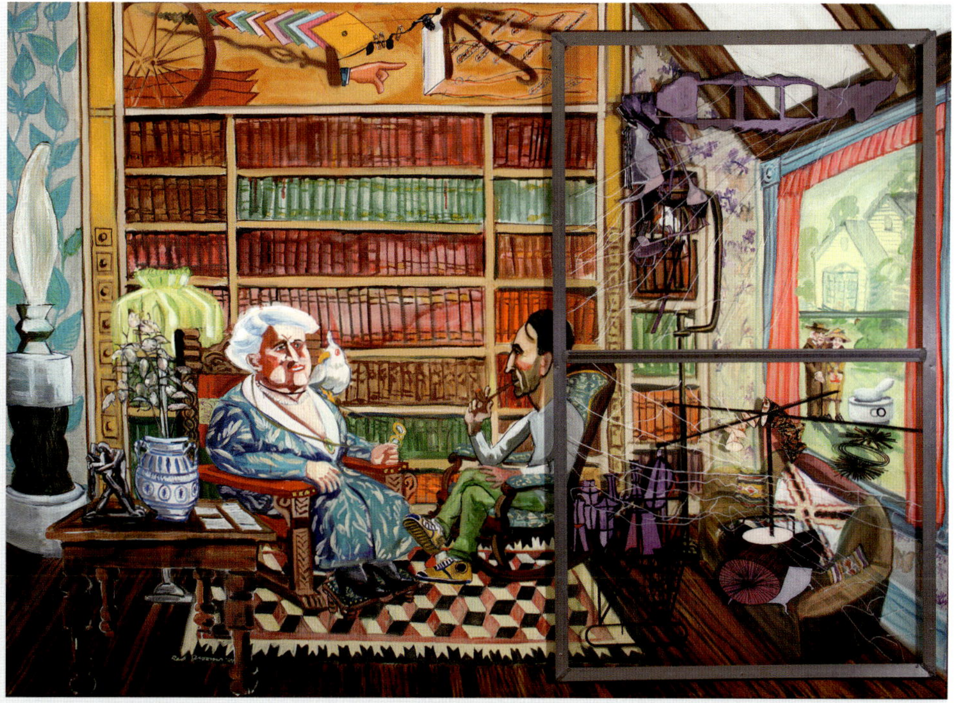

exhibition of painting and sculpture and awarded the artist the J. Henry Schiedt Memorial Prize at the 1946 annual, it did not mount a retrospective during the artist's lifetime. The superb painting *John Brown Reading His Bible*, 1942, included in the current exhibition, was among the works in his 1994 retrospective (plate 52).

Critic Edward Sozanski got straight to the heart of Pippin's public appeal: "Pippin is the real thing. His work may not be polished but it's completely honest and often surprisingly sophisticated in its design and use of color. Pippin is America's Henri Rousseau—if he doesn't validate the model of the self-taught artist, no one else ever will." He adds, "This may be the best art exhibition Philadelphia will see this year."[20]

In 1999, expanding the boundaries of inclusion once more, the Pennsylvania Academy mounted the exhibition *Maxfield Parrish, 1870–1966*. Beloved for his illustrations for magazines, advertisements, posters, and books, Parrish was the most popular artist of his day. In her catalogue essay that reexamines Parrish's *oeuvre*, curator Sylvia Yount noted that in 1925 the House of Art, a New York printing company, estimated that a reproduction of Maxfield Parrish's *Daybreak* could be found in one of every four American homes.[21] Parrish was an Academy graduate whose career in illustration outshone many of his fellow students and an artist who embraced the new mass-media technologies of the twentieth century. As critic Holland Cotter affirmed, "Everything Parrish did was an exercise in conspicuous virtuosity. He developed his expertise at the Pennsylvania Academy itself, where he was enrolled from 1892 to 1894, and even as a student he was fixated on the challenges of the craft.... And he genuinely relished his role as popular artist, never viewing himself as a genius painter condescending to do graphic work."[22] Huge crowds of all ages visited the Academy, enchanted to journey through the fantastic magical world of the illustrator.

Let us return to the questions initially posed by the 1908 art critic at the beginning of this essay: "Does American art represent the ideals of the American people? Is it national: is it modern; is it living?" While the 1908 critic's response was, at the time, quite negative, he did raise a most relevant issue about how Americans are keenly interested in the process of painting. "American artists as a class seem to be lacking in both ideas and ideals," he said. "They are absorbed in the questions of technique until they forget what technique is for. They practice their arpeggios in pigment and expect the public to applaud. They think of a picture as merely a rectangular surface covered with masses of color harmoniously placed. If that were all we

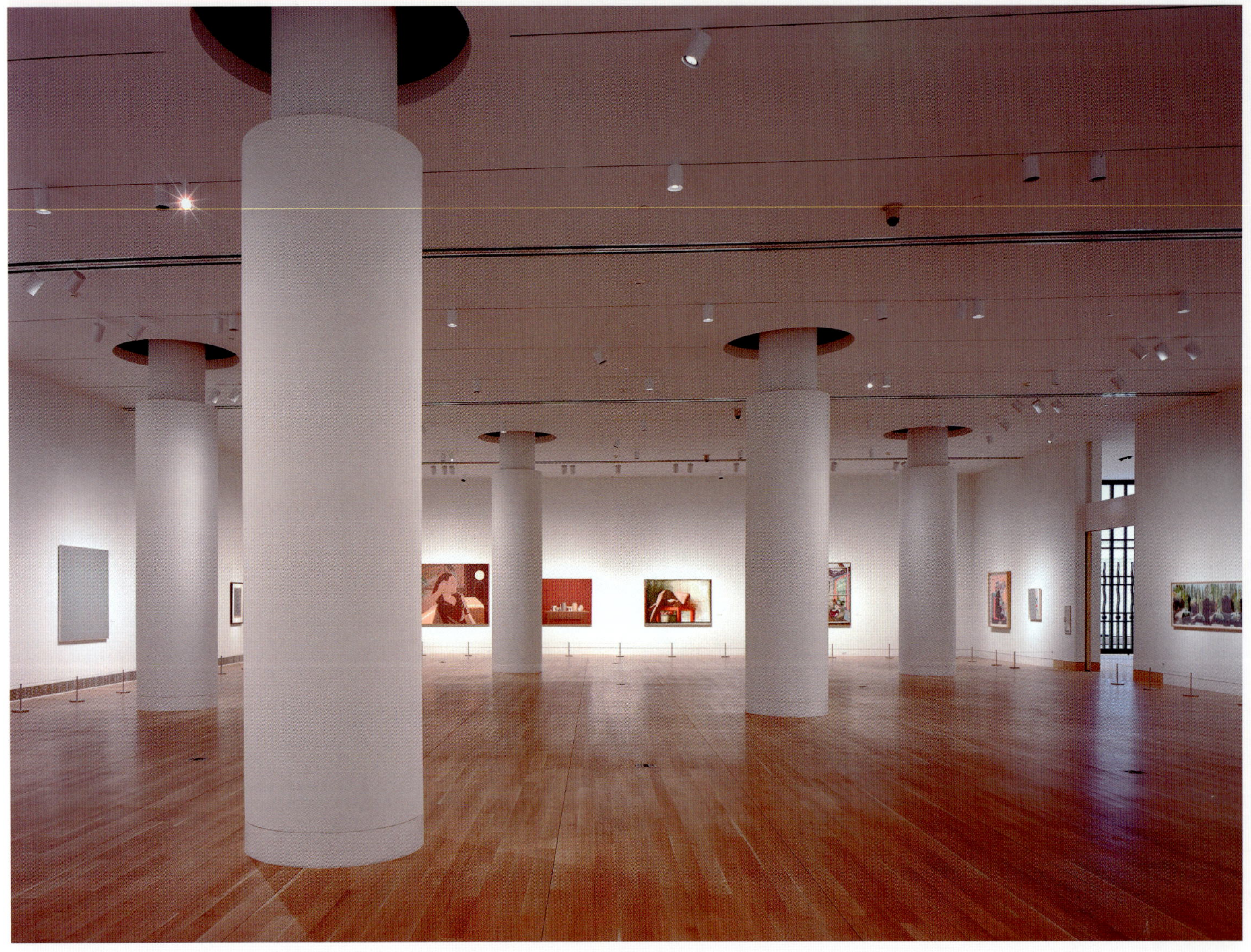



wanted we would spend our 50 cents for a kaleidoscope instead of an academy ticket."[23] One can reflect on how these same questions can be applied to art in the first decade of the twenty-first century. Since the mid-twentieth century, New York has become the center of the art world. With the triumph of Abstract Expressionism, American art became the cynosure and was internationally renowned.

American art has always been a reflection of our democratic ideology, as a nation of many immigrants. As a nation we are not really a melting pot but rather a mixing bowl of diverse cultures, with many distinct voices. The current polyphony of American art is perhaps one of its greatest strengths; however, national art has been eclipsed in the last ten years as globalization (not just in technology but also in art) has gained supremacy.

How does the oldest art school and museum in America fit in all of these changes? "The Pennsylvania Academy of the Fine Arts represents a kind of heart line in the history of American art.... Its existence as a center for artists and a home for art has lent strength and stability to a mobile scene, not only in Philadelphia but for American art in general," wrote Joshua C. Taylor, Director of the National Collection of Fine Arts in 1976.[24]

In 2005 the Academy celebrates its 200th anniversary with the inauguration of its expanded campus—the spectacular Samuel M. V. Hamilton Building (fig. 13) and the newly restored Historic Landmark Building. With renewed vigor, the board of trustees, led by chairman Donald

R. Caldwell, set the goal of bringing the institution back to pre-eminence as one of the great centers for education in the fine arts. Another goal for the Academy's bicentennial was to organize a once-in-a-lifetime exhibition to celebrate two centuries of American painting drawn exclusively from private collections. *In Private Hands: 200 Years of American Painting* is the result of that ambitious goal. Fifty-four American collectors, each with an acute eye and remarkable artistic instincts, have generously lent their spectacular paintings to this exhibition. With this milestone event, these men and women of vision will help to inaugurate the third century of educating, exhibiting, and collecting at the Pennsylvania Academy of the Fine Arts.


NOTES

1. "Growing Pains of American Art," *Current Literature* 44, April 1908, p. 393.

2. Alan Wallach, "The Voyage of Life as Popular Art," *Art Bulletin* 59, no. 2 (June 1977), pp. 234–41.

3. *Powers' Statue of the Greek Slave, Exhibiting at the Pennsylvania Academy of the Fine Arts* (Philadelphia: T. K. Collins and P. G. Collins, 1848), p. 1.

4. Letter from Hiram Powers to E. W. Stoughton, Photostat in New York Public Library, scrapbook on Hiram Powers.

5. Linda Hyman, "The Greek Slave by Hiram Powers: High Art as Popular Culture," *Art Journal* 25, no. 3 (Spring 1976), p. 219.

6. J. Eugene Reed, "American Pictures at the Philadelphia Academy," *National Baptist* 17, no. 47 (November 24, 1888), whole no. 882. Pennsylvania Academy of the Fine Arts clipping scrapbooks, microfilmed by the Archives of American Art, roll P 53, frame 0274.

7. *Evening Telegraph*, October 9, 1881. Pennsylvania Academy of the Fine Arts clipping scrapbooks, microfilmed by the Archives of American Art, roll P 53, frame 0270.

8. "The Philadelphia Art Exhibition," *Harper's Weekly*, December 10, 1881.

9. Charles Henry Hart, *Catalogue of the Thomas B. Clarke Collection of American Pictures* (Philadelphia: Times Printing House, 1891), p. 3.

10. "American Art Exhibit," *The Press*, October 15, 1891.

11. *Catalogue of the Exhibition of Paintings by Ten American Painters*, April 11–May 3, 1908 (Philadelphia: J. B. Lippincott Company, 1908), p. 4.

12. William Howe Downes, "The Ten Painters," *Boston Evening Transcript*, May 9, 1908, p. 2.

13. "New Art Salon without a Jury," *New York Herald*, May 15, 1907.

14. James B. Townsend, " 'The Eight' Arrive." Loose clipping from the archives of the Pennsylvania Academy of the Fine Arts.

15. "Growing Pains of American Art," *Current Literature* 44 (April 1908), pp. 394, 397.

16. In 1996 Academy curator Sylvia Yount and art historian Elizabeth Johns organized *To Be Modern, American Encounters with Cézanne and Company*, an exhibition that partially re-created the 1921 *Exhibition of Paintings and Drawings Showing the Later Tendencies in Art*. In the accompanying catalogue, their essays present a wider cultural context for the three pivotal Academy exhibitions of the 1920s and clarify the impact they had on the modernist art world.

17. Cheryl Leibold, "A History of the Annual Exhibitions of the Pennsylvania Academy of the Fine Arts: 1914–1968," *The Annual Exhibition Record of the Pennsylvania Academy of the Fine Arts, 1914–1968*, ed. Peter Hastings Falk (Madison, CT: Sound View Press, 1989), p. 25.

18. Ronald DeGraw, "Visited by 173,000," *Philadelphia Inquirer*, November 27, 1966.

19. "222 Works by Andrew Wyeth," *Today's Art*, January 1967, p. 12.

20. Edward J. Sozanski, "Horace Pippin, Folk Artist and Storyteller," *Philadelphia Inquirer*, January 30, 1994, p. H1.

21. Sylvia Yount, "Day Dreams: The Art of Maxfield Parrish," in *Maxfield Parrish, 1870–1966* (New York: Harry N. Abrams, 1999), p. 15.

22. Holland Cotter, "Lush Idylls in Never-Never Land," *New York Times*, June 18, 1999, p. E29.

23. "Growing Pains of American Art," *Current Literature* 44 (April 1908).

24. *In This Academy* (Philadelphia: The Pennsylvania Academy of the Fine Arts, 1976), p. 6.

*Nicolai Cikovsky, Jr.*

# Painting for the Many:
# American Art during the Nineteenth Century

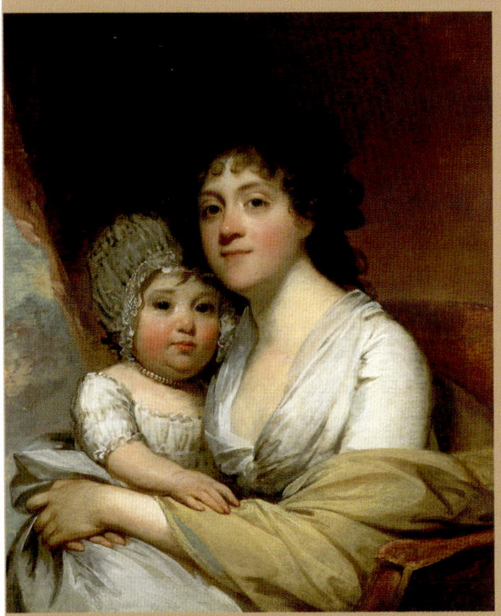



Gilbert Stuart (1755–1828)
*Mrs. Samuel Gatliff and Daughter Elizabeth*, ca. 1798
Oil on canvas, 29¼ x 24 inches
Pennsylvania Academy of the Fine Arts,
Bequest of Dr. Ferdinand Campbell Stewart, 1899.9.2

**OPPOSITE**

William Sidney Mount, *The Painter's Triumph*
(detail, fig. 17)

In the first half of the nineteenth century, nationalism guided the enterprise of American painting. In the United States, more than elsewhere in the Western world, it was believed that the more or less consciously conceived and acted upon political, social, and cultural circumstances of American existence should shape the country's art. National consciousness, moreover, stimulated and gave coherent purpose to the growth of American artistic culture in ways greater than found in Canada, South America, or Australia, where such a consciousness was slower to develop.

Just what form artistic Americanness should take, however, was a problem to which there was no simple answer. Neither the history nor theory of art provided guidance for what kind of art could or should be made in America's unprecedented conditions of republican government and democratic society. Nothing directed what subjects would be most fitting nor what language of style should be used to depict them.

How seriously problematic this was can be measured by the unusually high rate of disappointment among those artists who in the early years of the new republic first coped with what nationality—and not merely nationhood—required of them, at least among those not content, like Gilbert Stuart (fig. 14), to paint portraits in the rich tradition of British portraiture. John Trumbull, Washington Allston (fig. 2), John Vanderlyn, and Samuel F. B. Morse were all thwarted in their ambitions and embittered by failure. "Better learn to make shoes or dig potatoes than to become a painter in this country," Trumbull advised an aspiring artist.[1] Morse, after years of unremitting disappointment, gave up art for the more practical field of invention, where with the telegraph he achieved the fame that painting never brought him.

The circumstances in which these artists found themselves in democratic and republican America were utterly different than the artistic culture they had known in Europe or gleaned from the history of art. Deeply embedded in their artistic inheritance were notions of the nobility and idealism of subject matter and style that, in the learning and sophistication they demanded of their audience, were incompatible with and even hostile to the political, social, and economic order of republican democracy. An almost pathetic example of how remote this generation of artists could sometimes be from what was artistically suitable in republican America was the fact that Washington Allston proposed the subject of the *Three Maries at the Tomb* as a theme for a mural in the U.S. Capitol.

As strange or unpalatable as their new cultural and political circumstances may have been, these artists attempted, if only grudgingly, to accommodate them. Trumbull, for example, painted subjects of national history like the *Declaration of Independence* (which did become a Capitol mural). He and Vanderlyn painted episodes from the Revolutionary War, Morse painted the interior of the old House of Representatives as a symbol of republican governance (fig. 15),

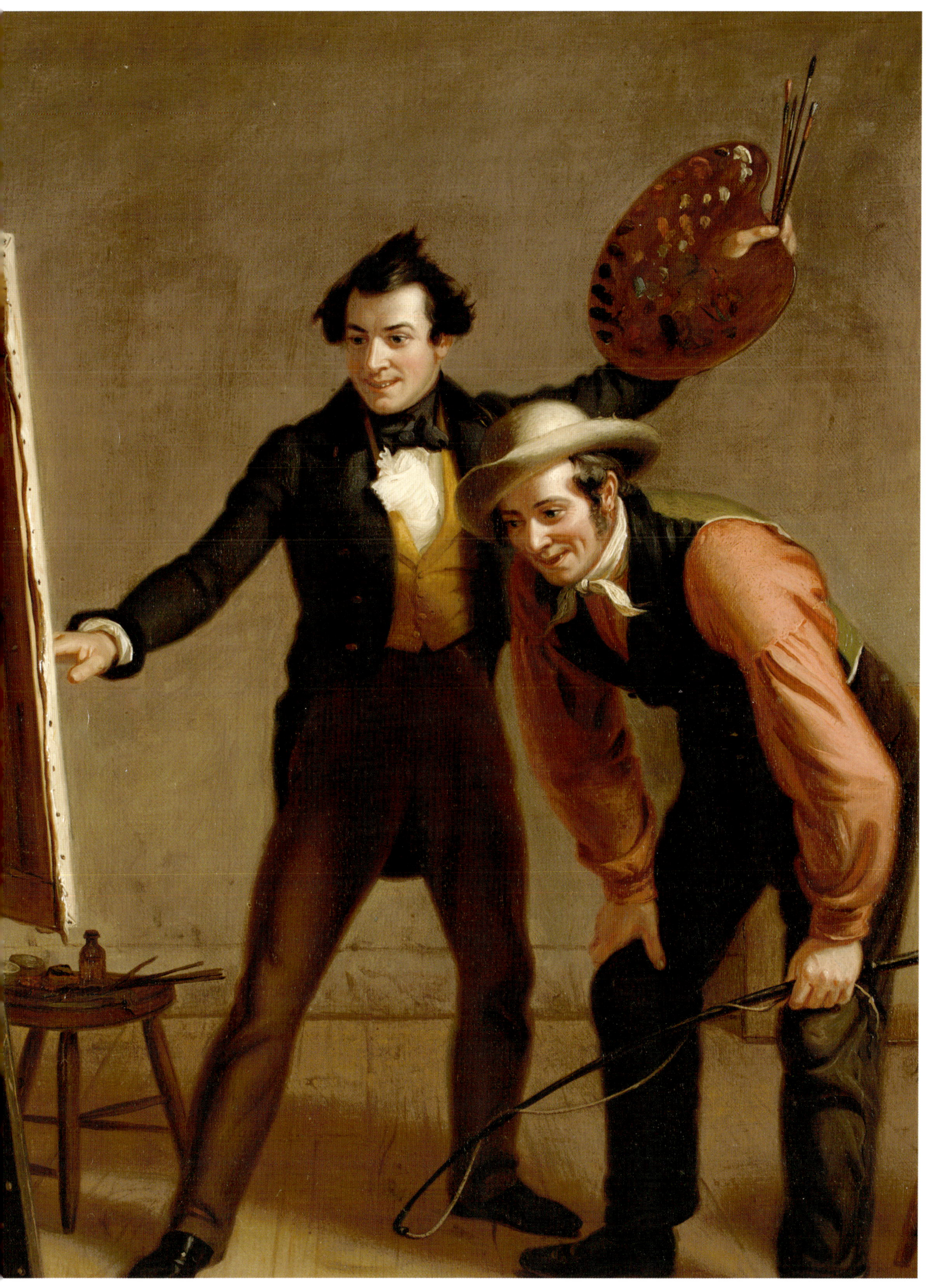

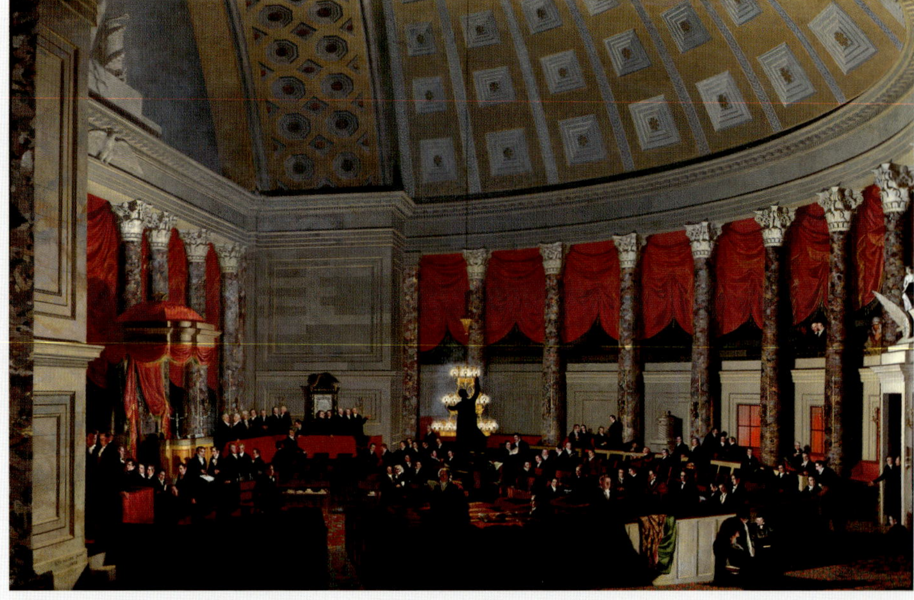

and Trumbull and Vanderlyn both painted what was already by the turn of the eighteenth century the canonically national landscape subject: Niagara Falls.

In addition to exploring such subjects of readily legible nationalism, artists of that generation tried their hand at styles of painting or exhibitions that were concessions to democratized taste and understanding. To do so they borrowed from low or popular art in various ways, as when both Trumbull and Vanderlyn painted panoramas.

Invented in the 1790s, panoramas were large, continuous, horizontal scroll-like images designed to be exhibited on the walls of circular buildings. By spatially filling the viewer's field of vision and by temporally "unfolding" for the viewer who followed the pictures around their exhibition space, panoramas were remarkably convincing, almost cinematic illusions. Their success depended chiefly on the extent of their physical and intellectual accessibility to all classes of spectators. Central to their popular appeal was the fact that they didn't require familiarity with the learned subjects and protocols of high art. When Morse painted *The House of Representatives* (fig. 15) and *Gallery of the Louvre*—these were not strictly panoramic, but they were painted on panoramic scale and strove in their style for a high degree of illusionism—he was appropriating that format's essential popular appeal. He also showed them in the kind of public exhibitions that panorama painters typically used to attract large popular audiences.

The artist who seems to have most purposely and persistently practiced a form of popular art at this time was Raphaelle Peale of Philadelphia. He painted still lifes (fig. 16), but as any serious artist knew at the turn of the eighteenth century, practicing this genre was to deliberately ignore the fact that still life was ranked lowest on the scale of artistic significance; thus he openly flouted the received artistic opinion. Still lifes were scorned because of their commonplace and unedifying subjects, as well as for their stylistic language of deceptive illusionism. In the art criticism of the time, such imitation was routinely referred to as "servile" and "mechanic" to characterize it as something made by servants and mechanics for an artistically illiterate audience, and to make it a popular style. So when artists who knew their art theory, such as Raphaelle Peale and Samuel Morse, painted illusionistically, it must have been with a clear sense of illusionism's democratic legibility.

About the time Raphaelle Peale died in 1825, clearer and more confident forms of national and democratic art were taking shape in America. That year Thomas Cole exhibited several landscapes in New York that caught the eye of John Trumbull and other young painters, establishing Cole as one of the most influential artists of early-nineteenth-century America. Landscape was Cole's subject—his only subject, and not, as it had been for Trumbull, Vanderlyn, or Allston, one subject among others. And Cole knew that his subject was a conventionally inferior one but one he pursued in an almost revolutionary way, to challenge and overturn the accepted ordering of the subjects of art.

Cole invented American landscape painting, and in doing so, he virtually invented American painting. He was the first to see that the special features of the American landscape formed a collective metaphor for America itself. "The most impressive characteristic of American scenery is its wildness," Cole proclaimed.[2] He saw that its Edenic newness and the heroic scale and uncorrupted purity of its virgin wilderness were the background against which America's redemptory historical mission was to be enacted and its national destiny fulfilled. Landscape was a field of unlimited future where, as Cole said, "mighty deeds shall be done"[3] (plate 5). He recognized it as a rich and deeply meaningful subject that was as elevating and inspiring as human history itself. It was largely due to Cole that this belief became as strongly orthodox, at least among Americans, as the one it superseded. Cole also understood that landscape was an inherently democratic subject, one that was the common property of all Americans. "Its beauty, its magnificence, its sublimity" were, Cole said, "an unfailing fountain of intellectual enjoyment, where all may drink."[4]

A whole school of landscape painters modeled itself on his example. Eventually named the Hudson River School, after the place Cole had identified, discovered, and sanctioned for artistic use, it was centered on the Hudson, as Cole himself had been, and its members repeatedly painted the subjects it supplied with a scale of vision, and often in the stylistic language, he had invented. When Cole's pupil Frederic Edwin Church built the house and studio he called "Olana" on the banks of the Hudson, he located it facing west, toward Cole's beloved Catskills and opposite Cole's house and studio. Church's younger contemporary Sanford Gifford was born near Olana, upriver in the town of Hudson. Out of his great admiration for Cole, Gifford roamed and painted the Catskills that Cole had made an almost sacred site for American landscape painters (plate 2). Jasper Cropsey also honored Cole, as Church had done, by building a house and studio on the Hudson, and in another way by openly and unabashedly imitating Cole's style, as if in that way he might share in Cole's achievement and proclaim his intimate



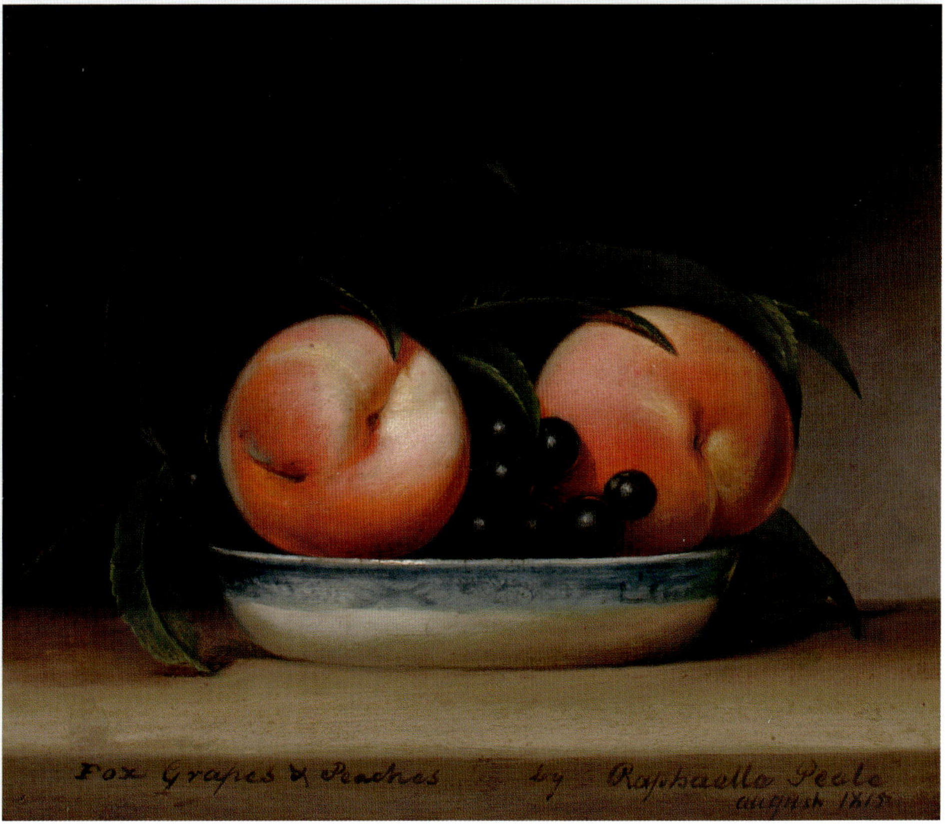

association with it (plate 18). Cole's example was instrumental in transforming his older contemporary Asher B. Durand from an engraver, figure painter, and portraitist into a landscape
painter who, after Cole's death in 1848, became the leader of the Hudson River School. There
are many such examples of Cole's inspirational power.

Cole and the artistic generation he inspired were clear about two things. One was the originality
of their invention and promulgation of a new kind of landscape. The other was how crucially
this depended on the novelty of American nature itself, on what Durand called "the virgin
charms of our native-land." As he asked rhetorically, "Where should this kind of painting
advance if not in this country?...Why should not the American landscape painter, in accor-
dance with the principle of self-government, boldly originate a high and independent style,
based on his native resources?"[5] As an example of the depth of this dependency, when
Worthington Whittredge, a slightly older contemporary of Church, Gifford, and Cropsey,
returned to America in 1859 after a decade abroad, he knew as though from some national
instinct or inbred national artistic ideology that in order to be able to "produce something new
and which might claim to be inspired by my home surroundings" he needed to immerse himself in American nature.[6] "I hid myself for months in the recesses of the Catskills,"[7] knowing
instinctively and ideologically that it was there where American nature could be experienced
most intensely and intimately.

However, the Hudson Valley and Catskill Mountains were not the only subjects for the generation of the Hudson River School. Its members traveled and painted in many other places—
Cropsey in England and Italy; Gifford in England, France, Switzerland, Italy, Greece, and Egypt;
Church in South America, the Arctic, the Near East, and Greece. No matter how widely they
traveled, however, the Hudson River and its tutelary deity, Thomas Cole, always remained their
inspirational center of gravity.

Not all American landscape painters were as centered, nor was the enterprise of landscape
quite as monolithic, as this might suggest. John F. Kensett worked in upper New York State
and in interior and coastal New England, especially Newport, Rhode Island (plate 11). Albert
Bierstadt (plate 14) and Thomas Moran found the subjects for which they are most admired in
the newly opened American Far West, though they painted elsewhere. Fitz Hugh Lane found
his subjects in his native New England; Martin Johnson Heade found his inspiration up and
down the East Coast, from New England to Florida, as well as in the Caribbean and Brazil.

Nor were these artists as bound by the stylistic example of Thomas Cole as their more orthodox Hudson River School colleagues had been. Bierstadt was influenced by European art and
the Alpine landscape, Moran (plate 29) by the English landscape painter J.M.W. Turner; Lane
painted with an almost classical precision and restraint (plate 6). But simply by being landscape
painters, in one essential respect they shared the legacy that Cole bequeathed to nearly all
American painters at work in the first part of the nineteenth century.

Yet there were some painters who took their subjects not from inanimate nature but from
human nature, making it their task to depict the life and types, the doings and the dress, the
modes and manners of American life. The two greatest of these were William Sidney Mount
and George Caleb Bingham, both younger contemporaries of Thomas Cole. Mount found his
subjects in the commonplaces of rural life in and about his home at Stony Brook, on New
York's Long Island; Bingham found his on the Western frontier in Missouri and on the
Mississippi and Missouri Rivers. Qualities and characteristics of place mattered greatly to both
of them, but their overarching subject was the workings and requirements of American
democracy. This subject was laid out most clearly in Bingham's election pictures, which depicted
the institution that more than any other lay at the heart of democratic self-government.

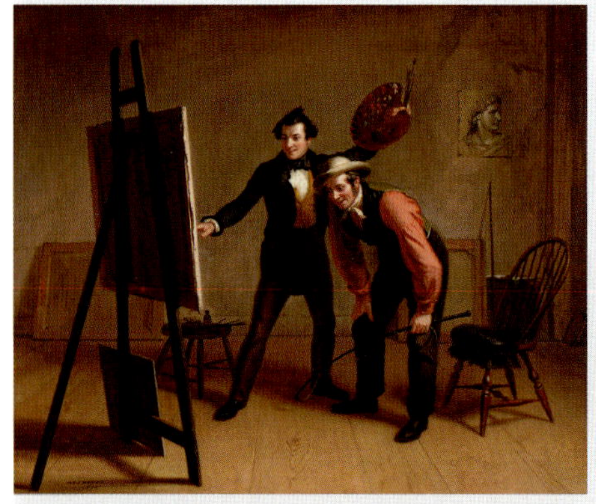

FIG. 17
William Sidney Mount (1807–1868)
*The Painter's Triumph*, 1838
Oil on canvas, 19½ x 23⁹⁄₁₆ inches
Pennsylvania Academy of the Fine Arts, Bequest of
Henry C. Carey (The Carey Collection), 1879.8.18

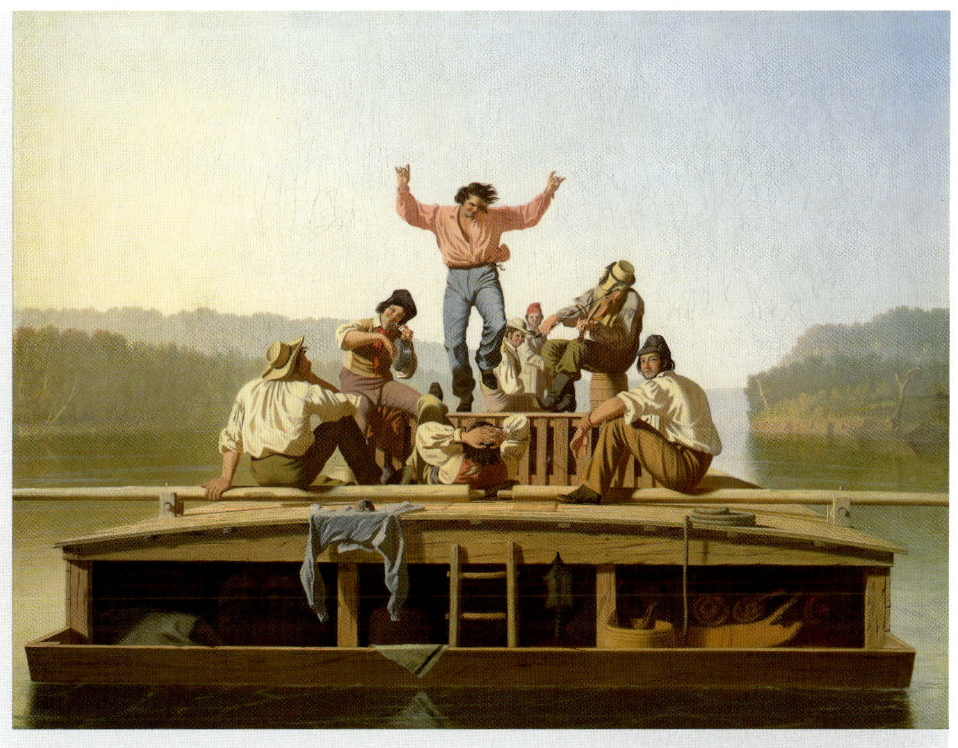

Mount was clearest about its requirements, particularly about the essential democratic obligation to be understood: "Never paint for the few, but for the many," he wrote.[8] "Paint such
pictures as speak at once to the spectator, scenes that are most popular, that will be understood
on the instant"[9] (fig. 17). In the case of both Mount and Bingham, that was a matter not only
of painting popular subjects, but of painting them in such a way that they would be the most
visually and imaginatively accessible. Mount implied that when he said of his pictures that one
could step inside their frame and walk about in them. Bingham, too, used form and gesture to
produce often urgent continuities between the viewer and the picture space that made the
latter almost physically inhabitable (fig. 18).

The Civil War and the decade of the 1860s were as much a watershed in American art as in
American life, one that sharply and irrevocably separated one epoch from another. It was a
profoundly disturbed time, one of uncertainty and tension, complexity and ambiguity, irony
and doubt. Yet for those reasons it was a period when things that had not been conceivable
before could be possible or necessary. The confident certainties and simple pieties that had
previously guided artistic enterprise were no longer operable. The limitations of earlier
American artistic culture became starkly apparent, as if with a sudden loss of innocence artists
came to see, for example, that the faithful depiction of American nature no longer self-
evidently guaranteed important art or national art. They could no longer see that landscape
painting was necessarily the American subject nor that the only material a true American artist
needed was what America itself supplied.

During the 1860s certain painters—although they remained landscape painters, if with flagging
commitment—began to regard landscape in a more critical light and with greater sophistication
and complexity. Martin Johnson Heade was a younger contemporary of Church, Gifford, and
Cropsey who matured artistically in the 1860s, much later than they had. But perhaps it was
only in this new climate where he could mature. Perhaps not until then his otherwise eccentric
and abnormal landscapes of lurid sunsets and eerily placed haystacks enshrouded by the dense
atmosphere of tidal marshes, or his seascapes with portentous black skies and moods of
ominous stillness, could finally become intelligible (fig. 19). And it was in the climate of that
decade that the simpler and more normative landscapes of the Hudson River School, an
expression of more settled times, were increasingly not intelligible.

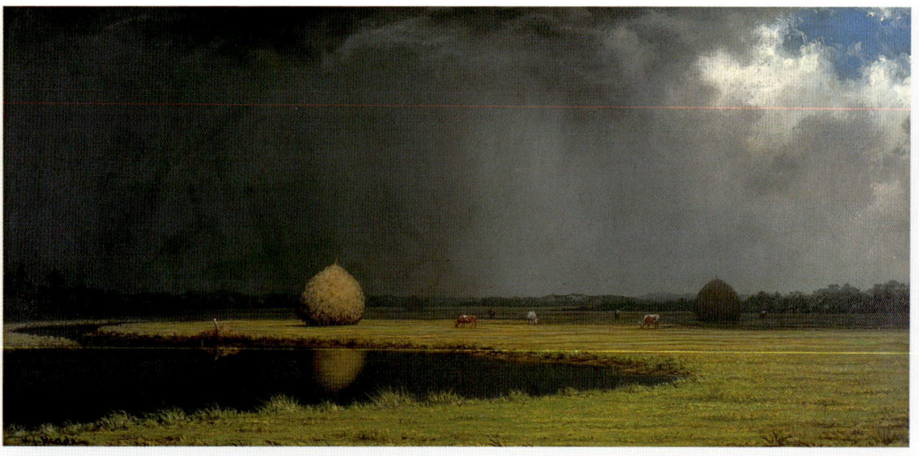

Another indication that in the 1860s American artists were beginning to lose their unquestioned devotion to landscape is seen in Heade's project of painting the hummingbirds of Brazil (plate 27). These paintings belong among the many nineteenth-century classificatory documents of natural history, the most famous being John James Audubon's *Birds of America*. Heade too had intended to publish his paintings, but he never did, so they survive instead as still lifes. The fact that he made so many of them, over an extended period of time, indicates that they were not an aberrant artistic undertaking but an essential part of his artistic production that had—as it could not have had before the 1860s—a weight and value equal to landscape.

George Inness, like Heade, first found his artistic voice and audience in the decade of the 1860s, and, like Heade, he deviated, though perhaps even more openly, from the accepted norms of American artistic behavior. He eagerly went to Europe (more than once), where he was openly influenced by what he saw, at a time when this was widely held to be an unnatural and unnational activity: "Go not abroad then in search of material for the exercise of your pencil, while the virgin charms of our native land have claims on your deepest affections,"[10] said Arthur B. Durand. Inness was one of the first Americans to absorb the broadly and suggestively painted landscapes of the French Barbizon School, particularly those of its most radical member, Théodore Rousseau. Following Barbizon examples, Inness developed a stylistic language that placed pictorial values over descriptive ones and the expressive powers of color and boldly applied pigment above the kind of accurate representation that had been the chief aim and almost the duty of the Hudson River School. He did so to such a radical extent that in the 1860s one of his works could be described, in terminology that could be applied to abstract art, as "more of a painting than a picture"[11] (plate 13).

If Inness's revisionist purpose was apparent in his style, it was even clearer in some of his subjects. By painting railroad trains—which had been for Cole the worst defilers of natural purity—puffing through cultivated fields (plate 7) or past the stumps of fallen trees or by depicting an artist—surely himself or his surrogate—painting in the midst of felled trees and before a pile of cut logs, Inness questioned the claims for the virtues of unspoiled wilderness that had for years been held sacrosanct by the Hudson River School. In landscapes that recorded every act of man, he painted the new civilized landscape of a less pure but more humanized America.

By publicly criticizing "the prevailing tendency of American landscape painting" for "what is *called* the real," by which is meant the local and particular, Inness tackled the American landscape tradition head-on. Landscape painting, he believed, did not consist of the mere delineation of places but freely used nature to express the "sentiment and feeling which flow from the mind and heart of the artist."[12] He argued through his art that an interpretive and self-expressive individuality was an alternative to the realism, localism, and particularism that had once prevailed in American landscape. His argument was increasingly heeded in the emotional climate of the 1860s, and which he expressed with a subtlety and allusiveness that both suited and was nourished by it. When Inness died, greatly honored, at the end of the nineteenth century, his contemporaries Church, Cropsey, Gifford, and Bierstadt were all but forgotten names and the Hudson River School was an irrelevant artistic relic. The form American landscape painting took was the one Inness had established a generation earlier (fig. 20).

The artist who in the 1860s made the most decisive break with what had gone before him was Winslow Homer. No other artist embraced as openly and intelligently the modern America that was formed during that decade, and no other artist saw as clearly nor argued as convincingly through his art that the most fitting and proper expression of modern America was no longer landscape but the human figure. The Civil War gave special urgency to the depiction of the figure. The canonical American landscape of the unpopulated wilderness could not express the resounding moral issues and human values that the war brought into such sharp and painful focus. Homer immersed himself in this intensely modern subject. He was by far the greatest interpreter of the war, but the contemporaneity he expressed also secured him as the greatest interpreter of modern America for more than a decade after the war ended. He painted figures —women as often as men—dressed in modern fashions, engaged in modern fads (new activities such as croquet or tourism), visiting newly popular places (the Adirondacks, the White Mountains, or Long Branch, New Jersey), and as perhaps the most salient types of newness, he painted children—boys and girls on farms or by the seashore, doing chores, going to school, idling, playing, or making mischief (plate 16).

The nationalism of Homer's art was particularly legible when he turned to the subject of children, but it was also evident in his style. From virtually the beginning of his career, but especially in the 1860s, his critics commented on his breadth, brevity, and persistent disdain for the conventional niceties of a painting's finish. While some voiced disappointment or disapproval, others perceptively saw signs of nationalism in the roughness and unpolished directness of his stylistic language. This was recognized above all in his watercolors, which expressed the "freshness, the crudity, and the solid worth of American civilization."[13] In mid-career, disillusioned by the rampant corruption of the Gilded Age that followed the Civil War and the discredit it cast on its ideals and on the nation, Homer changed his artistic course. He withdrew from the depiction of public life and turned increasingly inward to give form to more private aspects. For the last thirty years or so of his life, he worked from a studio on the coast of Maine, where he lived alone for much of the year, purposely remote from society and in closely guarded privacy and interiority. His inwardness was most profoundly and movingly expressed in the series of large, serious, enigmatic, and often brooding pictures that he painted in the final years of his life (plate 31).


George Inness (1825–1894)
*Woodland Scene*, 1891
Oil on canvas, 30 x 45 inches
Pennsylvania Academy of the Fine Arts,
Gift of John Frederick Lewis, Jr., 1954.22.3

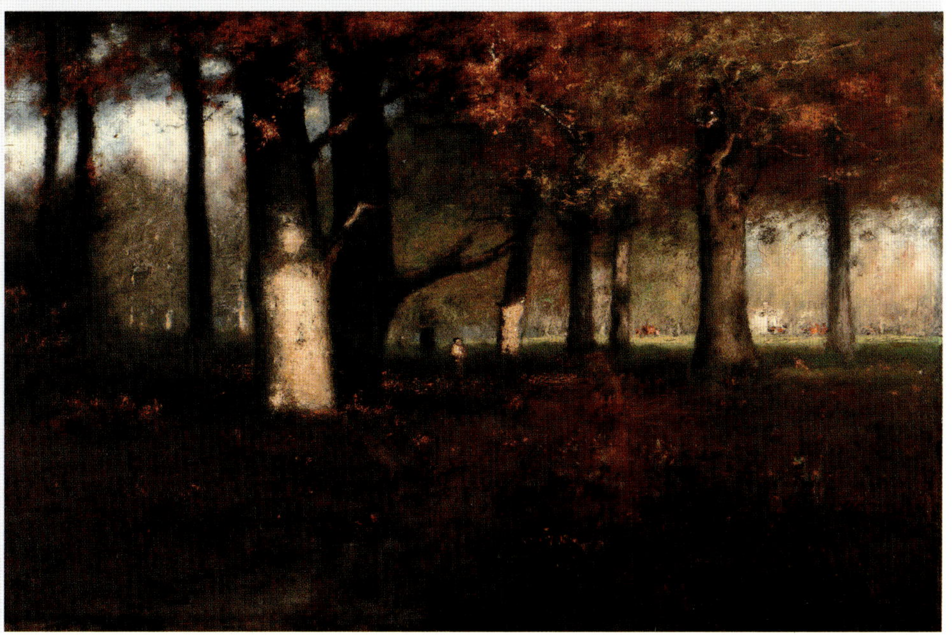

It was only after the Civil War that the earlier generation of American landscape painters came to be called the Hudson River School. It was a term of derision, intended as a critique of what postwar eyes saw to have been the provincialism of earlier American art. To shed that burden, American artists, with an almost audible collective sigh of relief, embraced cosmopolitanism as eagerly as they had once embraced insularity.

James Abbott McNeill Whistler, Homer's slightly older contemporary, led the way. Enacting one of his central tenets that art is of no nationality, he had gone to Europe even before the Civil War, settling in England and often visiting France, but never returning to America. Others soon followed him. The younger Thomas Eakins of Philadelphia studied in Paris and Spain for three years. He returned home and settled in Philadelphia for the rest of his life, but his experiences in France would lastingly remain his greatest intellectual and artistic influences. His French masters Gérôme and Bonnat shaped his style, and French scientific positivism, at the height of its influence when Eakins was in France, shaped his artistic making and thinking in ways that were essentially European, despite the fact that after his death he was cast as the most American of American artists (fig. 21).

Eakins's slightly younger contemporary William Merritt Chase best expressed the cosmopolitan longing of most American artists following the Civil War when he said that he would rather go to Europe than go to heaven. Chase did not become an expatriate, as did his sometime friend Whistler. But when he returned to America, he brought as much of Europe with him as he could. He lavishly filled his New York studio with imported art and artifacts, and he unashamedly borrowed artistic language from European models, especially from his idols the seventeenth-century painters Diego Velázquez and Frans Hals. Because he was an immensely popular teacher, he vividly represented European culture to many young American artists (plate 30).

No one embodied the cosmopolitan ideal as well as John Singer Sargent. Born to expatriate American parents in Florence, he spent much of his life traveling widely in Europe—Venice was one of his favorite places—and found his chief artistic exemplars among European artists. He too admired Velázquez and Hals (plate 20). But commissions for portraits and murals frequently brought him to America, and by moving so easily between Europe and America, he blurred, if not erased, the lines of nationality in both his life and his art and showed his countrymen (he always maintained his American citizenship), even more than Whistler had done, how freely, largely, and even imperially an American artist—the contemporary of Theodore Roosevelt—might move in the world.

American artists discovered Impressionism about 1890, almost twenty years after it was first developed in France. In its early French form, Impressionism stressed the rigorously objective depiction of transient sensations and effects of light and color, rendered though systems of broken brushstrokes. By 1890 it had developed into an international style that encompassed a variety of newer and diverse forms, which is what Americans first encountered and experimented with. Mary Cassatt used the broken brushwork of Impressionism but emphasized draftsmanship and linear design (at which she was wonderfully adept), reflecting the form of Impressionism practiced by her friend Edgar Degas. Childe Hassam's Impressionism was, in a restrained way, the most French in its palette and handling of paint (plate 26). William Merritt Chase, on the other hand, was more strongly influenced by the more delicate and almost brittle manner of the Spanish artist Mario Fortuny, while John Twachtman was decisively influenced, as were many other Americans, by the delicately tonal allusiveness of Whistler (plate 15). By taking Fortuny and Whistler as their models, they signaled that Impressionism was no longer ruled from France as it once had been. Theodore Robinson, although he was close to the Impressionist Claude Monet during the four years he was his neighbor in Giverny, painted

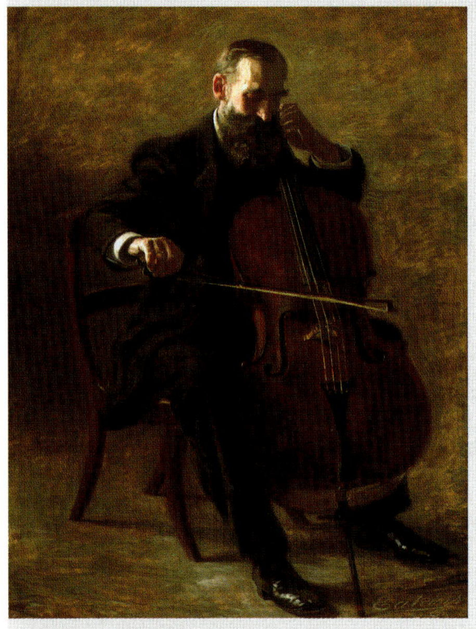


Thomas Eakins (1844–1916)
*The Cello Player* (Rudolph Hennig, 1845–1904), 1896
Oil on canvas, 64¼ x 48⅛ inches
Pennsylvania Academy of the Fine Arts,
Joseph E. Temple Fund, 1897.3

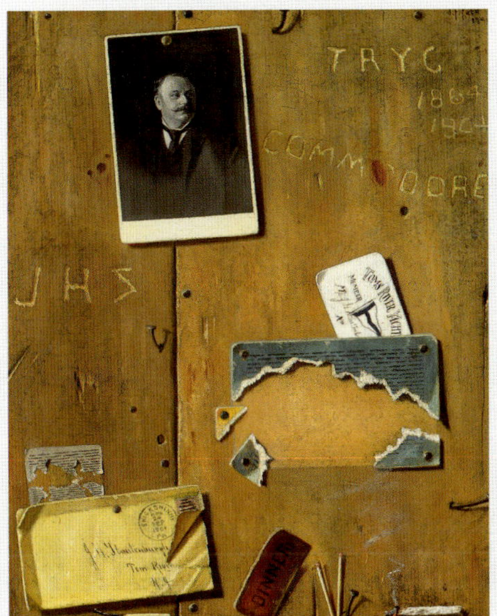



**FIG 22**
John Frederick Peto (1854–1907)
*Toms River Yacht Club*, 1904
Oil on canvas, 20 x 16 inches
Pennsylvania Academy of the Fine Arts, Purchased with
Funds from the Bequest of Henry C. Gibson, 1989.1

with rigorously structured patterns of design and brushwork that were less Impressionist than Post-Impressionist—more like Cézanne and Seurat than Monet.

Impressionism still carried an aroma of novelty and daring; that was surely one of its greatest attractions. Particularly as the twentieth century approached, and particularly in America, to be identified with Impressionism was to wear the badge of modernity.

The epidemic of *trompe l'oeil* ("fool the eye") still-life painting in the late nineteenth century stands out with curious singularity amid the wave of cosmopolitanism, and even more the stirrings of modernity that overtook America at that time. It did so in two ways. One was that it was a phenomenon with no counterpart in the styles and subjects of contemporary European painting. Another was that successful *trompe l'oeil* illusionistic deceptions depended on close imitation that was utterly antithetical to the allusive and suggestive qualities central to so much other late-nineteenth-century painting, much of it broadly influenced by Impressionism.

This singularity does not, however, imply that *trompe l'oeil* was an American invention. On the contrary, its sources—which go as far back as antiquity—had a recent legacy in seventeenth-century Dutch still lifes and the later Enlightenment fascination with such simulacra as panoramas and mechanical automata. But there had been an active tradition of *trompe l'oeil* still-life painting in America, for the paintings of such artists as William Michael Harnett, John Frederick Peto (fig. 22), and John Haberle (plate 24) seem by certain similarities of style to have descended from the illusionistic still-life style of Raphaelle Peale that had flourished in Philadelphia among other members of the Peale family earlier in the nineteenth century.

Both Harnett and Peto had Philadelphia connections, suggesting that a tradition of *trompe l'oeil* painting survived there into the late nineteenth century. But it is also conceivable that the popular appeal and accessibility of *trompe l'oeil* subjects—indicated in one way by the fact that such paintings were more often seen in shop windows or barrooms than more rarified "artistic" spaces—continued in the late nineteenth century. Those qualities that made such an extreme realism so accessible were also the features that made it so suited to the taste and understanding of republican America. It is fitting that with the number of styles and movements that took place in nineteenth-century America, art would come full circle at the end of that century to the naturalism of the Peale family heritage.

**NOTES**


1.  Asher B. Durand, "Letters on Landscape Painting" (1855), in John W. McCoubrey, ed., *American Art 1700–1960: Sources and Documents* (Englewood Cliffs, NJ: Prentice-Hall, 1965), p. 113.

2.  Thomas Cole, "Essay on American Scenery" (1835), in John W. McCoubrey, ed., *American Art 1700–1960: Sources and Documents* (Englewood Cliffs, NJ: Prentice-Hall, 1965), p. 102.

3.  Ibid., p. 109.

4.  Ibid., pp. 98, 99.

5.  Durand, "Letters on Landscape Painting," pp. 112, 113.

6.  Worthington Whittredge, "Autobiography," in John W. McCoubrey, ed., *American Art 1700–1960: Sources and Documents* (Englewood Cliffs, NJ: Prentice-Hall, 1965), p. 119.

7.  Ibid., p. 119.

8.  Diary of William Sidney Mount, entry of February 1856, archives of the Long Island Museum of American Art, History and Carriages, Stony Brook, New York (formerly the Stony Brook Museum).

9.  Ibid., entry of July 1, 1850.

10. Durand, "Letters on Landscape Painting," p. 111.

11. "Some Living American Painters: Critical Conversations by Howe and Torrey," *Art Interchange* 23 (April 1894), p. 102.

12. See Nicolai Cikovsky, Jr., "George Inness: Sense or Sensibility," in *George Inness: Presence of the Unseen* (Montclair, NJ: Montclair Art Museum, 1994), p. 19.

13. Samuel G. [Green] W. [Walter] Benjamin, *Art in America: A Critical and Historical Sketch* (New York: Harper, 1880), p. 117.

*Robert Rosenblum*

# American Painting in the Twentieth Century: Ruptures and Continuities



Traditionally, the history of twentieth-century American art is split into two separate parts, B.C. and A.D. In the wake of the apocalyptic conclusion of World War II, the great divide is the advent of Abstract Expressionism, conventionally celebrated as the first emergence of an American art that finally freed itself from the presumed provincialism of being a minor outpost of European modernism. The sense was that, at last, with the ongoing wartime migrations of European refugees, the mantle of progressive art had crossed the Atlantic in 1945, and the first era of American supremacy had begun. In fact, the signature styles of these revolutionary artists seemed to proclaim a total rebirth of painting. One saw a vertical line stretching across a field of color, tinted clouds afloat in a void, chaotic fields of oceanic turbulence, vast expanses of pigment that seemed to map a newly discovered continent. These were abstract images that might have illustrated a new version of the Book of Genesis.

This reading of history is one, in fact, that is not only deeply embedded on this side of the ocean, where pre-1945 American art seems to belong to national history and post-1945 American art to international history, but even more so throughout the rest of the world. Whether in Asia or Europe, museums and private collections have abundant representations of the best American art of the last half-century, from Pollock to Koons; but with perhaps only one exception, Madrid's Museo Thyssen-Bornemisza, they draw absolute blanks on what happened between 1900 and 1945, not to mention the nineteenth century. This situation of both ignorance and indifference may well be changing slowly, given the recent enthusiastic European receptions of Edward Hopper and Georgia O'Keeffe (fig. 23) as well as of the awe-inspiring nineteenth-century landscapes now placed under the rubric of the "American Sublime." But for all practical purposes, the first half of the twentieth century is terra incognita abroad. Nevertheless, thanks to the huge international recognition of postwar American art, it may still seem peripheral to the grander accounts of the evolution of modern art. It is with *In Private Hands: 200 Years of American Painting*, this sweeping anthology of two centuries of American art that ignores the presumed rupture between the first and second halves of the last century, that we may begin to discern continuities that weave these parts together, as well as echoing back into the nineteenth century.

There are countless ways of pointing to recurrent forms and themes in American art, and the rich diversity of this bounty from American collections can open many fresh vistas. Think, for example, about the importance of the city, especially the grit and energy of New York, as an ongoing stimulus for twentieth-century artists. Here, around 1900, paintings shift drastically from the territory sighted in the most remote, unpolluted American landscapes, whether Albert Bierstadt's *Wind River Wyoming* (ca. 1870) (plate 14), with its sense of prehistoric sublimity; Thomas Moran's *Stranded Ship on East Hampton Beach* (1894–95) (plate 29), a far cry from the Hamptons beaches we know today; or Winslow Homer's moonlit view of unspoiled

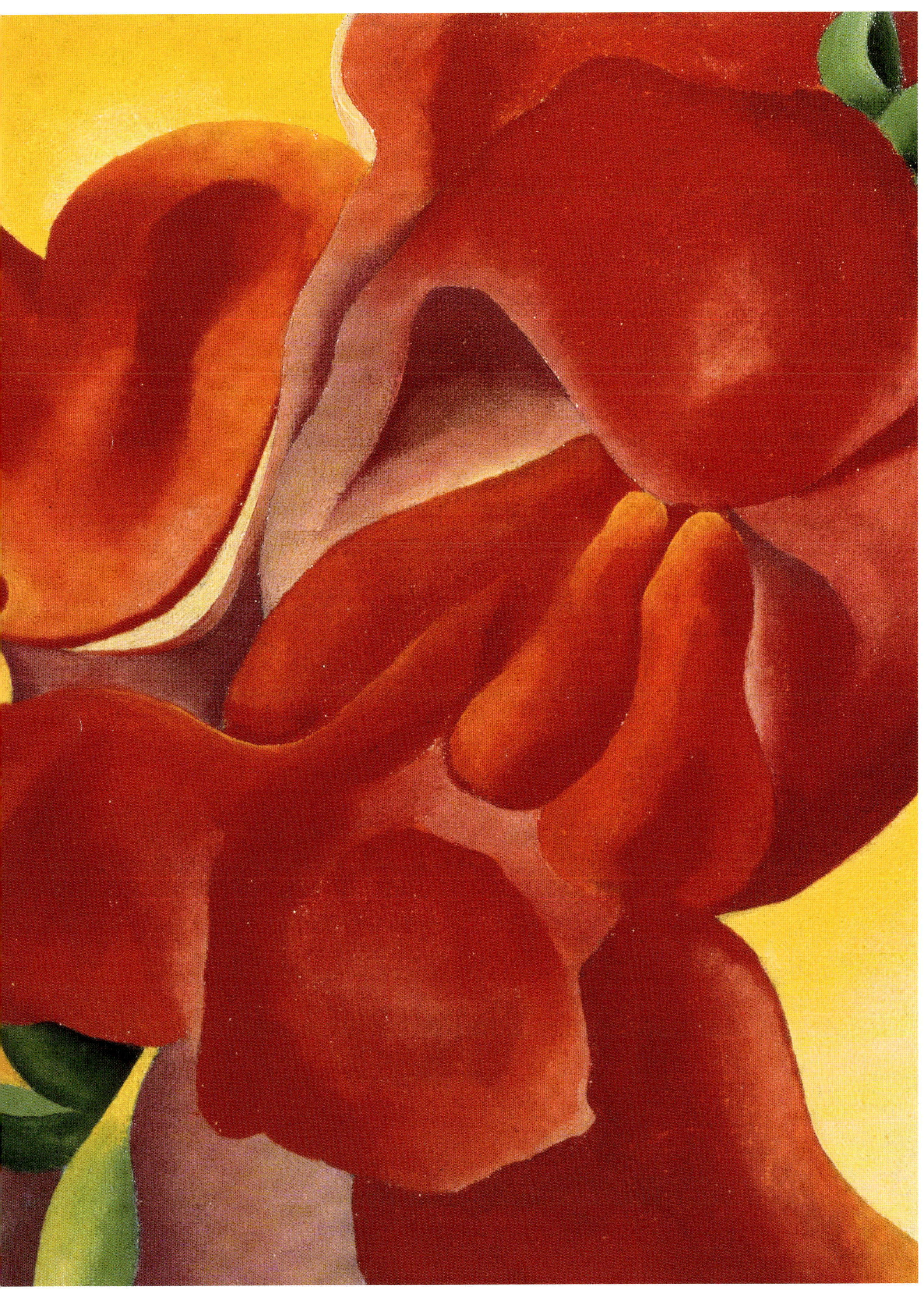

Canadian sea and rock, *Cape Trinity, Saguenay River Moonlight* (1904) (plate 31), with its sense of hermetic seclusion from the modern world.

But abruptly, in the same decade, these belated visions of a still primeval continent were countered by the excitement of the modern city, at first in the work of the Ashcan School, whose members reveled in glimpses of rough-and-tumble urban life. A perfect specimen is George Luks's *Thompson and Bleecker Streets* (ca. 1905) (plate 33), where we are totally immersed in the animated and regimented rhythms of Lower Manhattan. In the foreground a row of pushcarts, cropped left and right, rhymes perfectly with the diagonal axis of the urban buildings, whose geometric patterns of windows, shades, and awnings echo the city's gridiron plan. Cut off on top at the third or fourth story, they even close off any glimpse of the sky above, as if nature had been totally expelled from this urban vignette. On a more upwardly mobile urban level for the Ashcan School, which usually gravitated toward the seamier aspects of city life, there is also John Sloan's *Gray and Brass* (1907) (plate 34), whose arty Whistlerian title (named for color harmonies, not the subject) is countered by the overtly modern-age depiction of an automobile, a new symbol of technological progress that, in fact, would rapidly replace horses as the means of urban transportation. Before the speed-crazed Italian Futurists, there were surprisingly few paintings of automobiles, a fact that underlines Sloan's originality in his choice of such an untraditional theme from the modern city. And for another glimpse of upscale New York at the turn of the century, there is William Glackens's *Little May Day Procession* (ca. 1905) (plate 32), where well-heeled families in their Sunday best seem to reincarnate in Central Park the aristocratic garden parties familiar to such French Rococo masters as Watteau.

The artists of the Ashcan School who documented the high and low facts of New York, the ultimate symbol of the modern city, still worked in more traditional styles that seem compatible with their American Impressionist contemporaries, who generally preferred to escape from urban stress and disorder in favor of the pleasures of unspoiled landscapes and nostalgic survivors of the sweeping changes wrought by the wheels of industry. Such is the case in Childe Hassam's vision of a rural country fair in New England (1890) (plate 25), complete with a Colonial church; in Daniel Garber's view of a lovely tourist spot like *Frog Hollow* (1918) (plate 39), or in Theodore Robinson's summery record of low tide at the Riverside Yacht Club (1894) (plate 28). But a younger generation would absorb far more completely the new, pounding excitement of the city. Max Weber's youthful embrace of New York's teeming energies is now distilled in his fantasy of 1913 (plate 37), painted four years after his return from avant-garde Paris and in the same year that the Armory Show shocked the American art world with its latest news about the Cubists' and Futurists' reshuffling of reality. Here, a forceful conflict of abstract vertical planes thrusts upward from a distant ground like skyscrapers towering over the earthbound depths of the city streets, as if seen in an aerial view.

These clashing abstract rhythms of urban life could be further purified in other works in this exhibition by those younger Americans who explored fresh languages of modern art, Georgia O'Keeffe (fig. 23), and Charles Demuth. In her extreme polarity between paintings of the awesomely infinite landscapes of the American Southwest and her equal passion for painting the sublimities of Manhattan skyscrapers, O'Keeffe seesawed between nineteenth-century visions of sublime nature, as in *Birch and Pine Trees–Pink* (1925) (plate 44), and a twentieth-century fascination with the modernity of New York's no less fantastic heights and depths. In her *Black Spot No. 2* (1919) (plate 40), an abstraction reduced to near illegibility, evocations of her obsession with vast spaces, whether in the city or in nature, are glimmered, as a skyward bolt of black soars high above a curving vista of earth below. No less abstract a response to what often seemed in the 1920s the epitome of modern urban music is Demuth's *Jazz* (1921) (plate

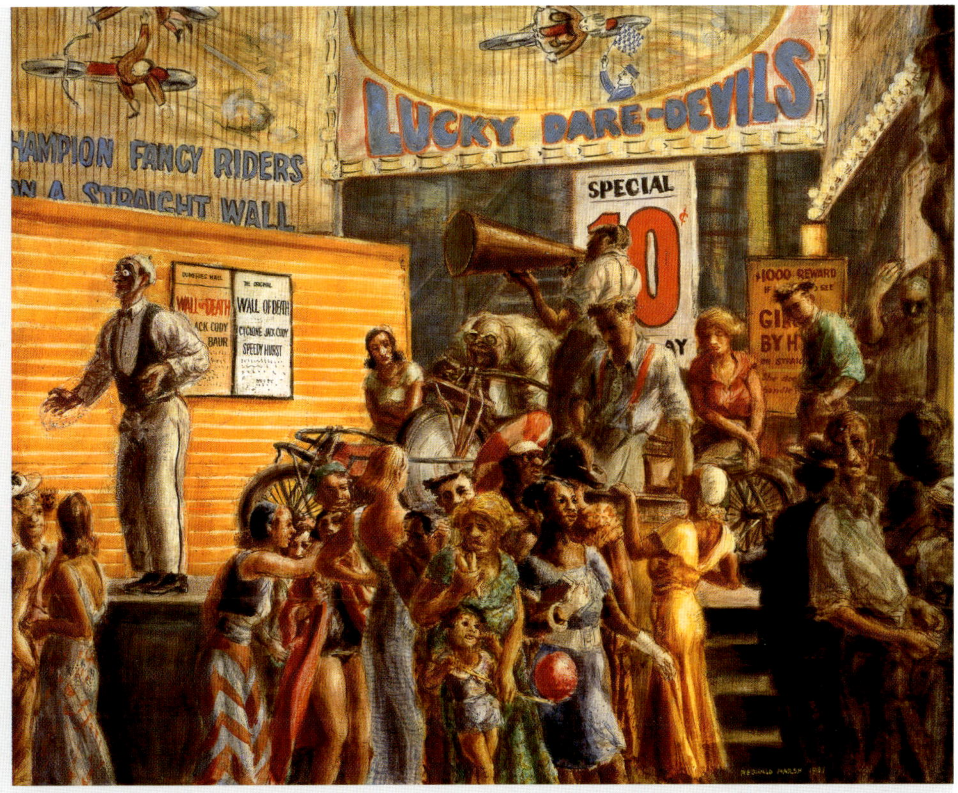

FIG. 24
Reginald Marsh (1898–1954)
*Lucky Daredevils* (*The Thrill of Death*), 1931
Egg tempera on panel, 30 x 36 inches
Pennsylvania Academy of the Fine Arts,
The Vivian O. and Meyer P. Potamkin Collection,
Bequest of Vivian O. Potamkin, 2003.1.6

41), which, like many twentieth-century paintings (such as Kandinsky's) attempts to translate pictorially the experience of the most abstract of the arts, music. Here the zigzagging lightning bolt (a counterpart to O'Keeffe's speeding rectangular trajectory) evokes the syncopated rhythms of jazz, a geometric patchwork quilt of bobbing, vibrant rhythms that prophesies Mondrian's own later infatuations with jazz, as exemplified in his *Broadway Boogie-Woogie* (1942–43, Museum of Modern Art, New York), painted in New York during the Dutch master's last years. The polarities of city and country, characteristic of O'Keeffe, are also apparent in the work of John Marin. His watercolor view of *Deer Isles, Islets, Maine* (1922) (plate 42), is exactly the kind of site that had earlier inspired Homer's confrontation with remote and savage nature. The work offers an upheaval of colliding, fractured planes that Marin had earlier used to seize the clashing energies of downtown Manhattan, whether the skyscraping heights of the new Woolworth Building or the agitated mixture of traffic and engineering that transformed the Brooklyn Bridge into a symbol of Machine Age speed and progress.

As for post-1945 American painters, life in New York continued to trigger more abstract responses. Franz Kline's *Untitled* oil painting on paper (1959) (plate 65) seems to carry on the legacy of Marin's style of crisscrossing velocities, a metaphor of the urban experience of crushing girders and intersecting streets jammed with cars and people that the artist often made explicit in such titles as *New York, NY* or *Wanamaker Block*. This energetic chaos can also be found abundantly in Robert Rauschenberg's works, such as *Drawing III for 700th Birthday of Dante*—one of thirty-four drawings published seven hundred years after the writer's birth in 1265—that would offer an updated version of this medieval vision of hell (plate 73). Rauschenberg, in fact, translates the inferno's infinite density and chaos into the language of contemporary reality, jostling together dozens of news photos, ranging from political leaders to athletes, in the kind of urban confusion familiar to newspaper stands and city walls covered with ads and graffiti. Like Warhol, Rauschenberg worked from actual clippings, integrating them into the language of painting and forever blurring the boundaries between photography and presumably higher forms of art. In this case, the images from newspapers and magazines were fixed onto the drawing paper with a solvent, a variation of the silkscreen technique that Rauschenberg had explored in the 1950s. This medium became Andy Warhol's trademark in the 1960s, as seen in his *Sixteen Jackies* (1964) (plate 68). Here, a multitude of press images of

the first lady, whether smiling for the public or mourning, are presented as a combination of
the original black-and-white news photos and a melancholic veil of tinted blue, laid out like
photo-booth or paparazzi snapshots in a tidy grid that mirrors the geometries of the modern
world, whether of supermarket displays or the monotonous fenestration of high-rise buildings.

There were, of course, other, less radical ways of depicting urban life. Reginald Marsh, for one,
loved the more tawdry aspects of New York (fig. 24), whether vignettes of rowdy crowds at
Coney Island or, as in the picture here, *Gayety Burlesque* (1932) (plate 46), of the landmark
(Gaiety) theater, now demolished, on 46th Street and Broadway, where both the strippers and
the audience are in your face, a complete immersion in the seedy reality of lowbrow entertain-
ment. We can easily imagine that the same crowds have ended up in a local bar, continuing
their revelry, an image perfectly captured in Paul Cadmus's *Hinky Dinky Parley Voo* (1939)
(plate 50), where we are again forced to join the proletarian crush. And also from the
Depression years, we can glimpse another part of Manhattan, Jacob Lawrence's *Christmas in
Harlem* (1937) (plate 48), once more a confusion of urban detail, filled with anonymous locals
and, in the foreground, a customer carrying a shopping bag from which a pair of chicken feet
stick out, just bought at the butcher shop behind her, its window adorned with plucked chickens.
Unlike Marsh and Cadmus, Lawrence mixes his realist vignettes with a poster-flat Cubist style
of intersecting planes, similar to other American modernists' interpretations of Cubism, as
exemplified here by Stuart Davis's *Eye Level* (1951–54) (plate 59) and Charles Sheeler's
*Lunenburg* (1954) (plate 60). Lawrence's collage-style realism, like a patchwork quilt of particular observations, is also used by another African-American artist of the same generation,
Romare Bearden, whose *Morning* (1975) (plate 81), a glimpse of domesticity, is literally a
collage of pasted papers.

There are endless ways of finding connections and genealogical tables in this diverse cornucopia
of two centuries of American painting. For example, it might be noticed that Luminism, one of
the modes of mid-nineteenth-century painting often singled out as particularly American in
character, had a much later afterlife following World War II. So it is that the vast luminous
expanses of sea and sky, as depicted say in John Frederick Kensett's *Coastal Scene at Newport*
(1864) (plate 11), often seem reborn a century later. Milton Avery's *Birds over Sea* (1957) (plate
63), for example, similarly transports us to the brink of our earthbound world, where we face
the infinite vistas of sky and water. It is a vision of an immaterial landscape that, in fact, has a
close counterpart in the contemporaneous abstractions of Mark Rothko, whose horizontal
tiers of lambent, floating color closely mirror a structure familiar to Avery's work (fig. 25).

Or consider an astonishing painting by a major American modernist, Arthur Dove, an artist
often overlooked in accounts of abstract painting after 1945. His *Hardware Store* (1938) (plate
49) is a far cry from his usual attraction to mystical landscapes, but it equally introduces a
new language of molten organic forms that, among other things, contrasts sharply with the
hard-edged contours of, say, Stuart Davis. What Dove depicts here is, in fact, an unexpected
counterpart to Davis's painting *Egg Beater* (1923) (plate 43), which, appropriate to its utilitarian
subject, is rendered in a mechanistic style. In Dove's painting, the hardware is almost illegible—
is that a four-bladed fan at the left?—for everything has begun to melt, blurring geometries in
a fluid, ambient space. It is a language that had enormous progeny. Arshile Gorky's *Central
Park at Dusk* (1936–42) (plate 47), despite its abundance of sharp-edged outlines, quivers with
the same impulse to turn the visible into a metamorphic world of constantly changing shapes
and colors, a search also registered in Willem de Kooning's abstract and figurative paintings. In
his ongoing series on the theme of *Woman* represented here in a canvas of 1966 (plate 74),
the contours and colors of the sitter's body and clothing seem to dissolve into the background,
leaving a ghostly mirage of churning flesh that eludes any material grasp.

Mark Rothko, (1903–1970)
*Untitled (Maroon over Red)*, 1968
Acrylic on paper mounted on canvas, 39 ⅛ x 26 inches
Pennsylvania Academy of the Fine Arts,
Bequest of Bernice McIlhenny Wintersteen, 1986.31.5

This pictorial language of molten, shifting forms and impulsive, ragged brushwork (modestly prophesied in many of Dove's prewar paintings) had become, in fact, a communal style in the postwar years. It can be found, for example, in Hans Hofmann's *Red Serpent* (1949) (plate 57), where an abstract reptile slithers through an equally animated and unstable background, and in works of equally imposing dimensions, such as Robert Motherwell's *In Ochre with Gestural Black* (1956) (plate 62) and Helen Frankenthaler's *Happiest New 1960* (ca. 1959) (plate 64), paintings that seem to burst all boundaries of calculated shapes, colors, and brushstrokes. And aspects of this formal inheritance can still be found in work from the 1980s and 1990s. Witness Jean-Michel Basquiat's *Untitled* (1981) (plate 85), where a humanoid, skeletal figure, echoing the powerfully brash images of city-wall graffiti, keeps disappearing into a constantly shifting ground of colored smudges of paint; Elizabeth Murray's *Flesh Table* (1986) (plate 91), where furniture and human anatomy are fused in serpentine coils; Robert Colescott's *April in Paris* (1998) (plate 96), with its cartoon-like explosion of multiracial figures having a ball below a distant sky dominated by the Eiffel Tower.

If this anthology can reveal evolutionary patterns that unite different generations, it can also underline the startling contrasts between artists who are working at exactly the same time but in totally different modes. Perhaps the most flagrant example here of such strange synchrony is a pair of major paintings of 1949 that, like red states and blue states, seems to offer a divisive view of the politics of culture. Here is a vintage Jackson Pollock, *Number 23, 1949* (1949) (plate 58), a perfect example of the artist's innovative techniques of pouring and splattering paint to create a new abstract language of impulse and energy set loose, but still controlled by a hand and mind that could map out a completely original universe from this unfamiliar vocabulary. But looking laterally in the same year, 1949, the archenemy of modern art, Thomas Hart Benton, was painting *Judgment of Paris* or *The Golden Apple of Discord* (plate 56), which, rather than looking forward into future transformations of abstract art, looked backward in both its mythological theme and in its legible depiction of fully modeled nudes to the Old Master traditions the artist tried to preserve in the face of what he thought was the international folly of modern art. Moreover, Benton, an aggressive isolationist who thought he should paint an American art for the American people, translated the classical myth into the language of grassroots America, as if the narrative were being replayed in a rural community somewhere in Missouri or Kansas. Of course, history has many ironies—in this case the curious facts that Benton was actually a youthful convert to European abstraction but then did an about-face to right-wing conservatism; and that Pollock, in 1930, had been a student of Benton's, whose sinuous pictorial rhythms, here apparent in the undulant landscape and contours of the nude Venus, left a strong mark on Pollock's early work and can still be sensed in his mature abstractions, such as *Search* (1955) (plate 61). And in terms of chronological ironies and surprises, it is worth noting that an artist such as Charles Burchfield, always associated with the early-twentieth-century avant-garde, was still alive and well in the 1960s, the decade of Pop Art and Minimalism. His watercolor *Dandelion Seed Heads and the Moon* (ca. 1965) (plate 70), rather than looking like an anachronism from a prewar world, seems to join forces with the organic, gyrating rhythms of Pollock himself, as if two very different generations of American artists had unexpectedly converged.

Generalizations, in fact, are constantly challenged in any broad anthology culled from the same time slots. Another irony of postwar art is that its most conspicuous early manifestation, Abstract Expressionism, was admired in part because of its universal antinationalist character that appeared to transcend the space-time coordinates of the realities of living in the United States after 1945. Who could tether Rothko's, Gottlieb's (fig. 26), or Pollock's paintings to any particular time or place? But some of the most revolutionary artists who followed in their avant-garde footsteps loudly proclaimed their American roots. As enigmatic as Jasper Johns's

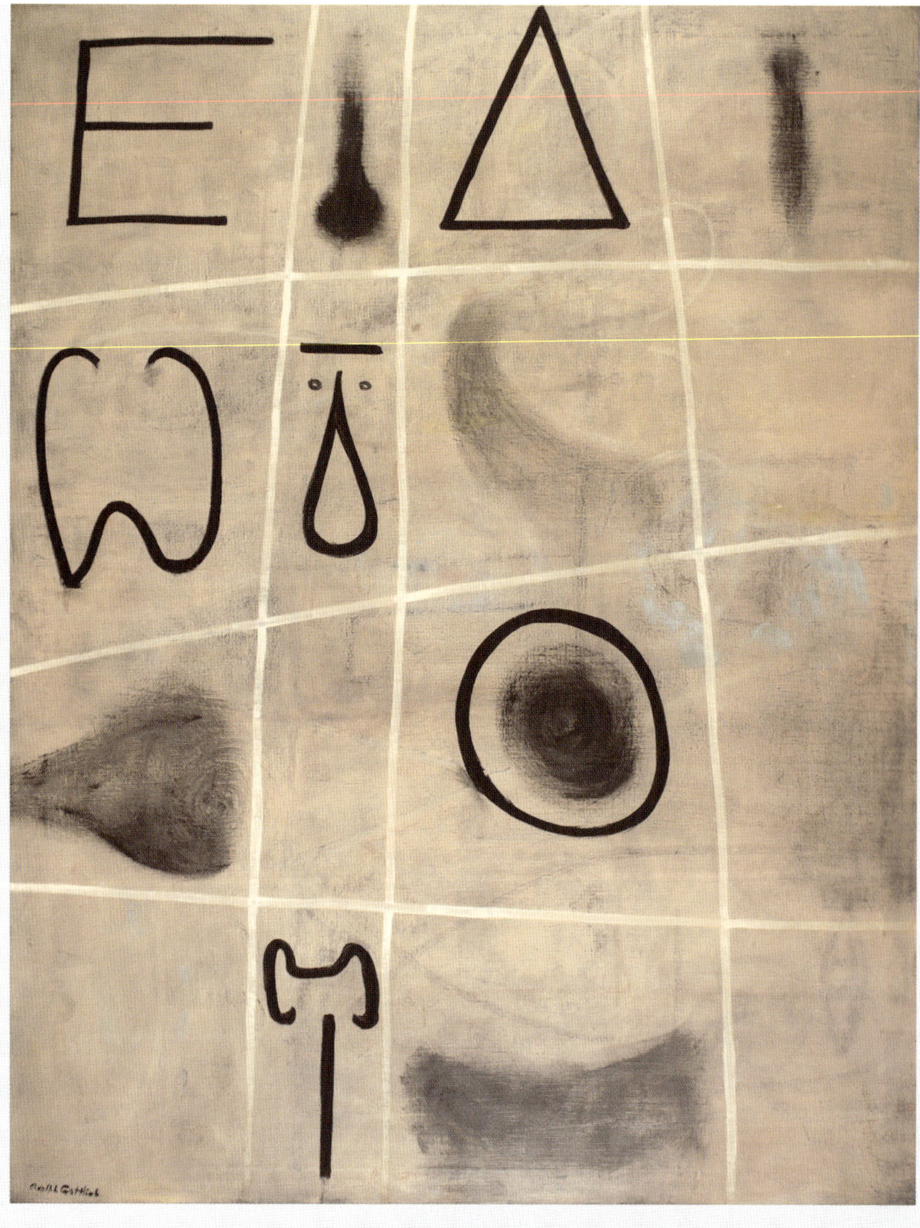

flags may be as meditations on the overlapping of commonplace images and pictorial fictions, it should also be remembered that they are the clearest possible declarations of the artist's nationality, even going on to register—as in the case of the *Flag* in this show made in 1965, ten years after Johns's first flag (plate 71)—the annexation of Hawaii and Alaska, a historic event that would update Johns's original forty-eight stars to fifty.

Pop artists in particular were intent on reflecting the specifics of American life, almost echoing, but with a new tone of parody, the isolationist program of such American scene painters of the 1920s and 1930s as Marsh and Hopper, Lawrence and Benton. So it is that two of the still lifes in the show (unlike say, the apples of Cézanne) shout out an American identity. Roy Lichtenstein's *Cape Cod Still Life II* (1973) (plate 80), with its boiled lobster centerpiece, lands us squarely in a picture-postcard vision of New England, complete with lighthouse and gull; Wayne Thiebaud's *Meringues* (1988) (plate 94) offers us a generic, germ-free display of factory-produced desserts and synthetic colors that we instantly recognize as archetypal American fare, available at countless cafeteria counters and bakeries.

Defying earlier concepts of a linear progression of modern art that moved from ism to ism, the later twentieth century, in retrospect, represents a triumph of diversity, with often contradictory viewpoints vying for equal time. A search for abstract purity, whether in shape or color, continued to provide, as it had in the earlier century, a lofty goal for younger and older artists. From the 1960s, we can see here not only a vertical slice of disembodied color, as caught by Jules Olitski in *Zore* (1966) (plate 75), but fusions of color and geometric pattern, as in Kenneth Noland's *Grave Light* (1965) (plate 72), with its marriage of parallelogram rhythms and pure hues, or in Frank Stella's 1968 *Saskatoon II* (plate 77), with its almost Islamic interlace of arcs, circles, and pastel colors. And looking ahead to the 1980s, such ambitions are still very much alive, whether in the work of an older-generation artist such as Ellsworth Kelly, whose *Dark Blue Curve II* (1982) (plate 86) looks like a further reduction of some of O'Keeffe's early-twentieth-century explorations of abstract shapes, or in such younger-generation artists as Robert Ryman, whose *Catalyst II* (1985) (plate 88) pushes modern art's recurrent impulse to begin with the cleanest slate to the extreme of a canvas covered only with white brushstrokes, and Sean Scully, whose *Morning* (1986) (plate 92) offers another variation on one of that century's most obsessive themes, the contrast and merger of horizontal and vertical geometries.

But realist currents, seemingly suppressed or even annihilated by the triumph of Abstract Expressionism, also persisted. There is the warts-and-all portraiture–as in the venerable Alice Neel, who, born in 1900, kept right on recording, seen in *Dennis Florio* (1978) (plate 84), the often gawky, specific facts of her friends' faces and bodies–or the fascination with sharp-focus, glossy photographic truth–as in Audrey Flack's 1976–77 allegorical still life *World War II (Vanitas)* (plate 82), with its revival, in modern translation, of Old Master symbolism about life's transience. Narrative painting continued, too, as in Leon Golub's 1987 *Threnody II* (fig. 27), or Eric Fischl's *Haircut* (1985) (plate 87), which, while looking backward to Edward Hopper's lone, alienated women in domestic interiors, updates this tradition with a shocking voyeurism that lets us glimpse what feels like a keyhole view of an anonymous young woman squatting on a bed while, with the help of a round mirror, she trims her pubic hair.

As all of us who live in contemporary America know, the twentieth century's earlier age of innocence had been buried by the 1960s, and a new age of sexual candor had begun. David Salle's split-screen paintings also belong to this liberated world of prosaic observation that often seizes surprising facts of modern life. *Wild Locust Ride* (1985) (plate 89) offers one of his many cropped and close-up studies of the female nude who, unlike studio models, is captured in an informal state of undress. But Salle, as usual, goes beyond this, juxtaposing his frag-

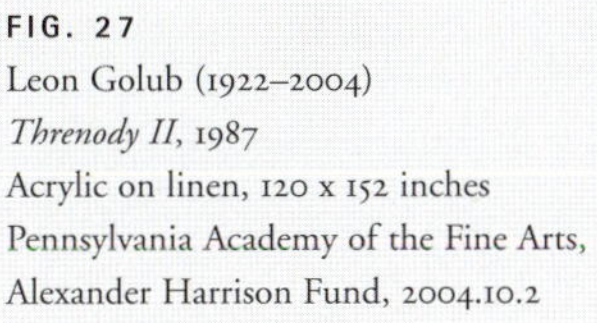

FIG. 27
Leon Golub (1922–2004)
*Threnody II*, 1987
Acrylic on linen, 120 x 152 inches
Pennsylvania Academy of the Fine Arts,
Alexander Harrison Fund, 2004.10.2

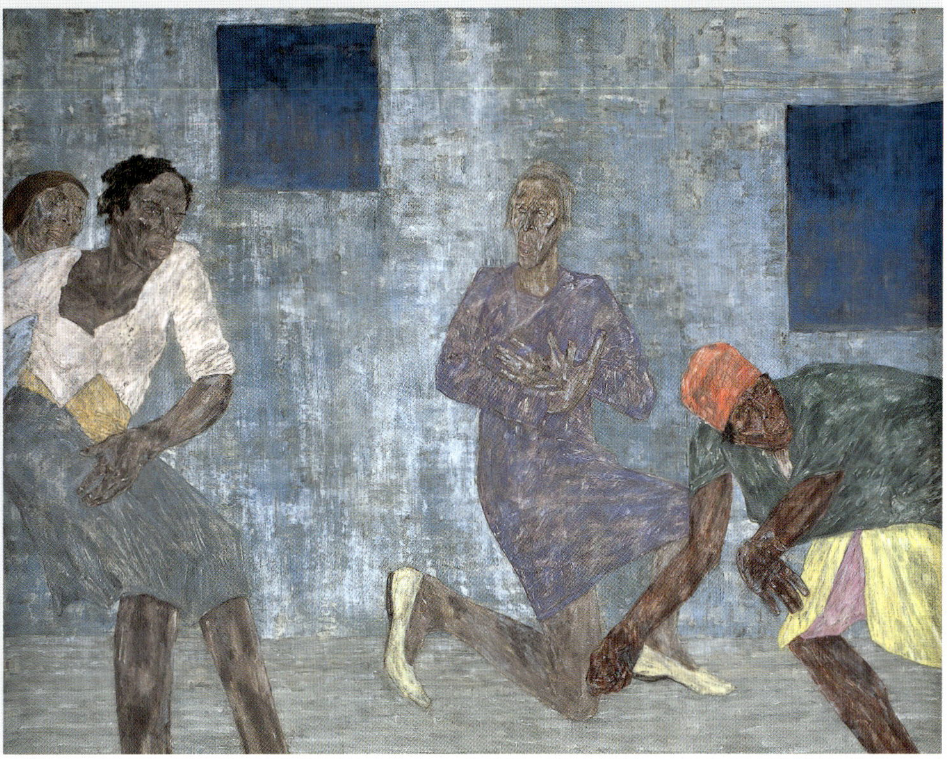

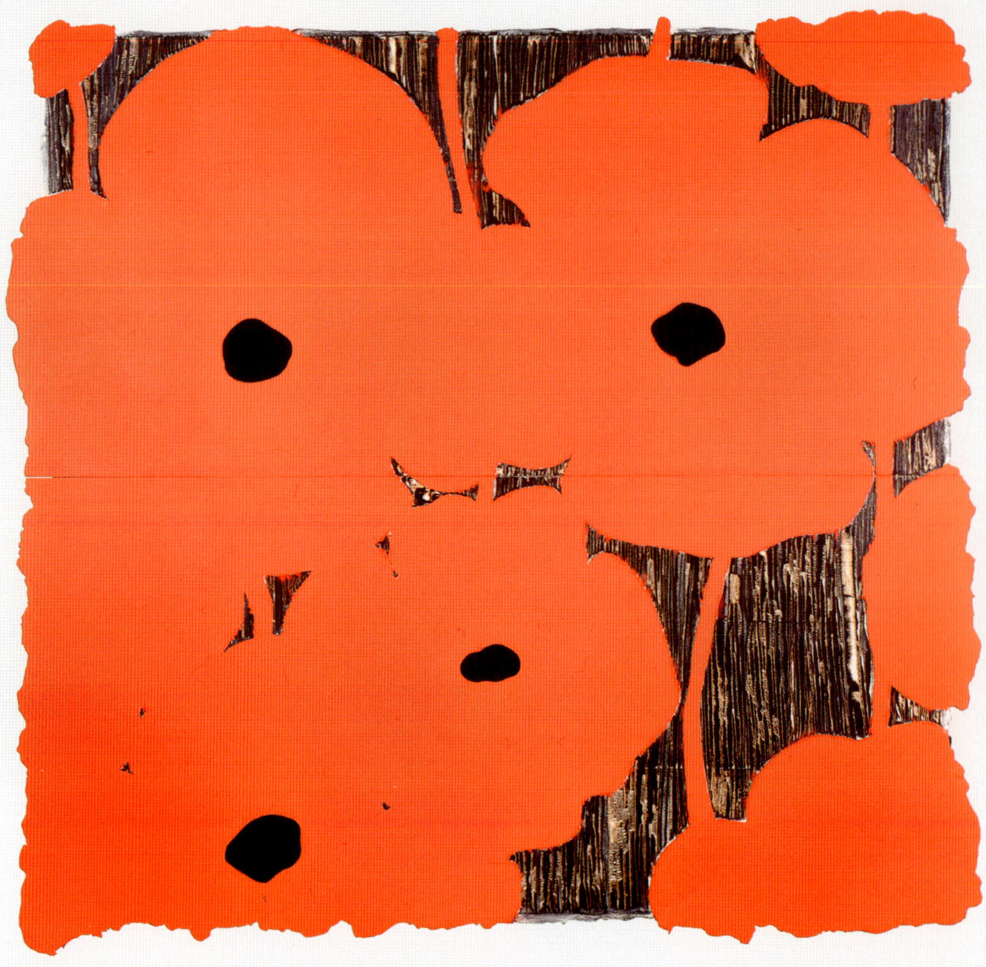

mented nude with an equally fragmented rectangle of a textile pattern, a multi-focus vision that recalls Rauschenberg's love of juggling the widest spectrum of commonplace images. And for a finishing touch, he puts a brightly colored Santa Claus head on top of the somber tones of the nude, adding a totally different point of reference. The simultaneous diversity of images here, like the split-screen format, is a perfect reflection of our new world of constantly shifting, often contradictory images that we keep staring at on our computers and TV screens.

Speaking of our new era, when artists are fascinated by the many ways in which we are immersed in images that are clones of reality, we might end with a version of portraiture that counters the veteran Alice Neel's view of her friends and family. Although Chuck Close's watercolor portrait of his wife, *Leslie/Watercolor II* (1986) (plate 90), may seem as "real" and confrontational as, say, Andrew Wyeth's hyperrealist *Drifter* (1964) (plate 69), it belongs to another world, one of pixels and Benday dots, the abstract units of electronic and photographic reproduction. These are the atoms that make up the replicas of reality surrounding us in newspapers, billboards (as in Donald Sultan's *Red Poppies* (2003) (fig. 28), movies, television, computers. Close has mimicked this means of simulating reality by creating his own system of small geometric particles that, abstract in themselves, suddenly fuse to become a facsimile portrait, stemming not from direct observation, as Wyeth and Neel had done, but from our ever more electronic environment. And looking at such a quantum leap in the way we see the world today, we can be sure that younger American artists of the early-twenty-first century will keep responding to the changing realities around us in equally new and surprising ways.

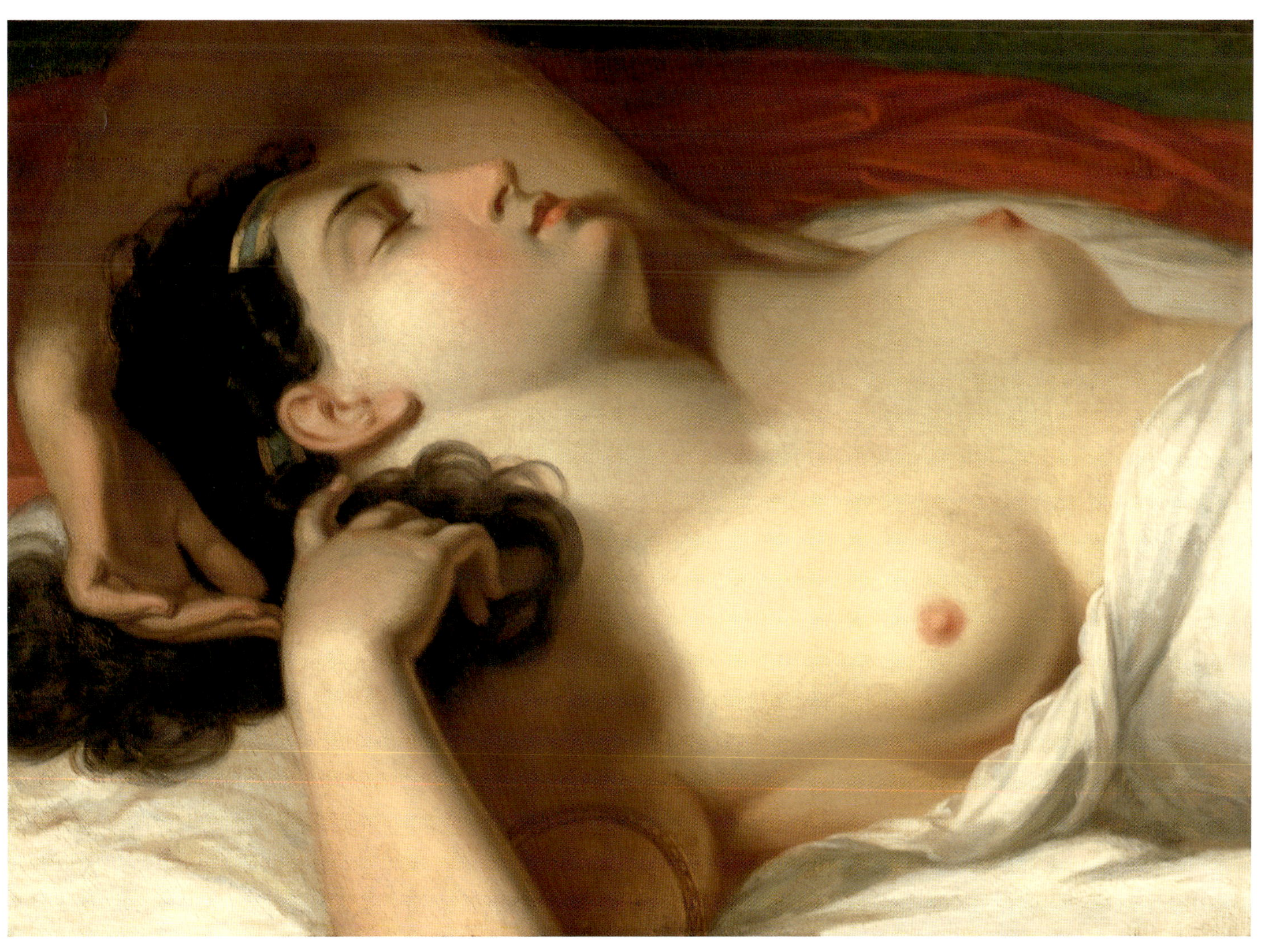

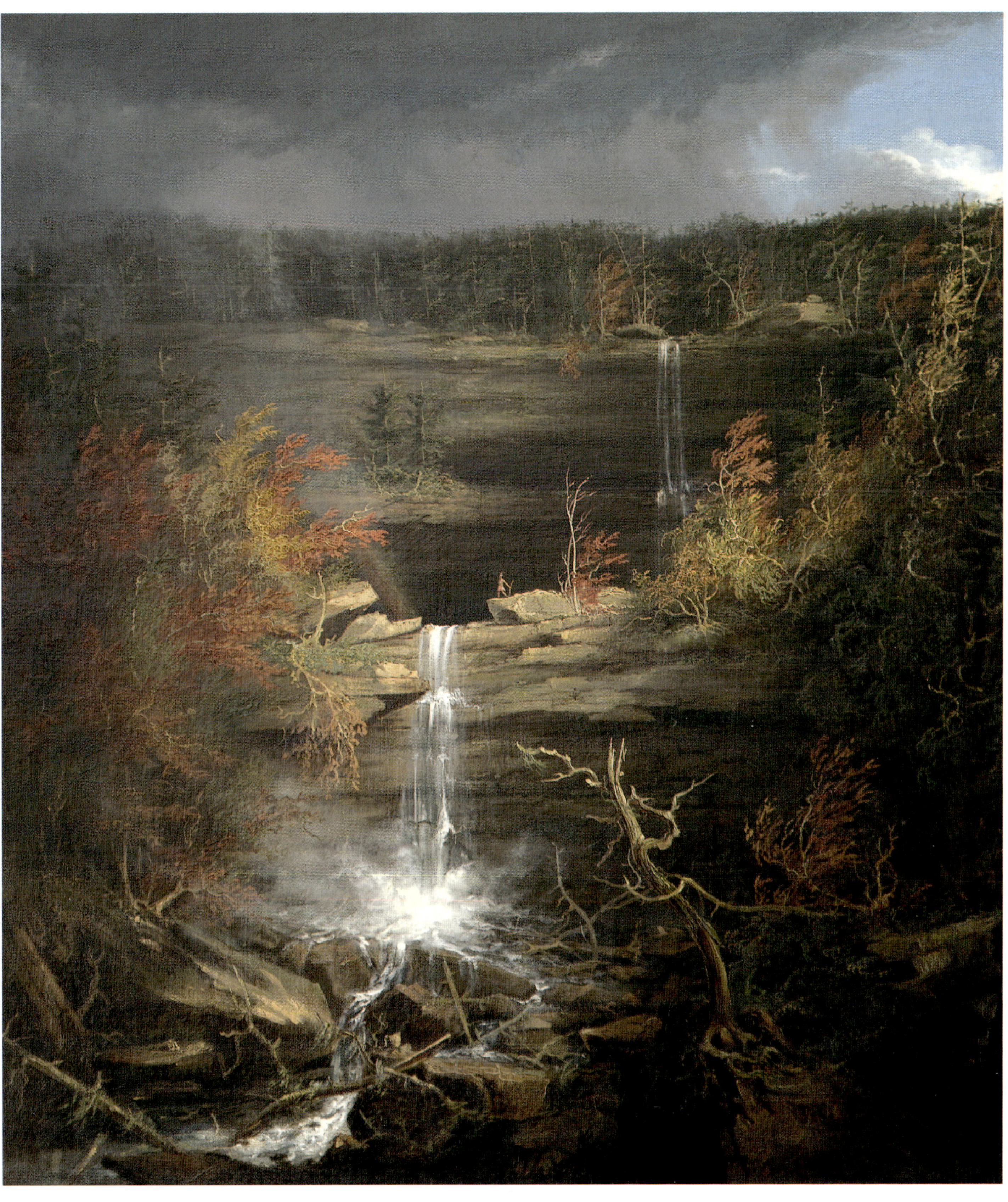

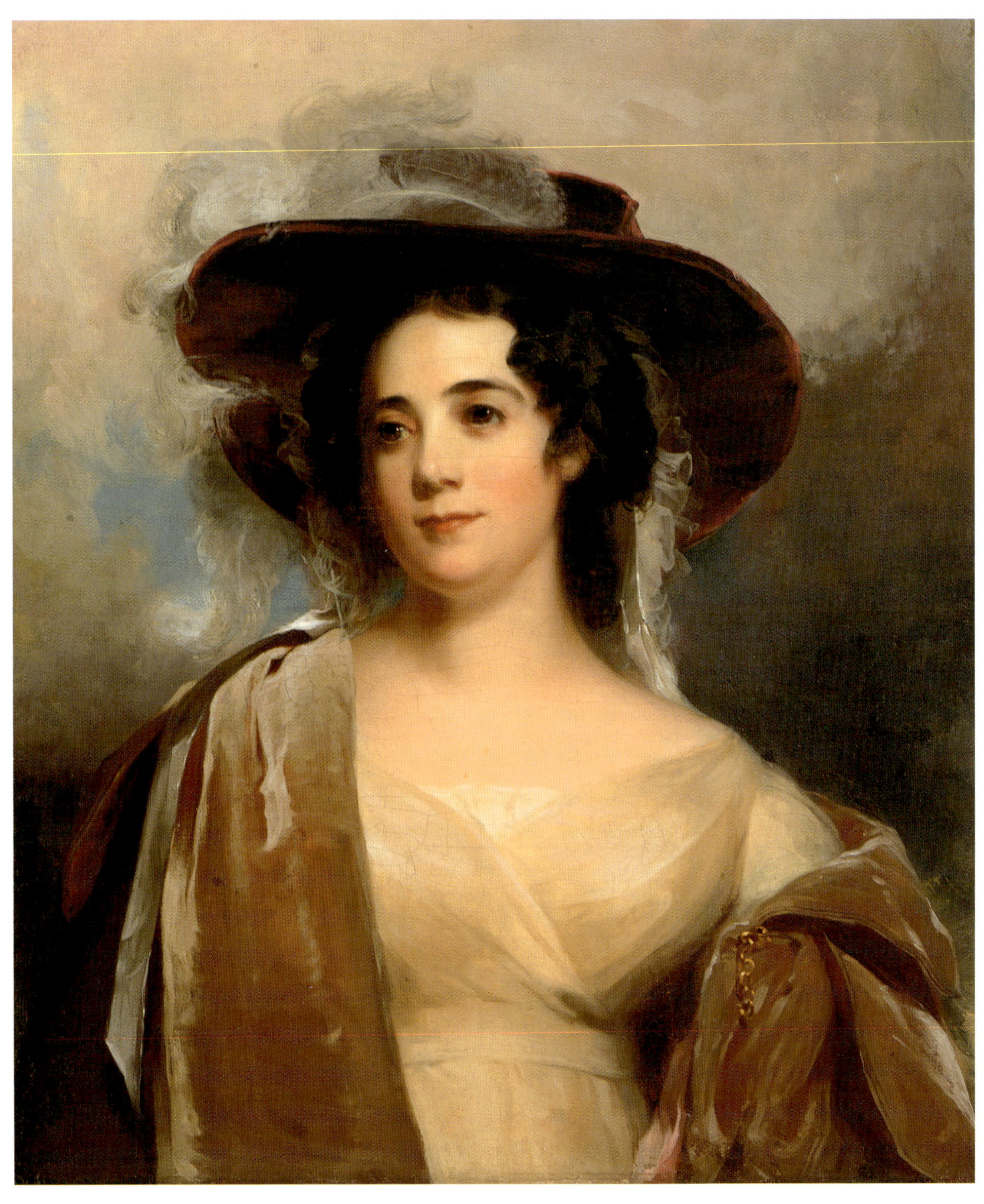

PLATE 3
Thomas Sully (1783–1872)
PENNSYLVANIA ACADEMICIAN  1812
HONORARY MEMBER  1812
BOARD  1816–32
FACULTY  1812–16
EXHIBITOR  1811–70
*Mrs. Nicholas Biddle (Jane) (1793–1856)*, 1826–27
Oil on canvas, 25 x 30 inches
The Andalusia Foundation

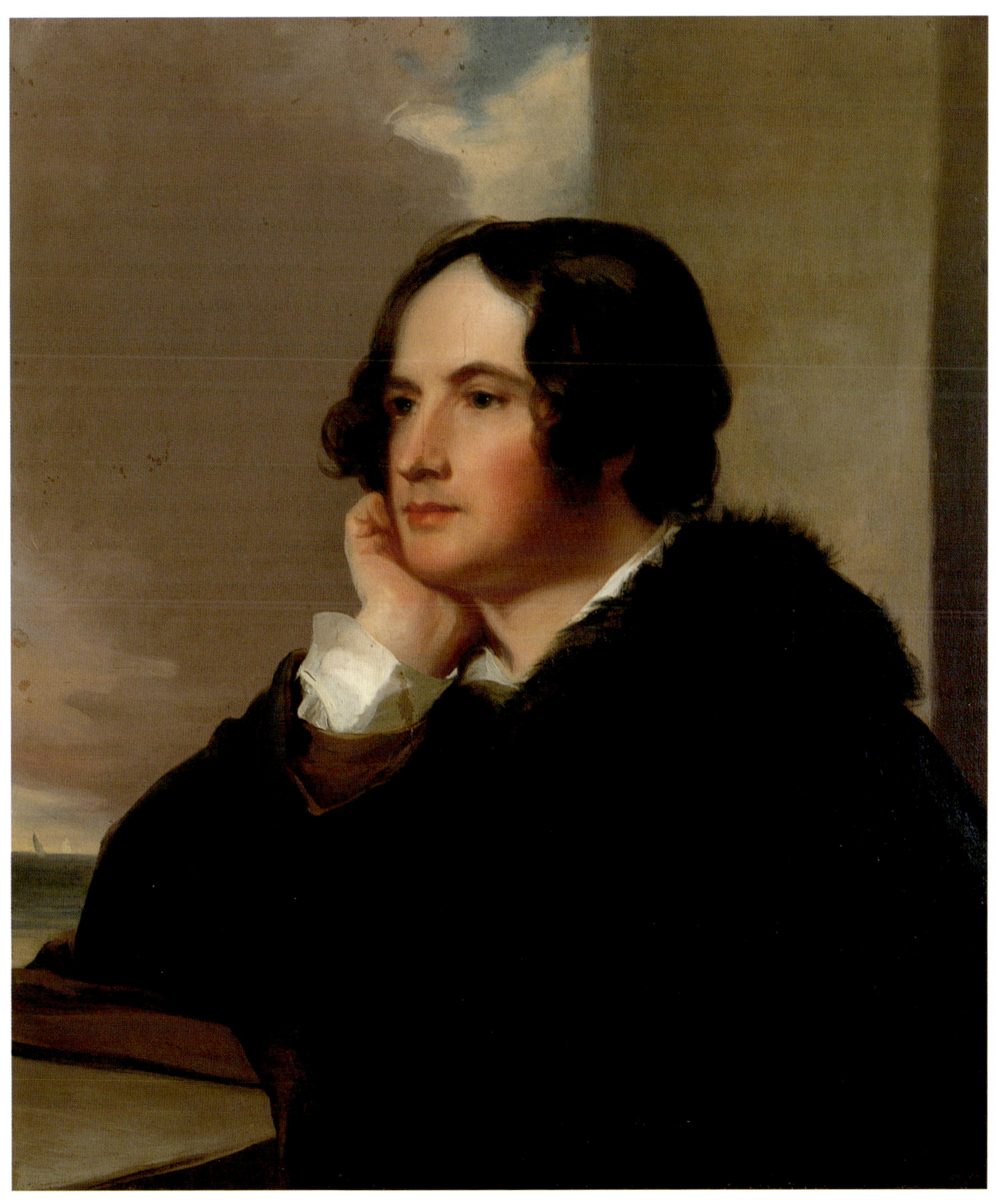



Thomas Sully (1783–1872)
PENNSYLVANIA ACADEMICIAN 1812
HONORARY MEMBER 1812
BOARD 1816–32
FACULTY 1812–16
EXHIBITOR 1811–70
*Nicholas Biddle (1786–1844),* 1836
Oil on canvas, 25 x 30 inches
The Andalusia Foundation

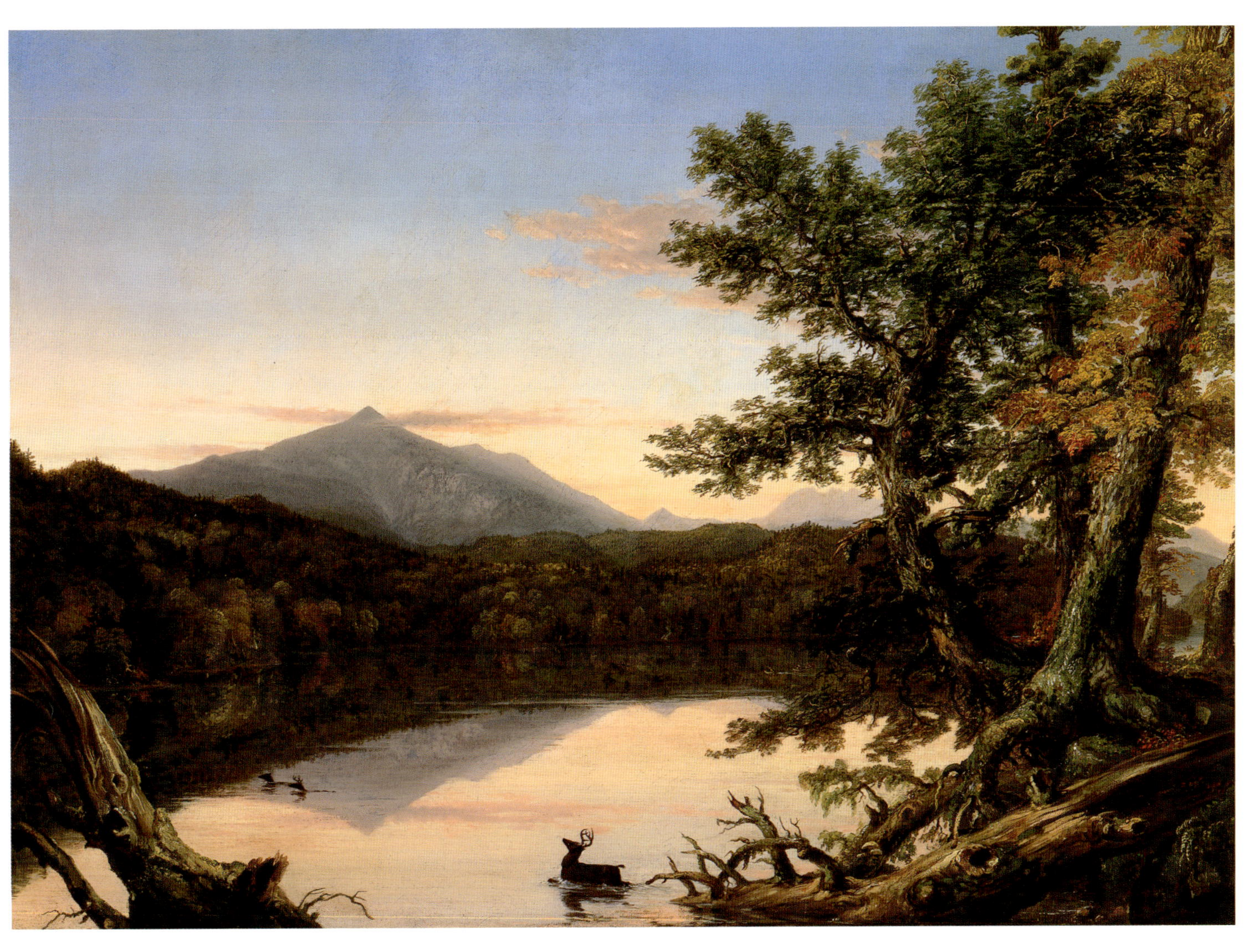

PLATE 6
Fitz Hugh Lane (1804–1865)
EXHIBITOR 1858
*Boston Harbor at Sunset,* 1853
Oil on canvas, 24 x 39 inches
Anonymous Loan

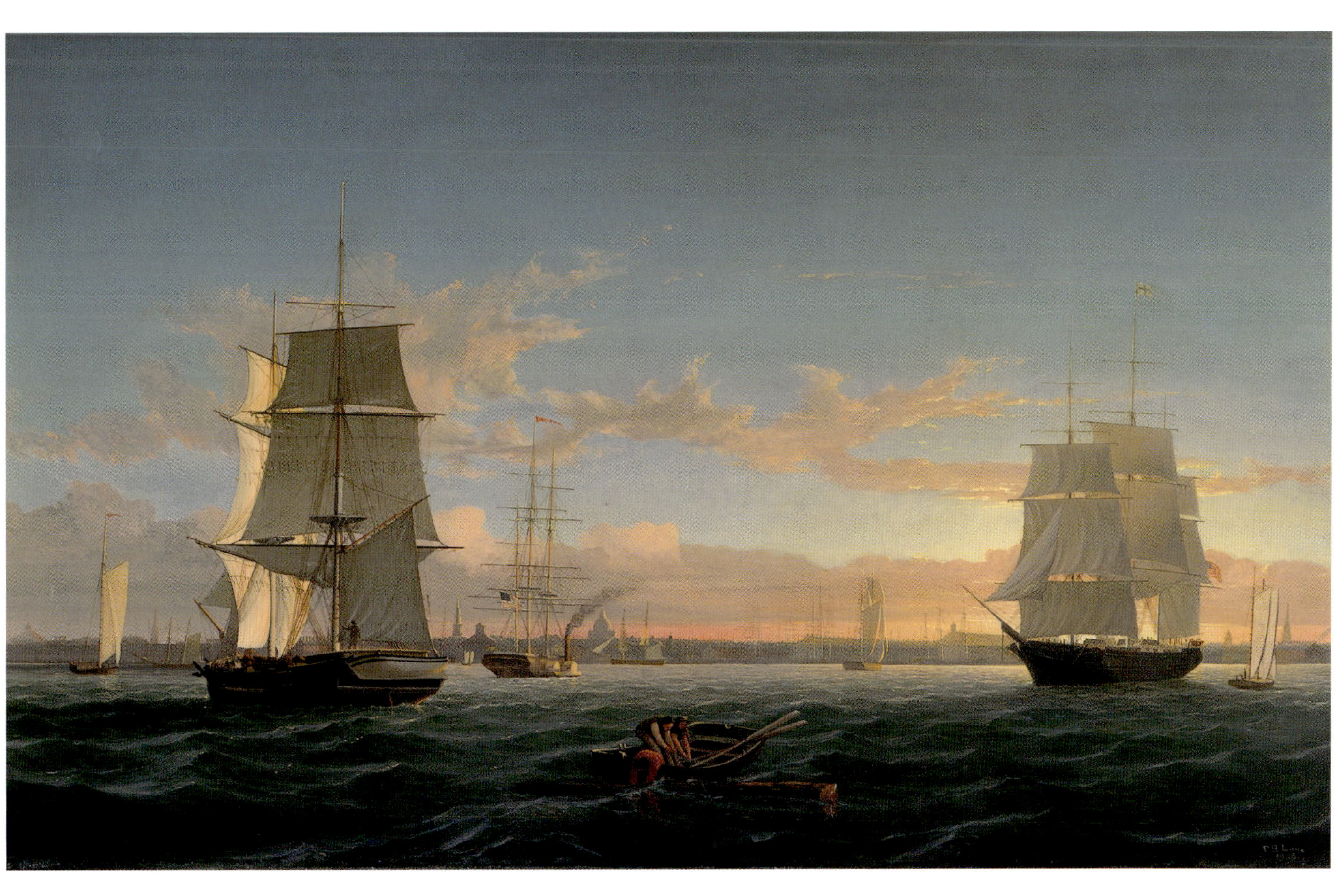

PLATE 7
George Inness (1825–1894)
EXHIBITOR 1879–94
*Delaware Water Gap,* ca. 1857
Oil on canvas, 32 x 52 inches
Private Collection, Washington, D.C.

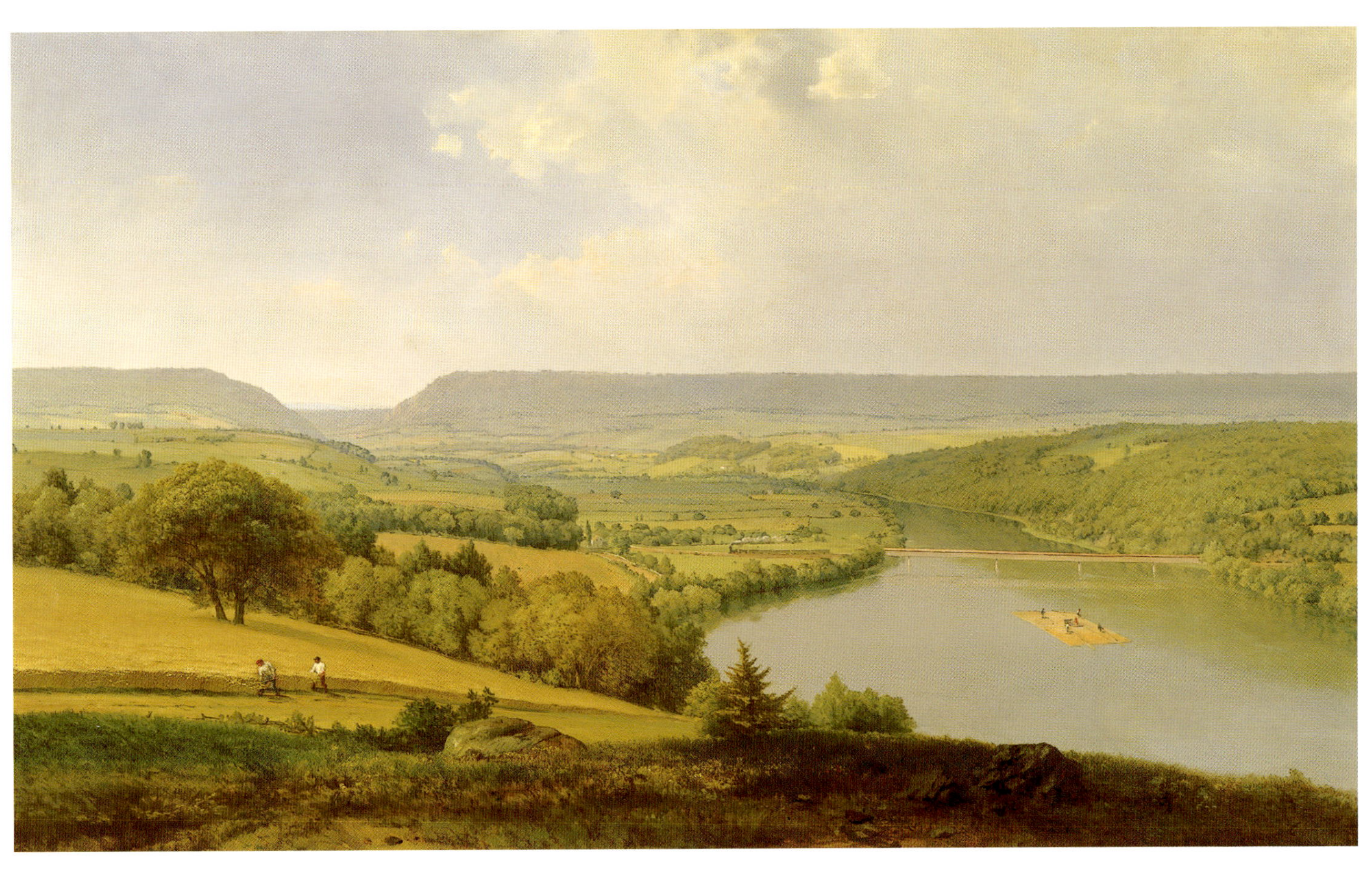

William Trost Richards (1833–1905)
PENNSYLVANIA ACADEMICIAN 1860
EXHIBITOR 1852–1905
MEDAL 1905
*Autumn in the Adirondacks,* ca. 1857–58
Oil on canvas, 24 ⅛ x 36 ½ inches
Private Collection

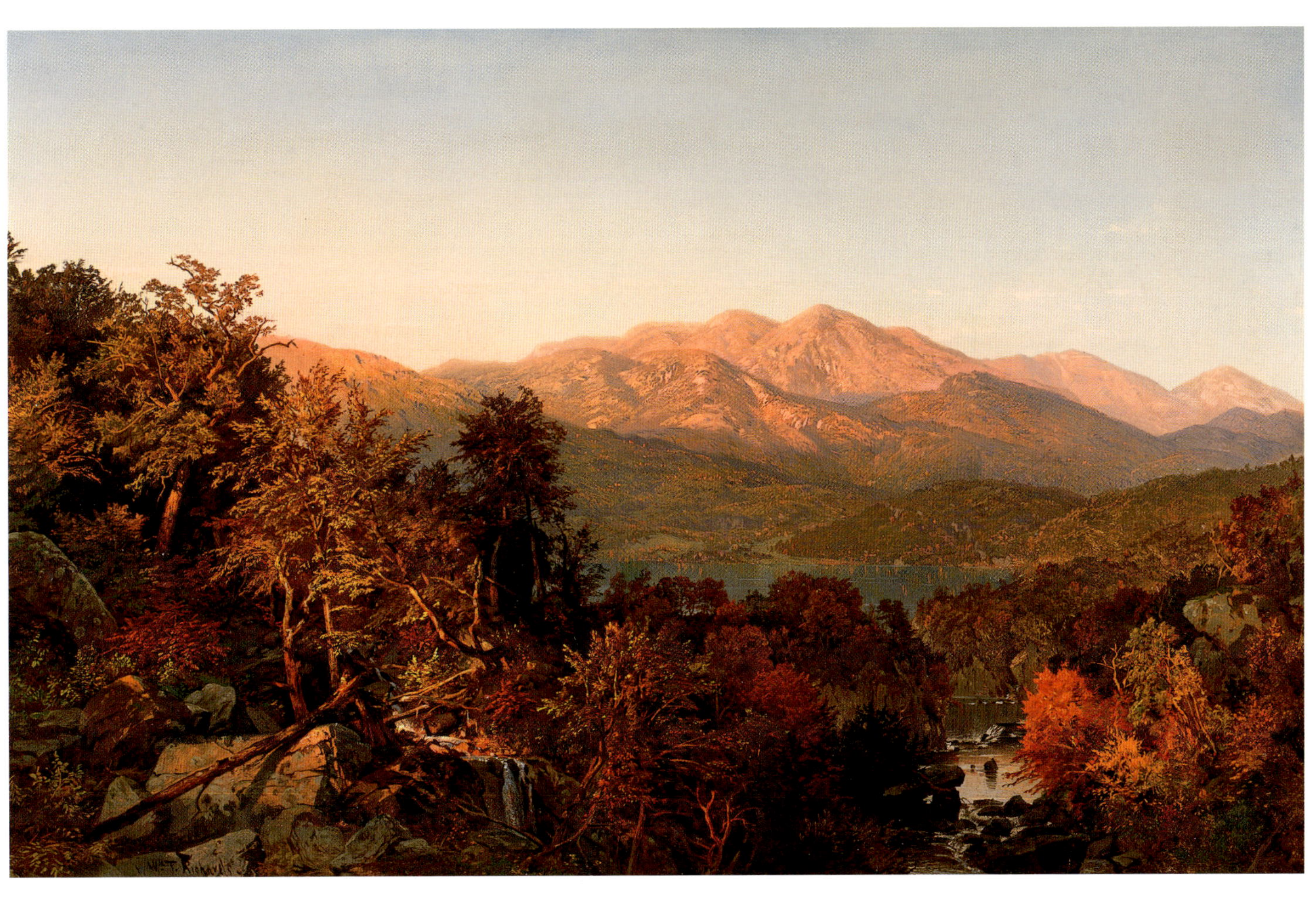

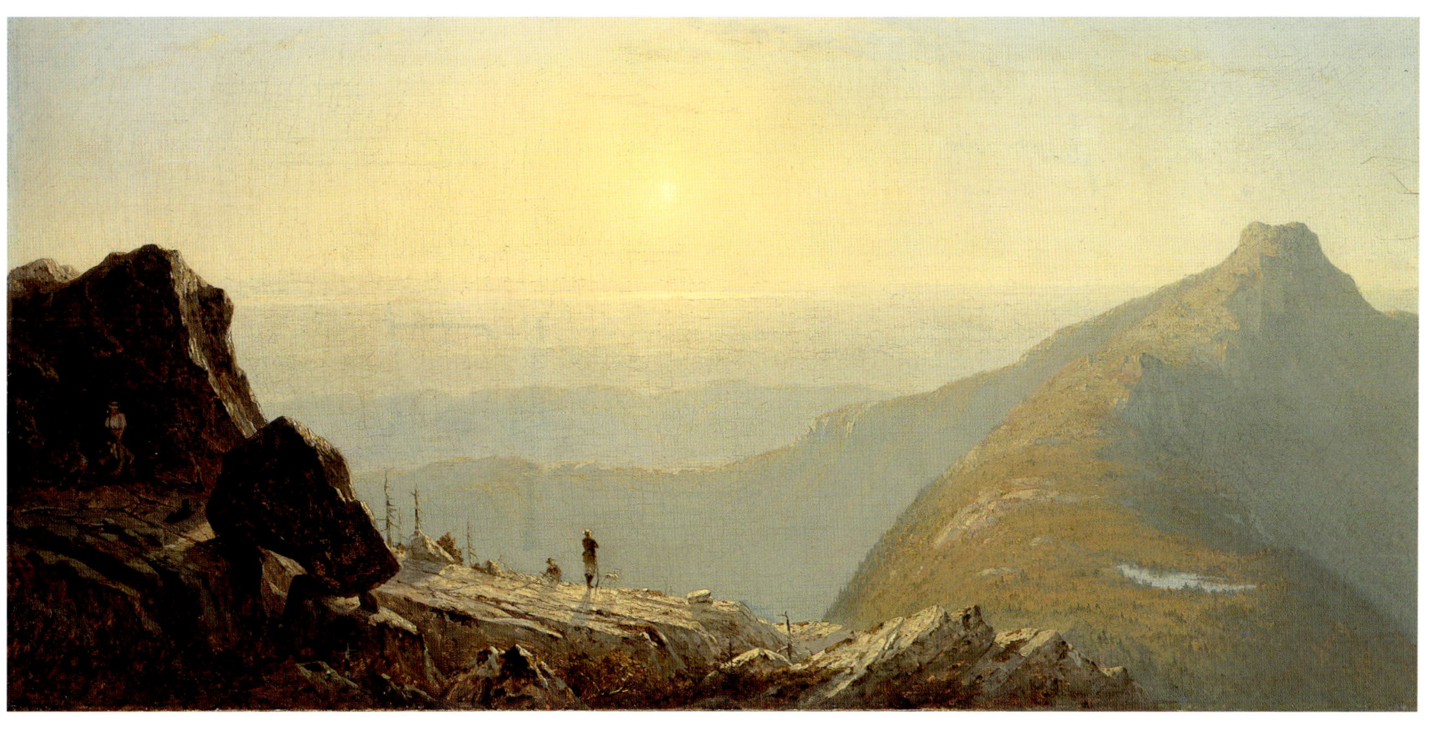

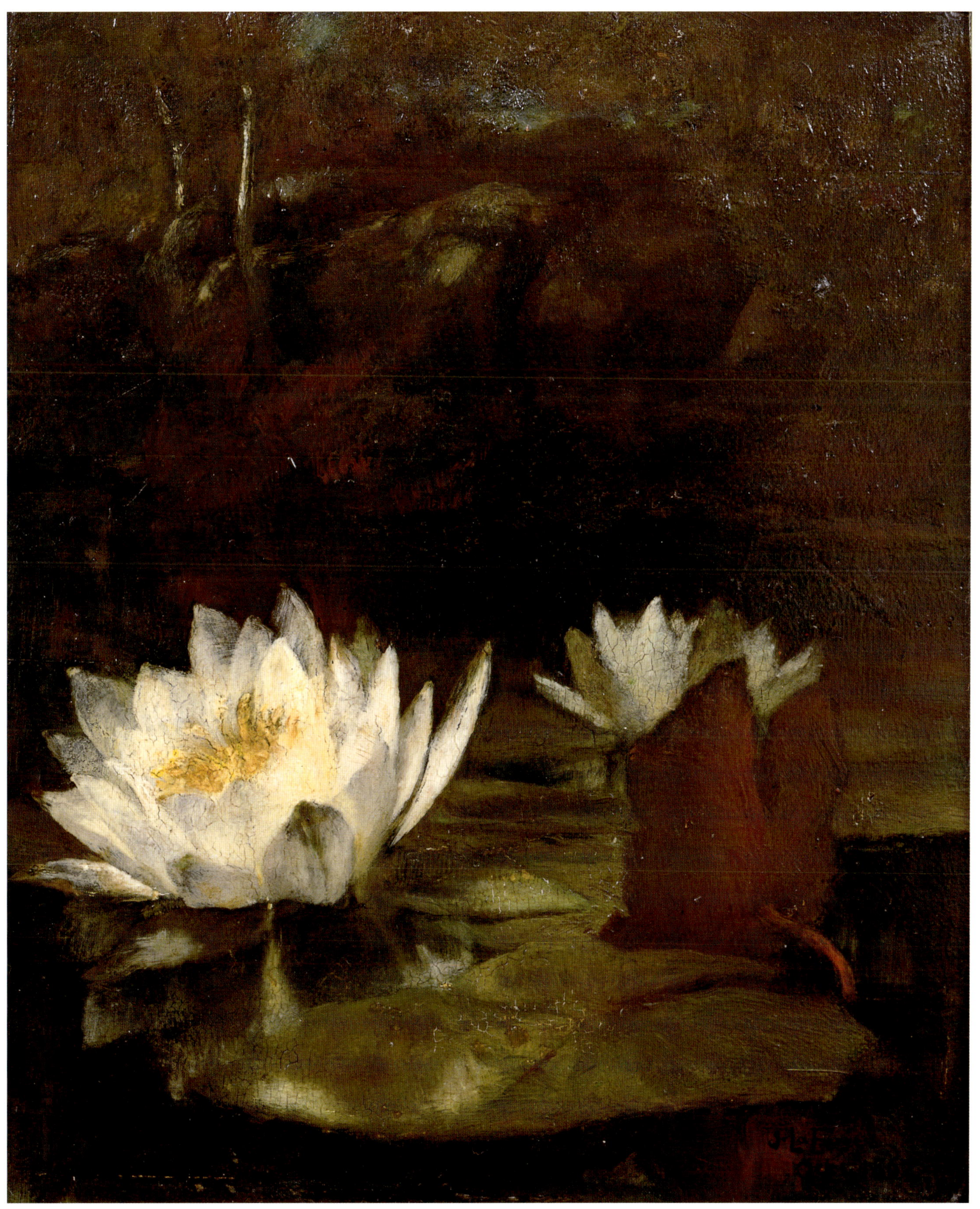

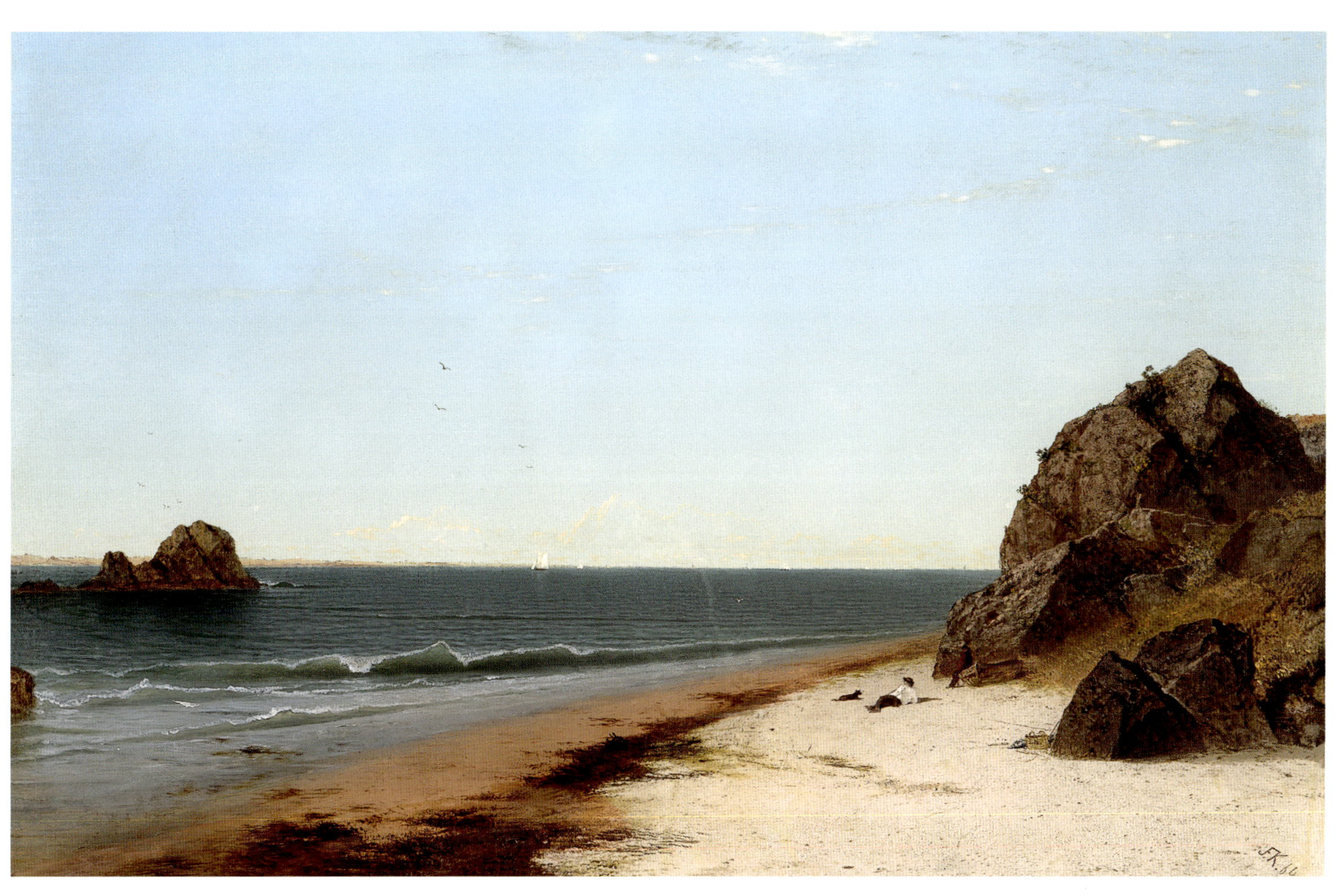

**PLATE 12**
William Trost Richards (1833–1905)
PENNSYLVANIA ACADEMICIAN 1860
EXHIBITOR 1852–1905
*Forest Interior in Autumn,* ca. 1861–65
Oil on canvas, 29 x 24 inches
Collection of Mr. and Mrs. Allan E. Bulley, Jr.

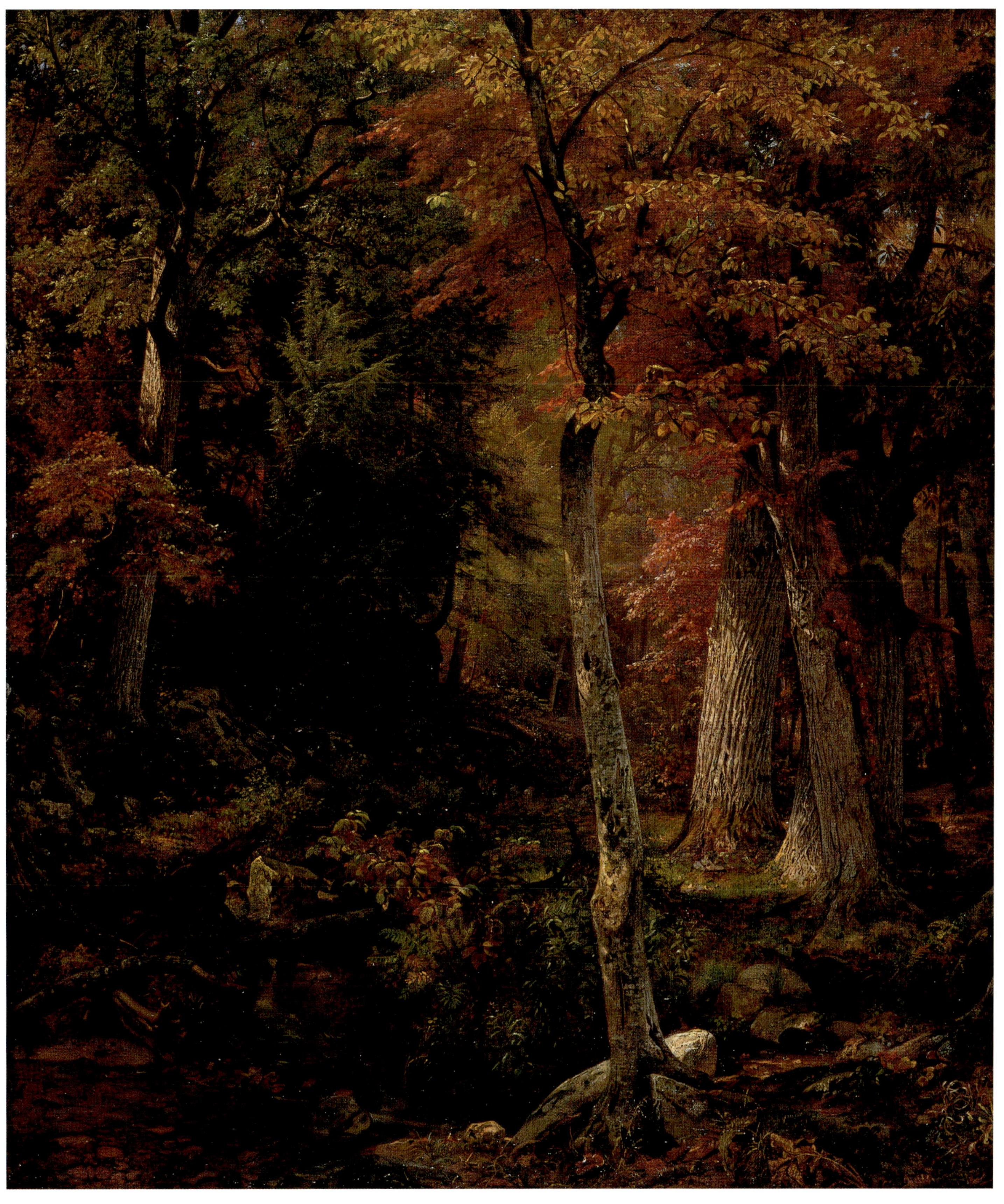

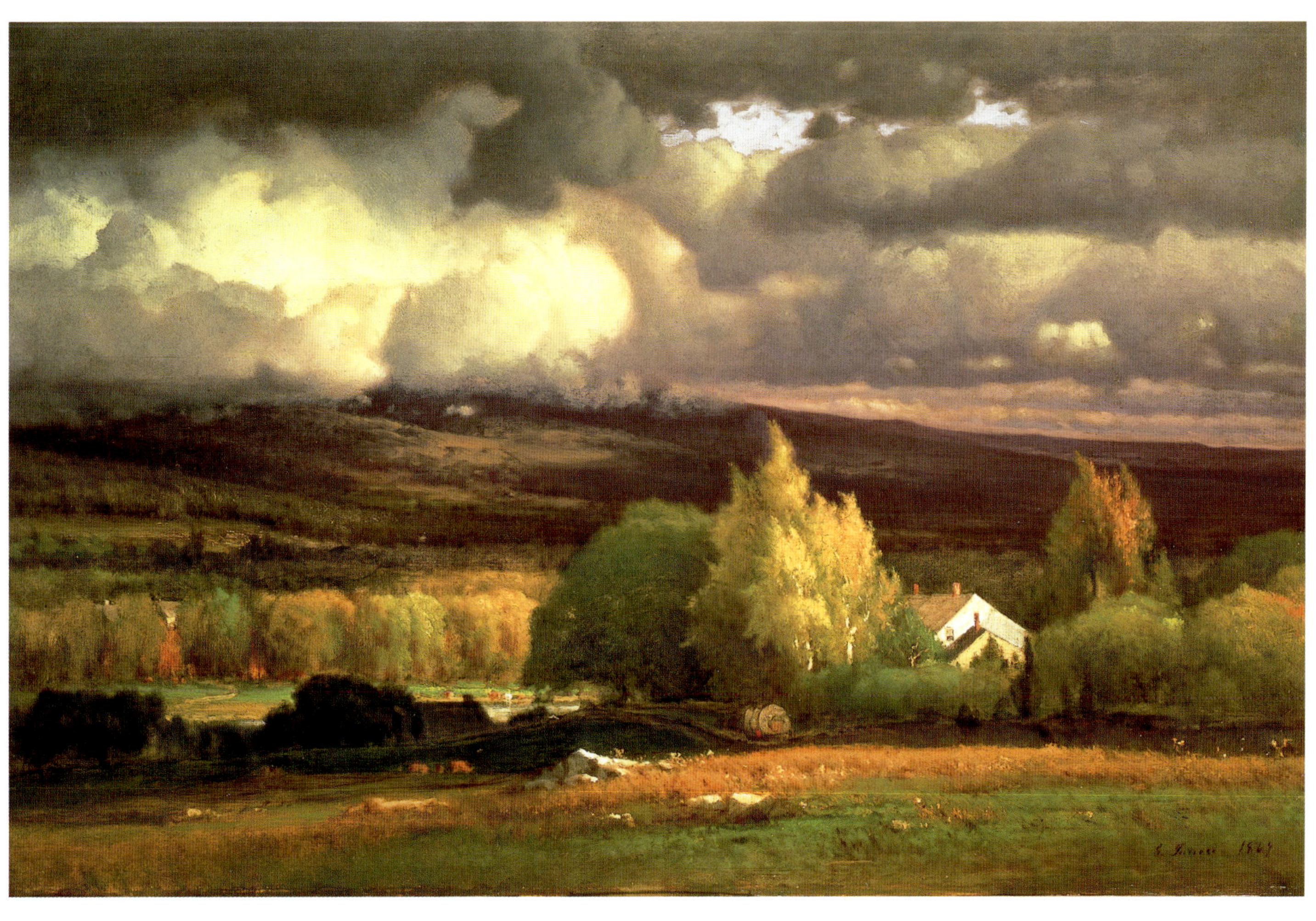

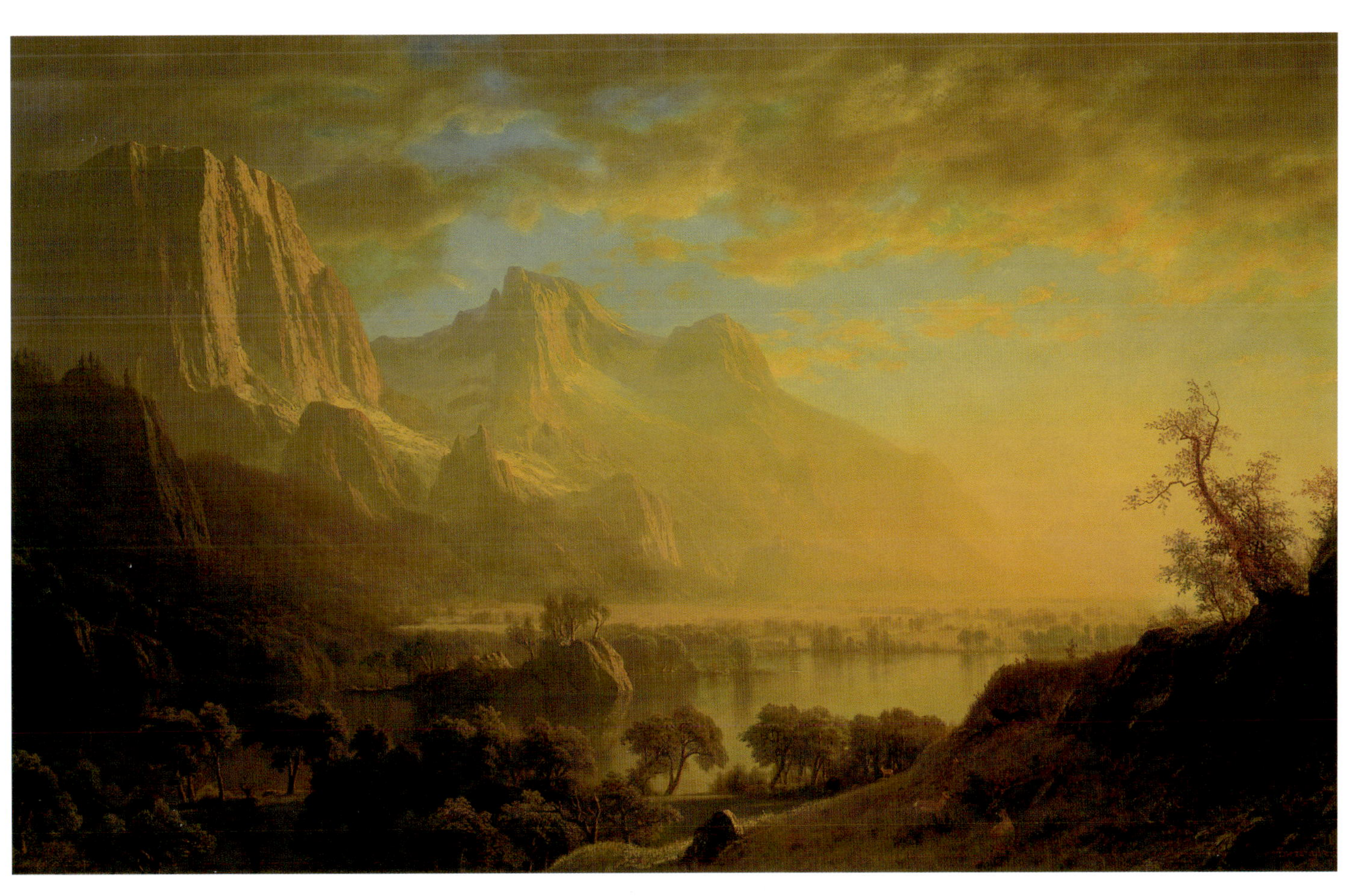

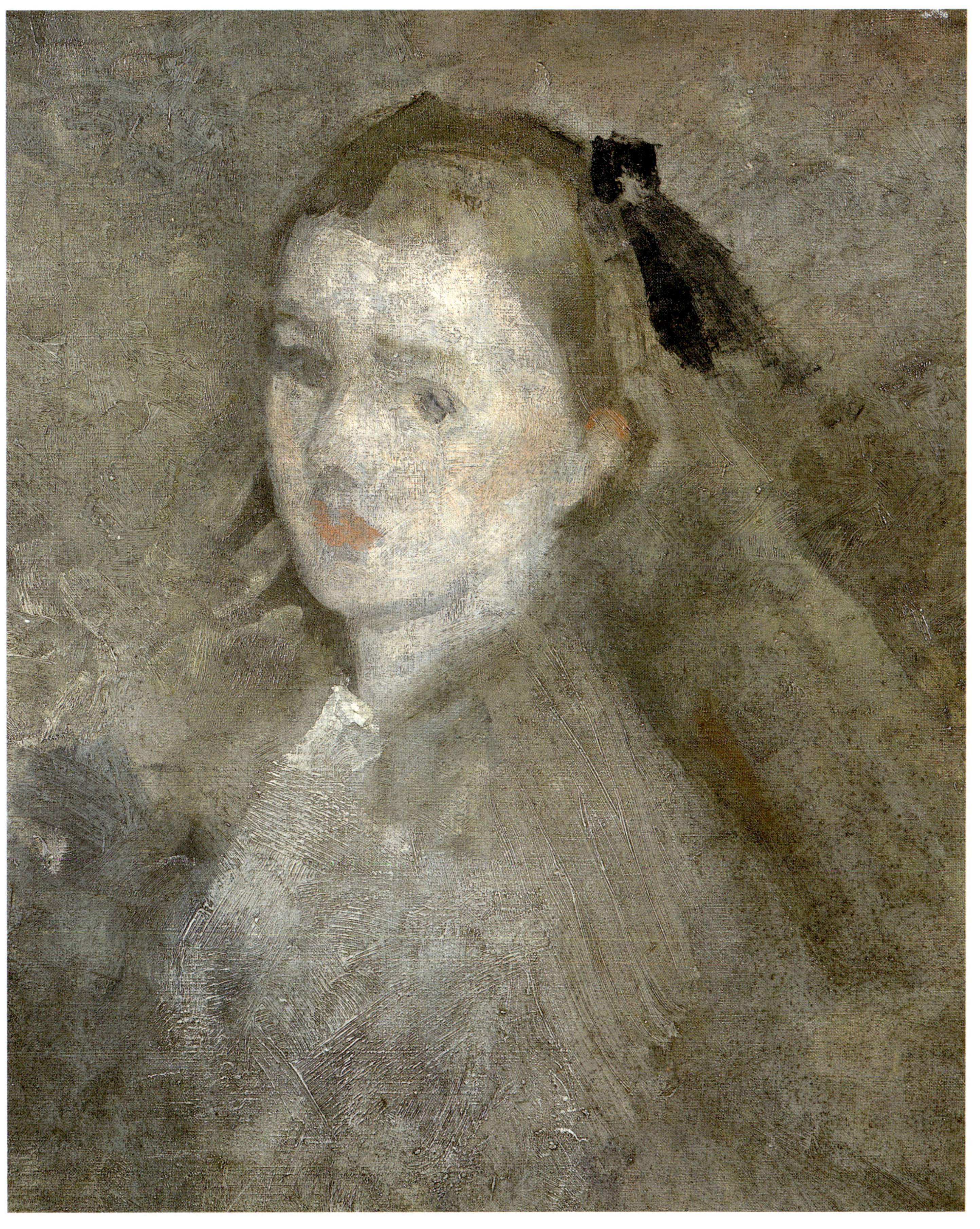

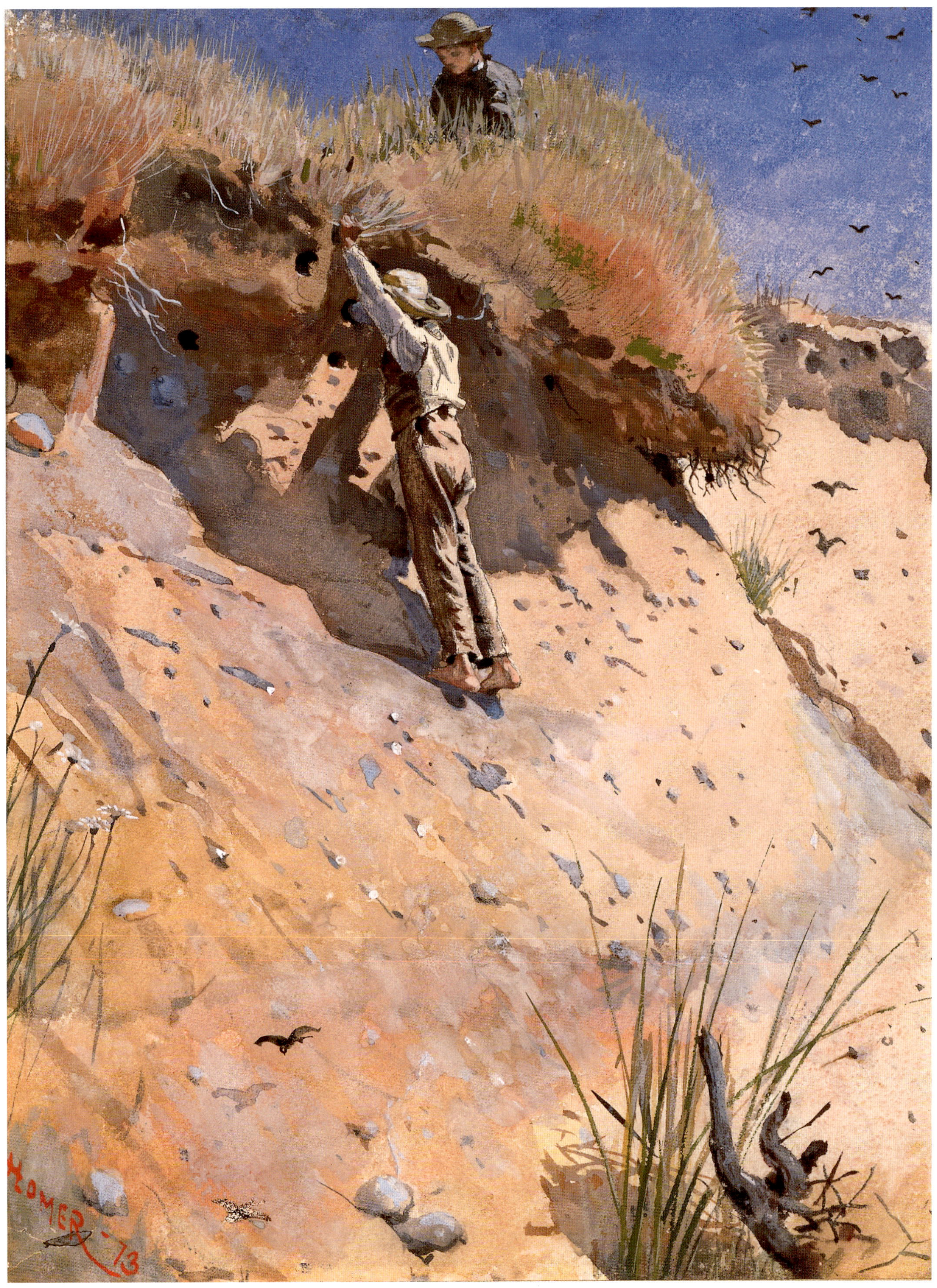

**PLATE 17**
Eastman Johnson (1824–1906)
EXHIBITOR 1862–63; 1893–1902
*The Cranberry Pickers,* 1875
Oil on paperboard, 22 ½ x 26 ¾ inches
Private Collection

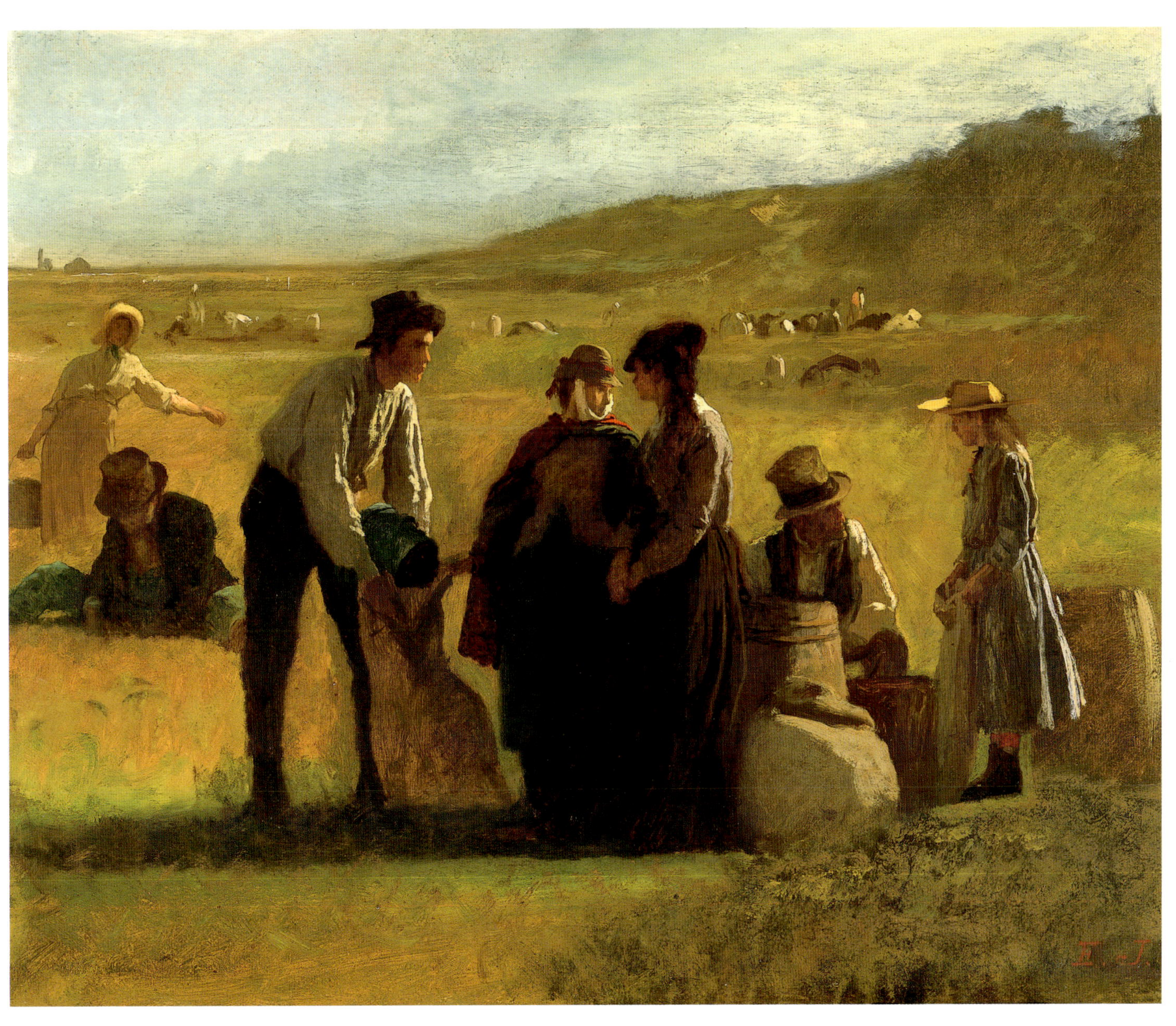

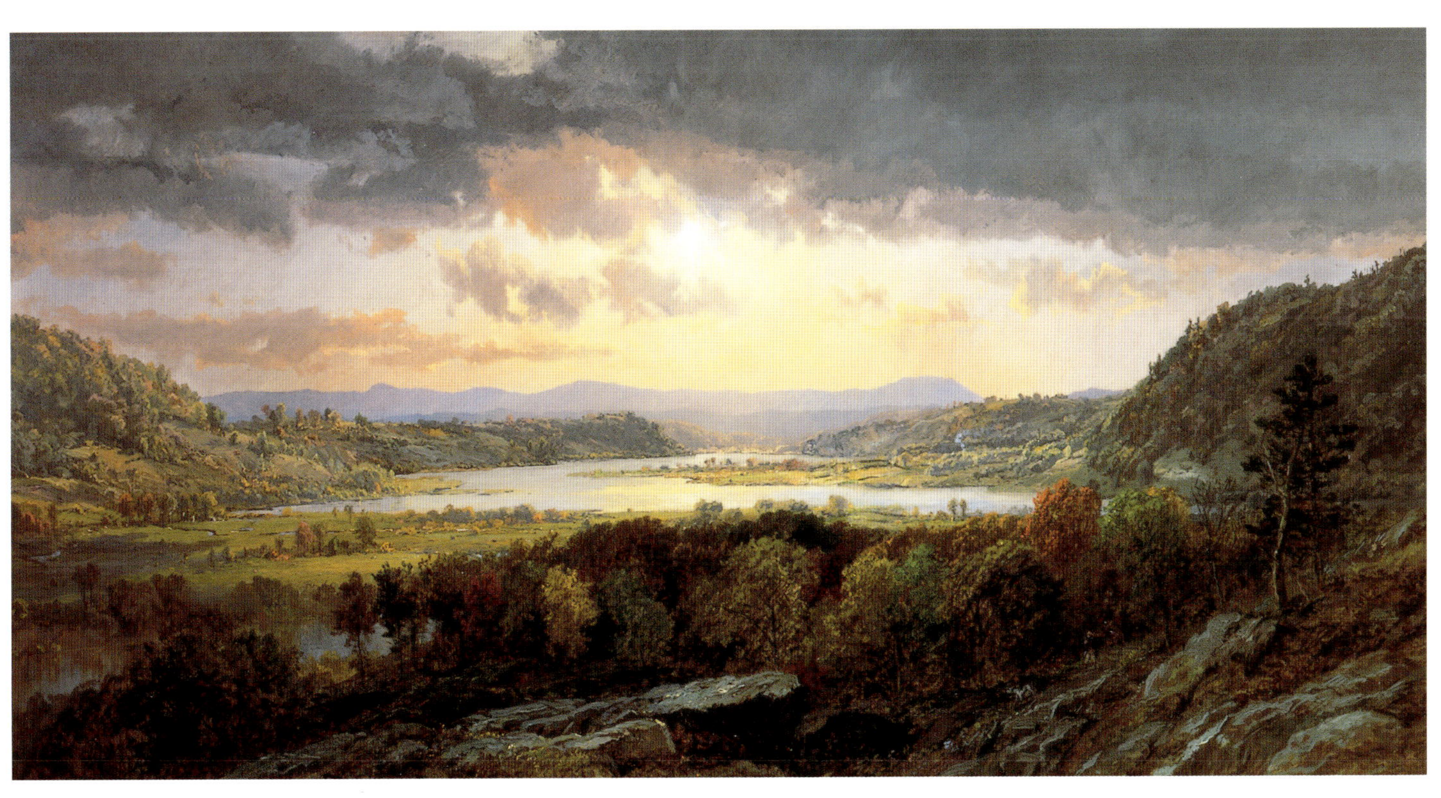

PLATE 19
Albert Bierstadt (1830–1902)
EXHIBITOR 1859–67
*The Shore of the Turquoise Sea,* 1878
Oil on canvas, 42 ½ x 64 ½ inches
Manoogian Collection

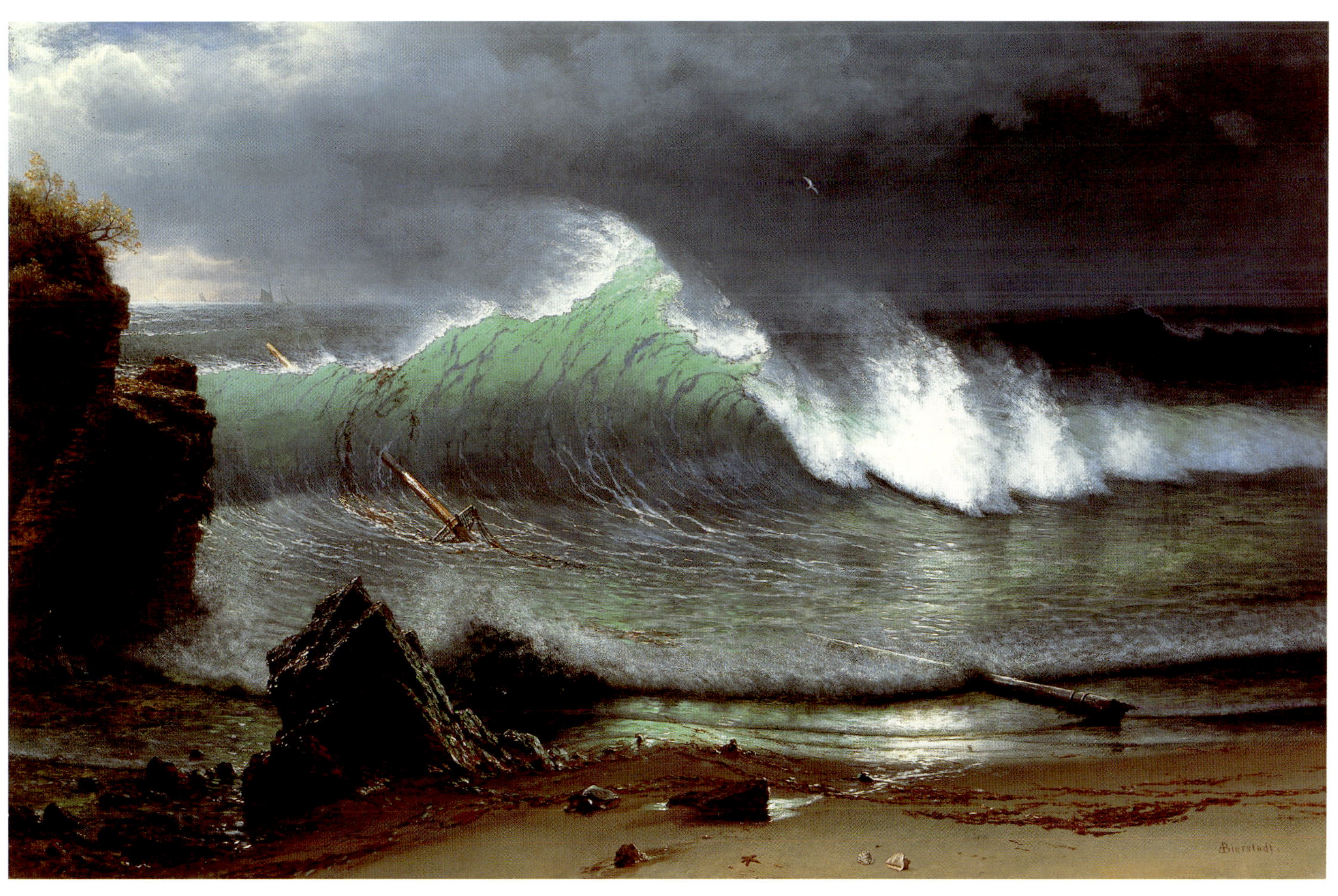

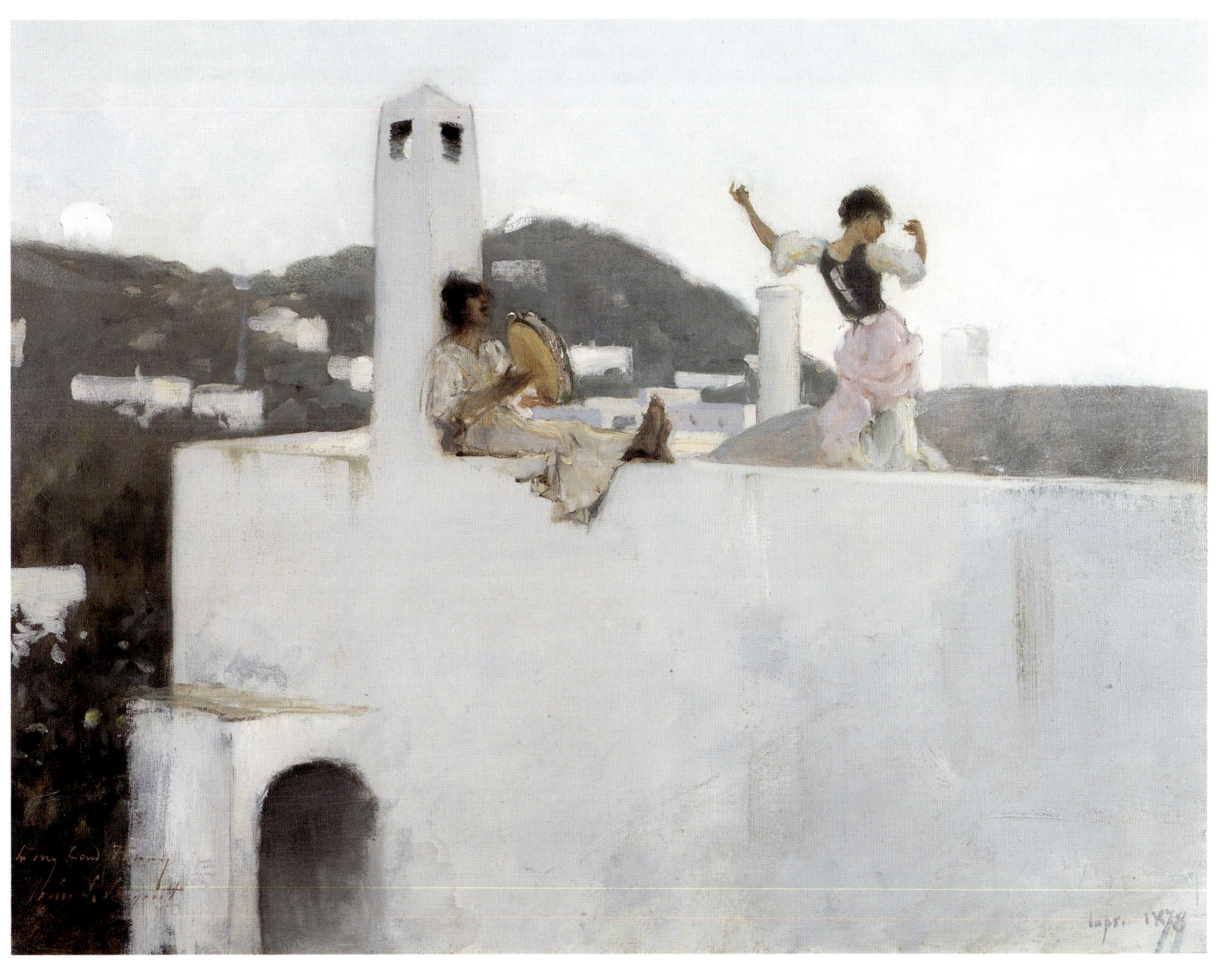

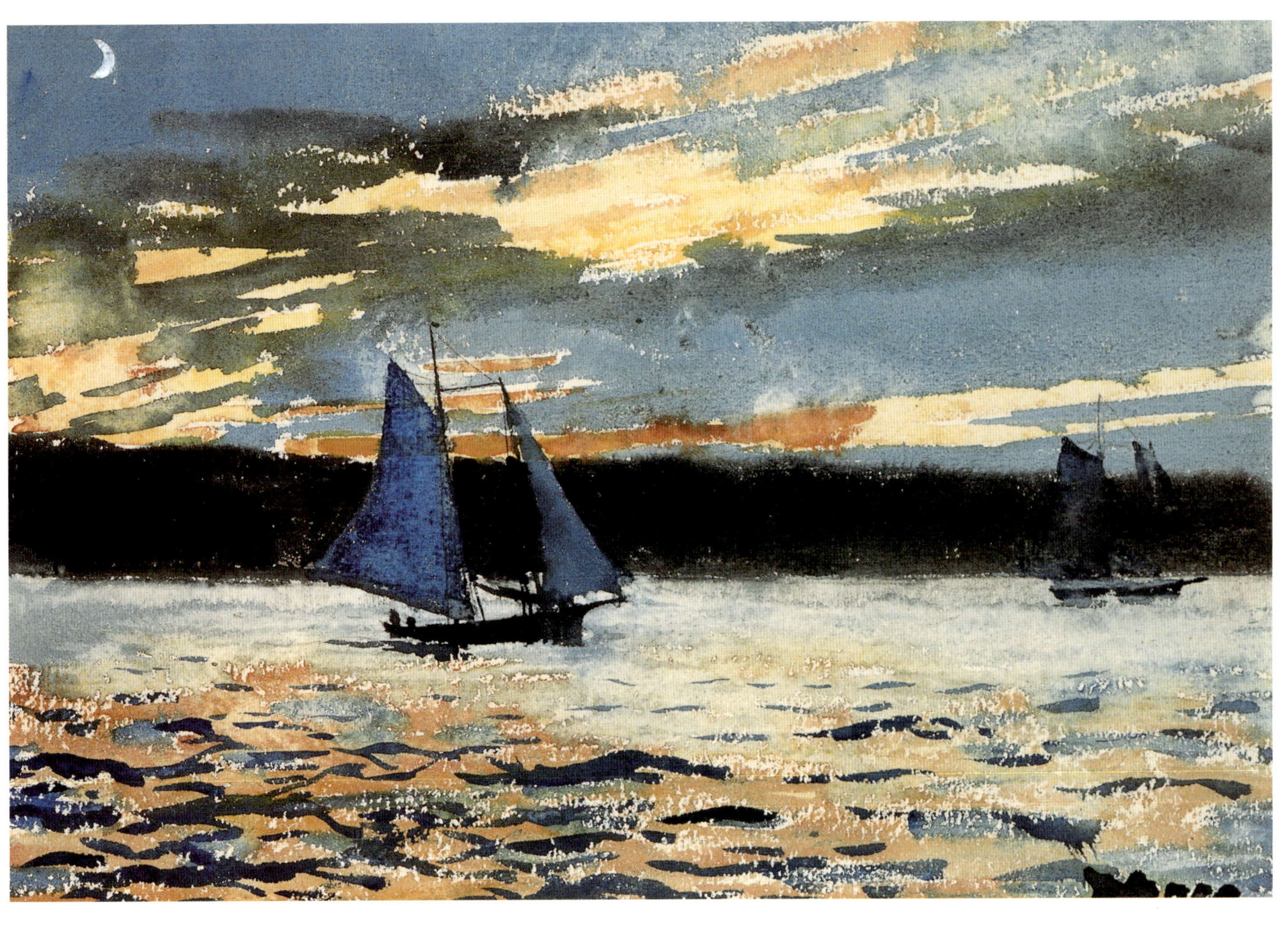

PLATE 22
William Michael Harnett (1848–1892)
STUDENT 1866
EXHIBITOR 1877–81
*Still Life with Tankard,* 1883
Oil on canvas, 5 x 7 inches
Private Collection

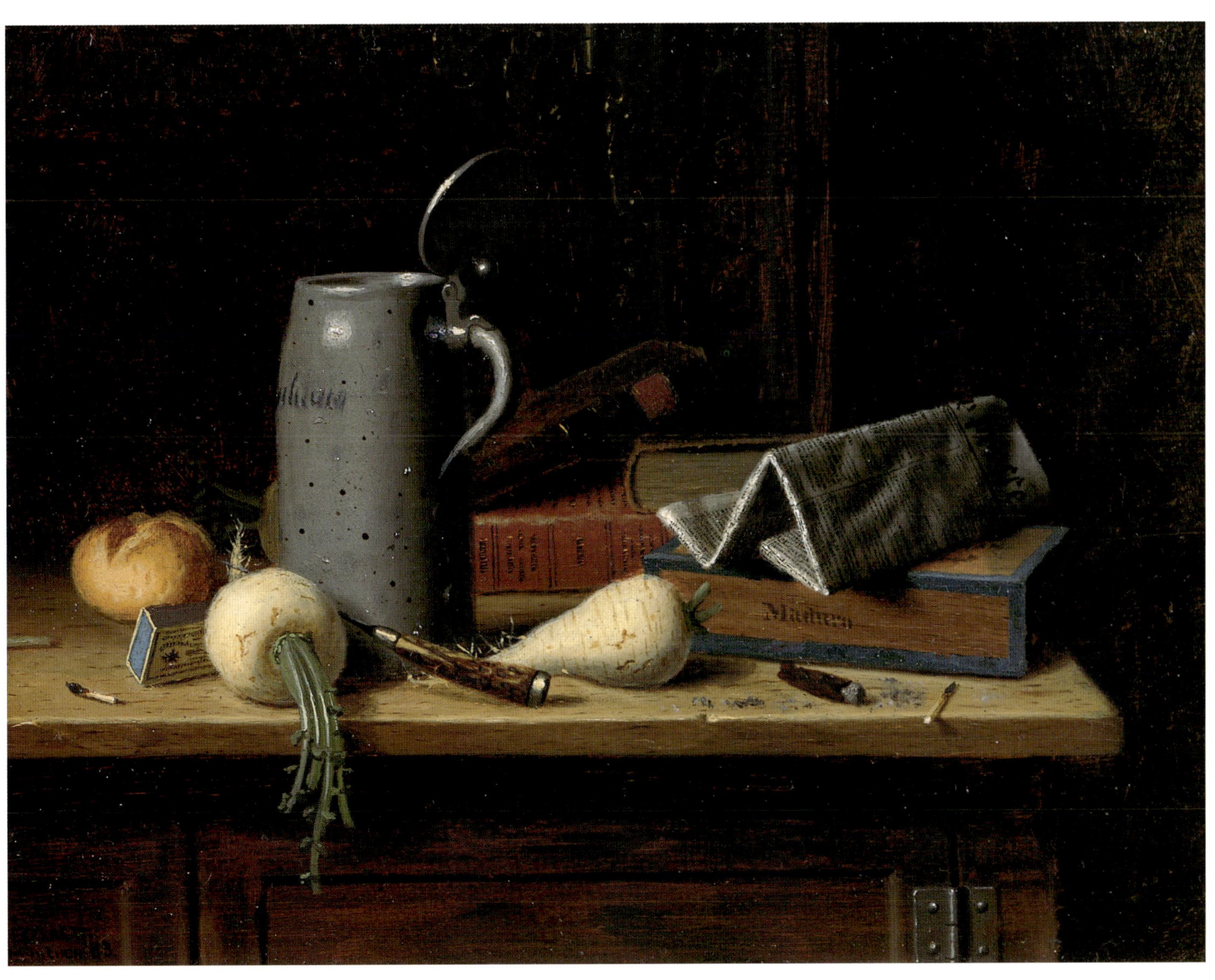

PLATE 23
Frederic Remington (1861–1909)
EXHIBITOR  1892–1910
*Return of a Blackfoot War Party,* 1887
Oil on canvas, 28 ½ x 50 inches
Courtesy of The Anschutz Collection

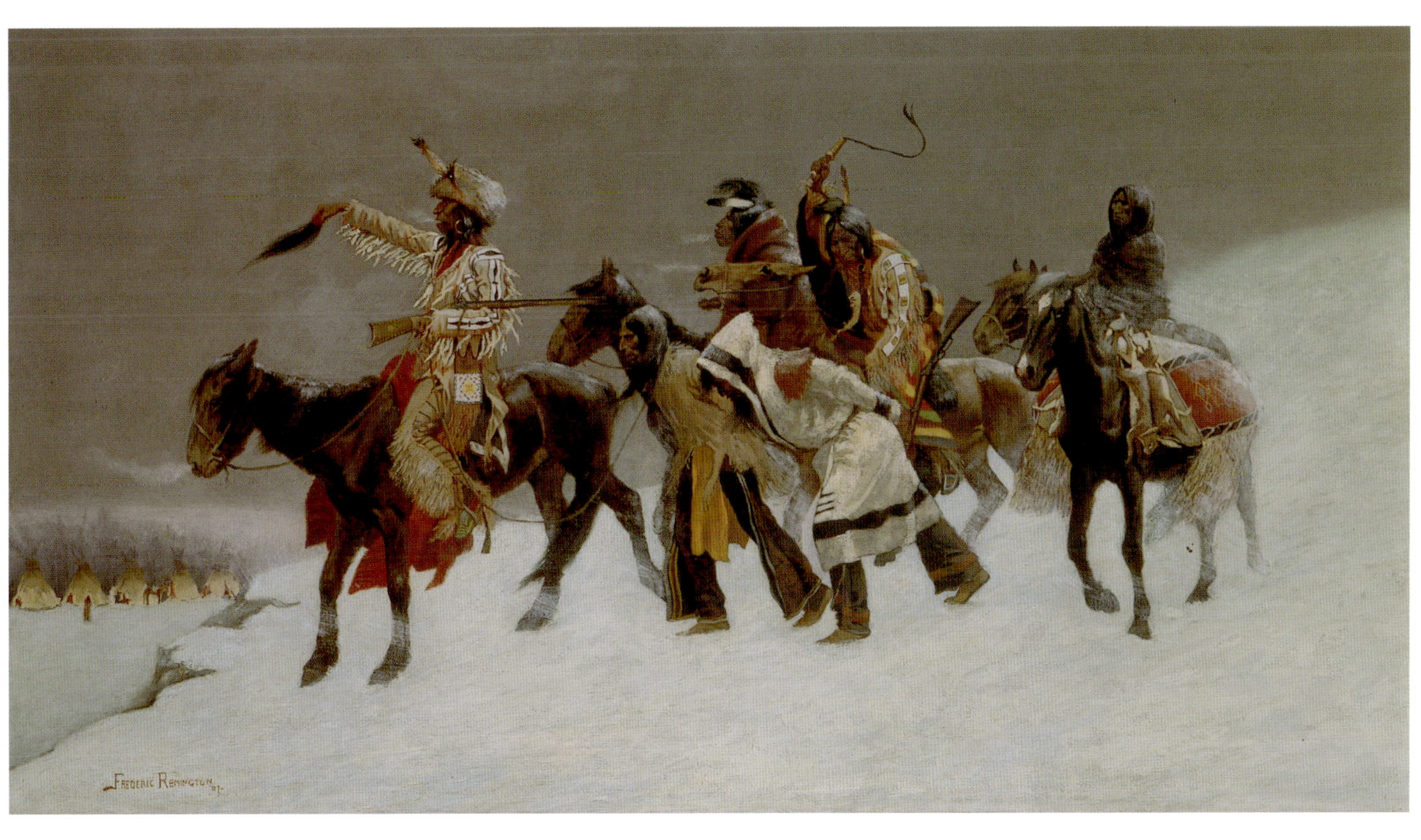

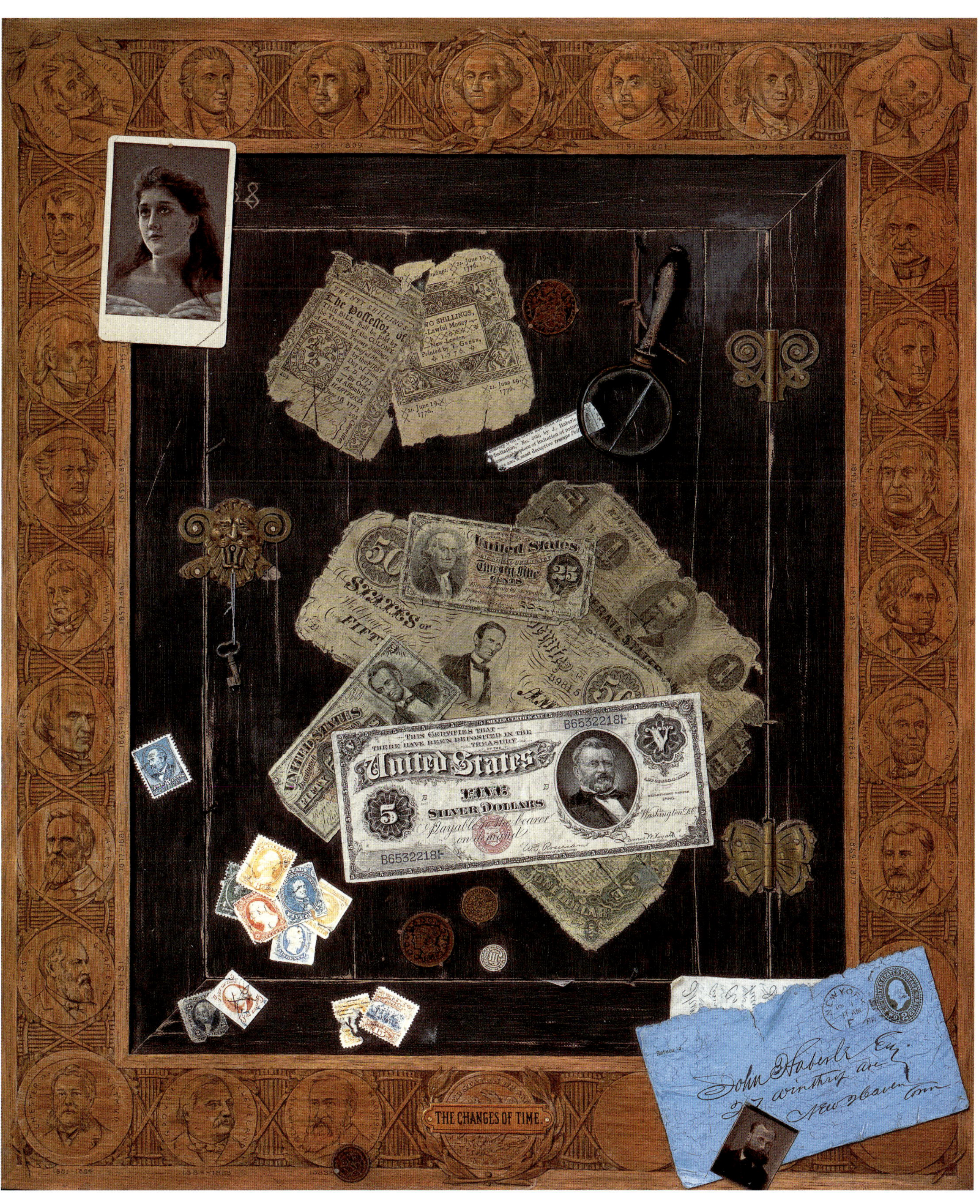

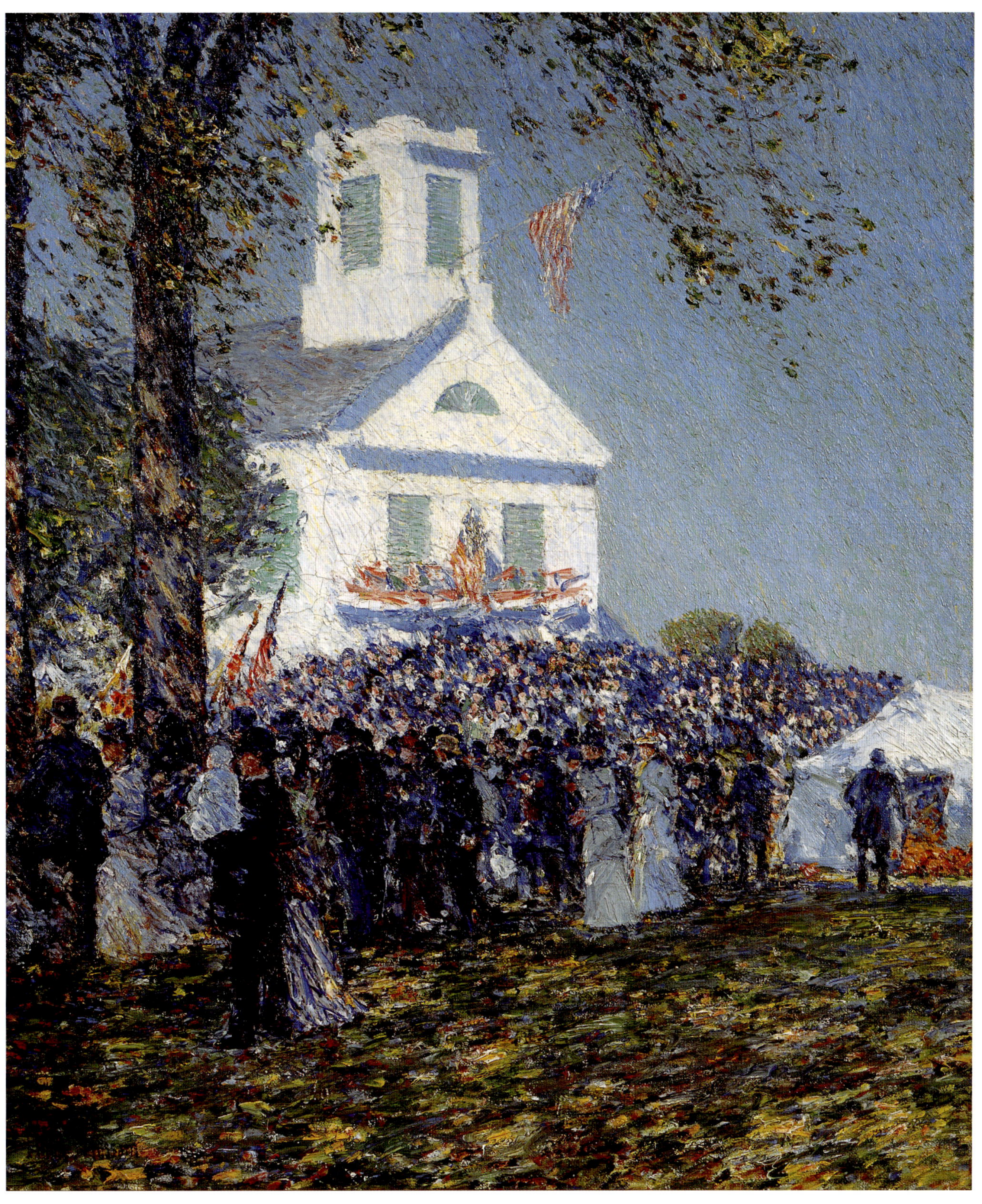

PLATE 26
Childe Hassam (1859–1935)
EXHIBITOR 1884–1936
MEDAL 1920
*Poppies,* ca. 1890–94
Oil on canvas, 18 x 25 ¼ inches
Private Collection, Washington, D.C.

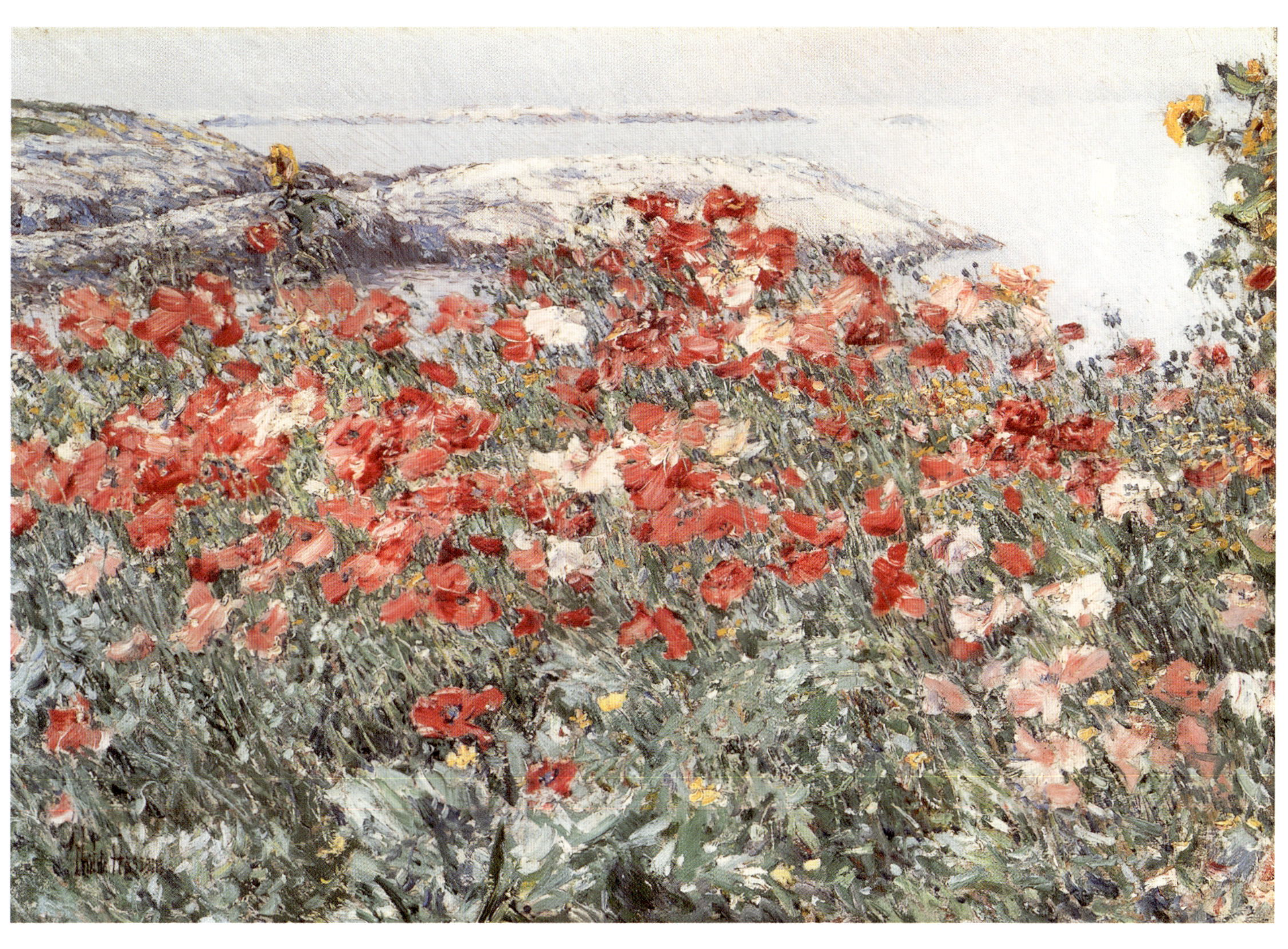

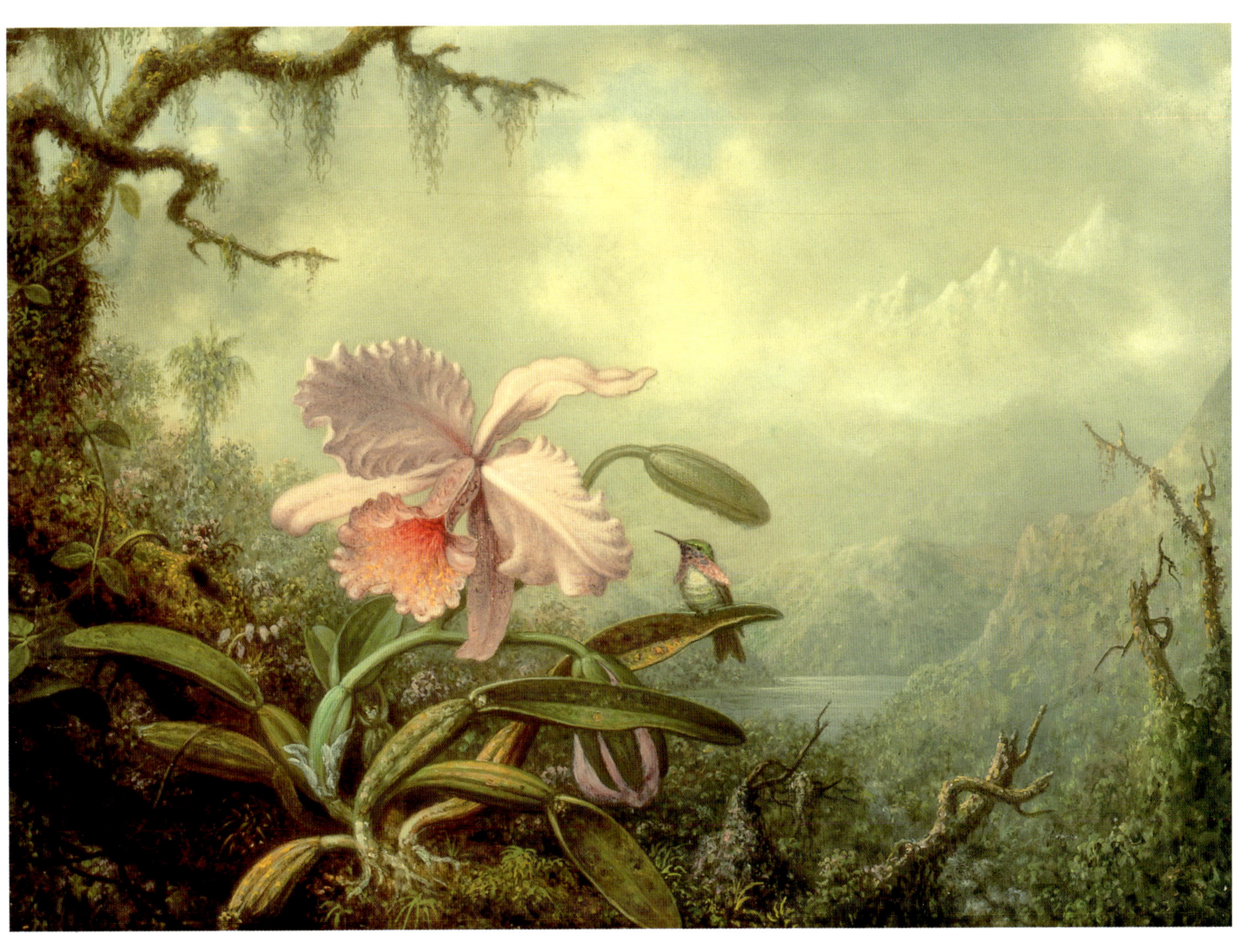

PLATE 28
Theodore Robinson (1852–1896)
FACULTY 1894–95
EXHIBITOR 1882–95
*Low Tide, Riverside Yacht Club,* 1894
Oil on canvas, 18 x 24 inches
The Margaret and Raymond Horowitz Collection

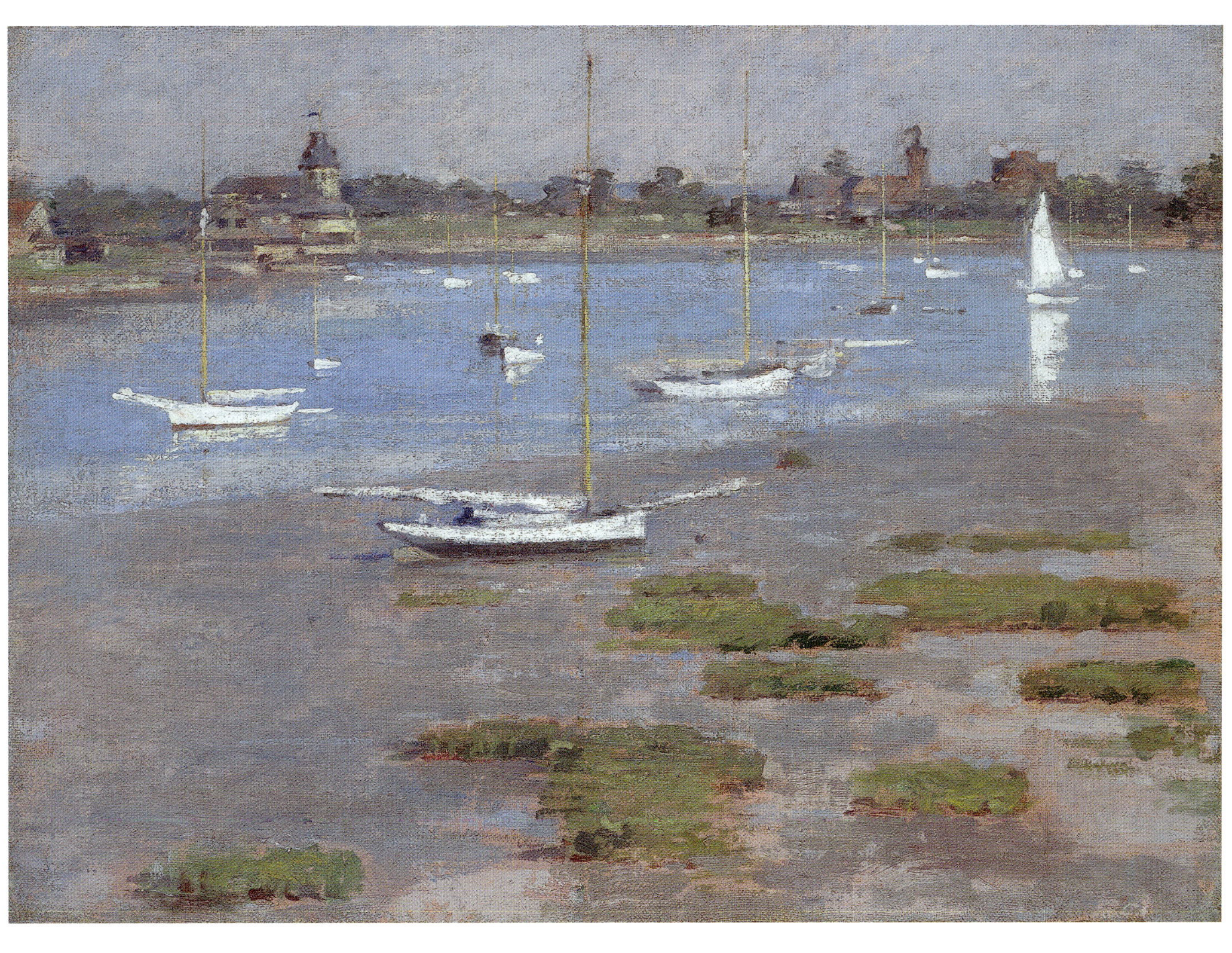

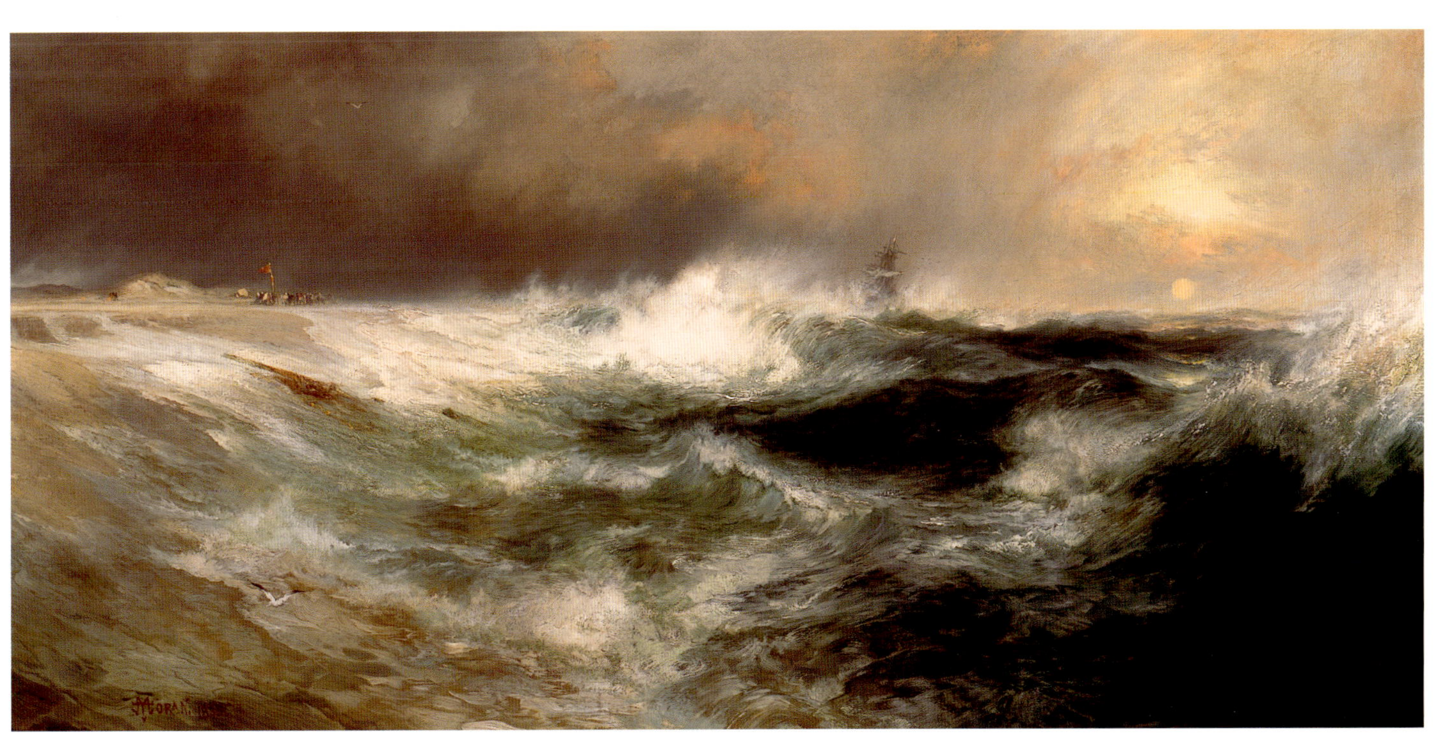

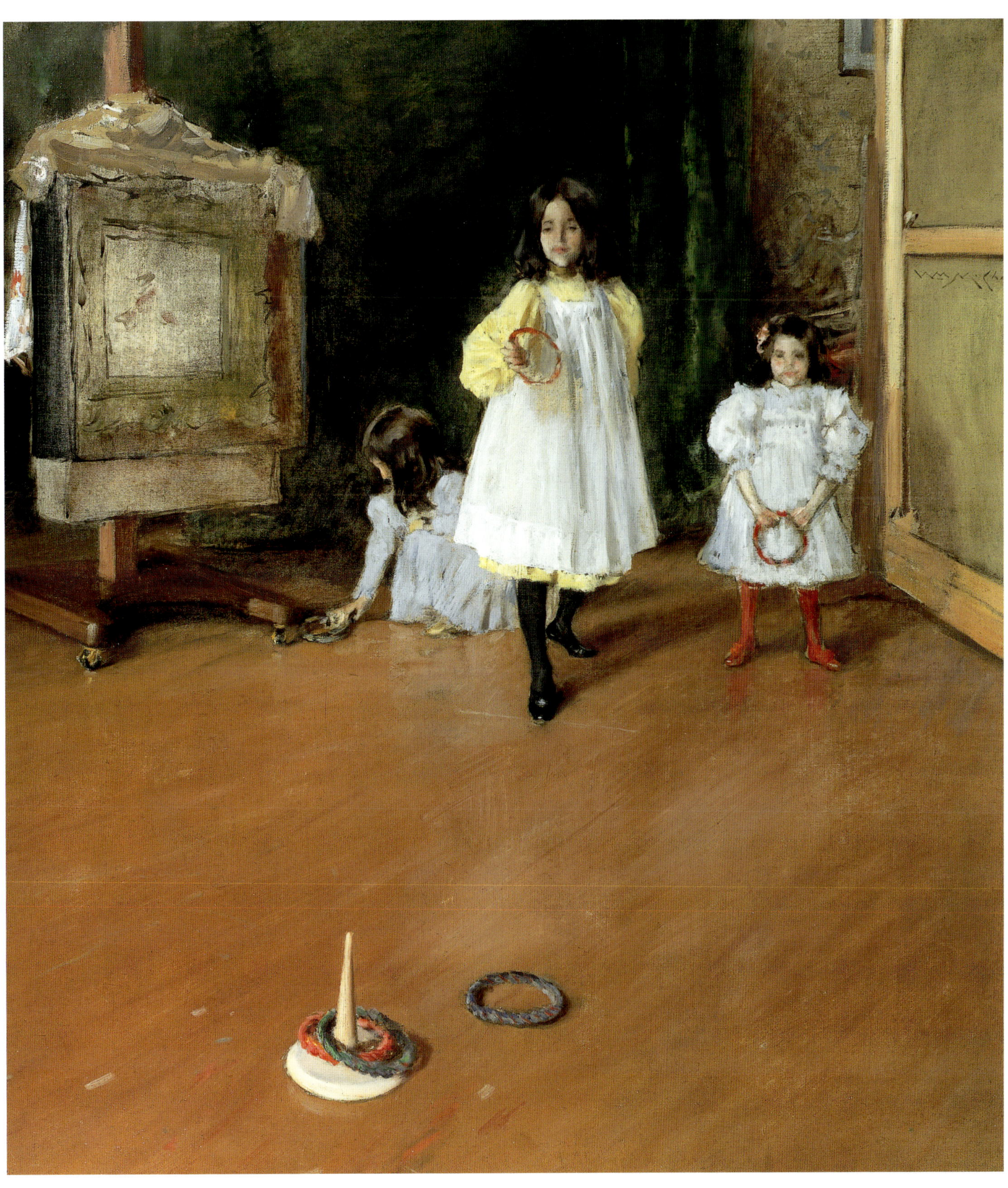

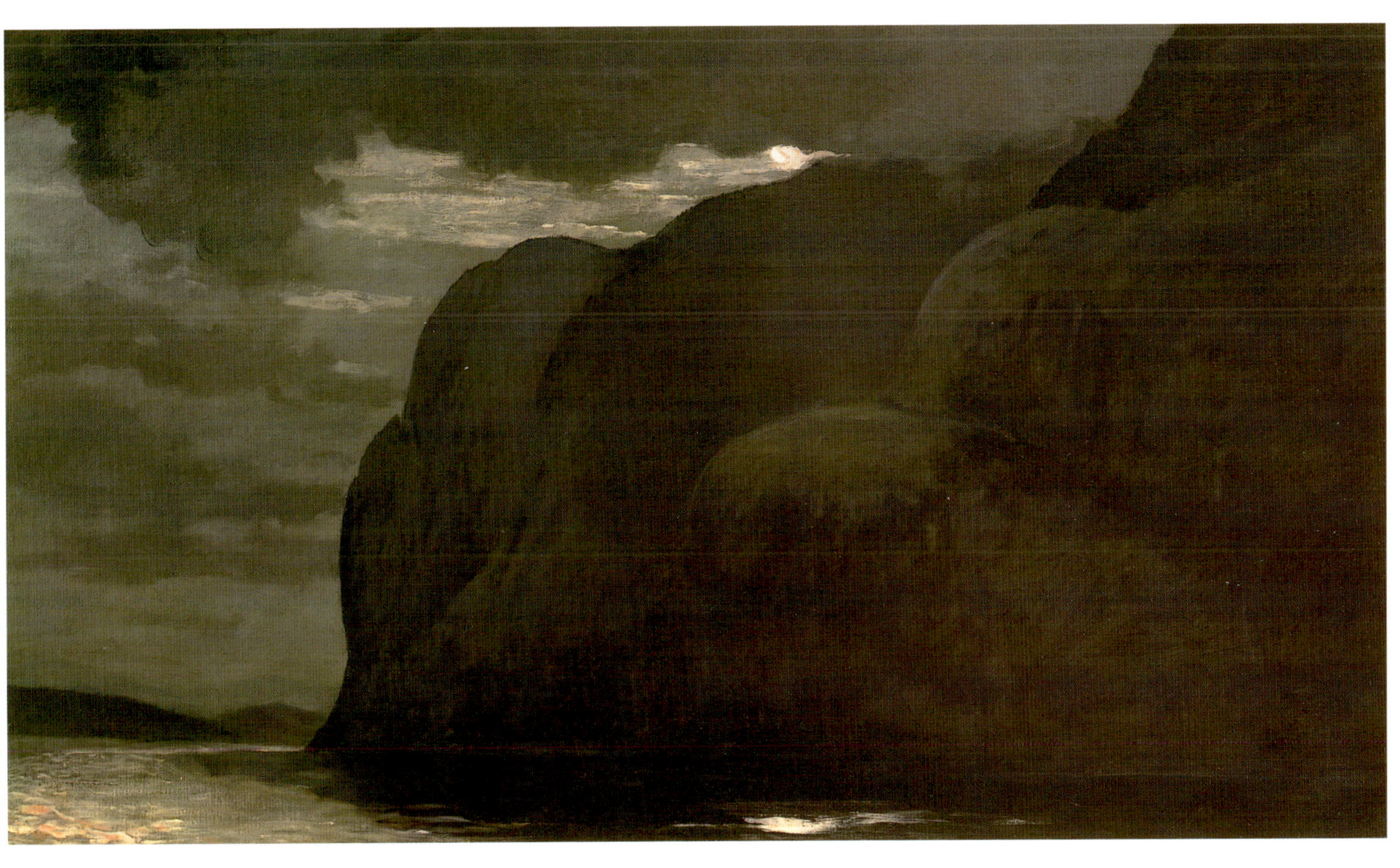

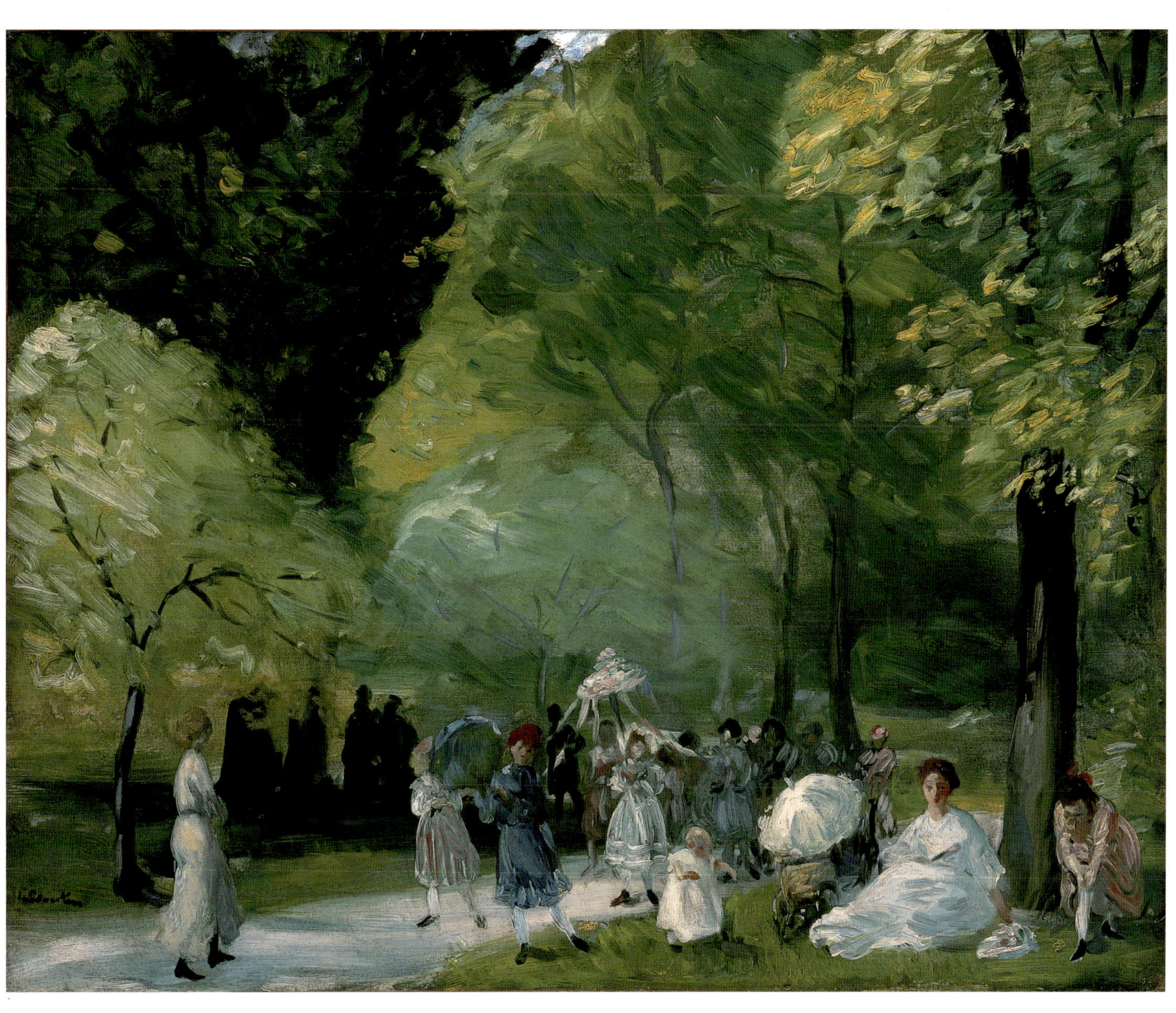

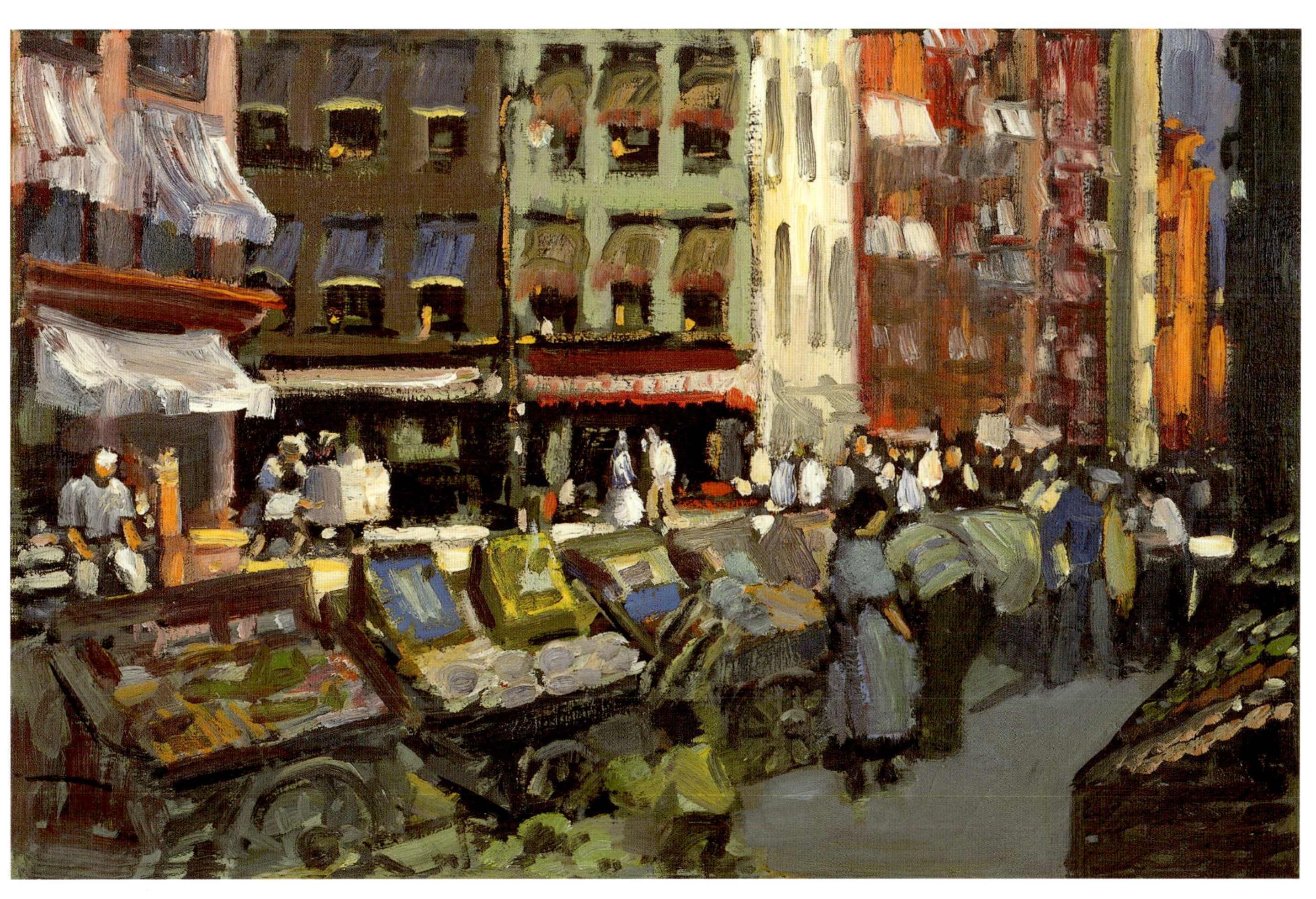

**PLATE 34**
John Sloan (1871–1951)
STUDENT 1893–94
EXHIBITOR 1901–51
*Gray and Brass,* 1907
Oil on canvas, 21 ½ x 26 ½ inches
Collection of Karen A. and Kevin W. Kennedy

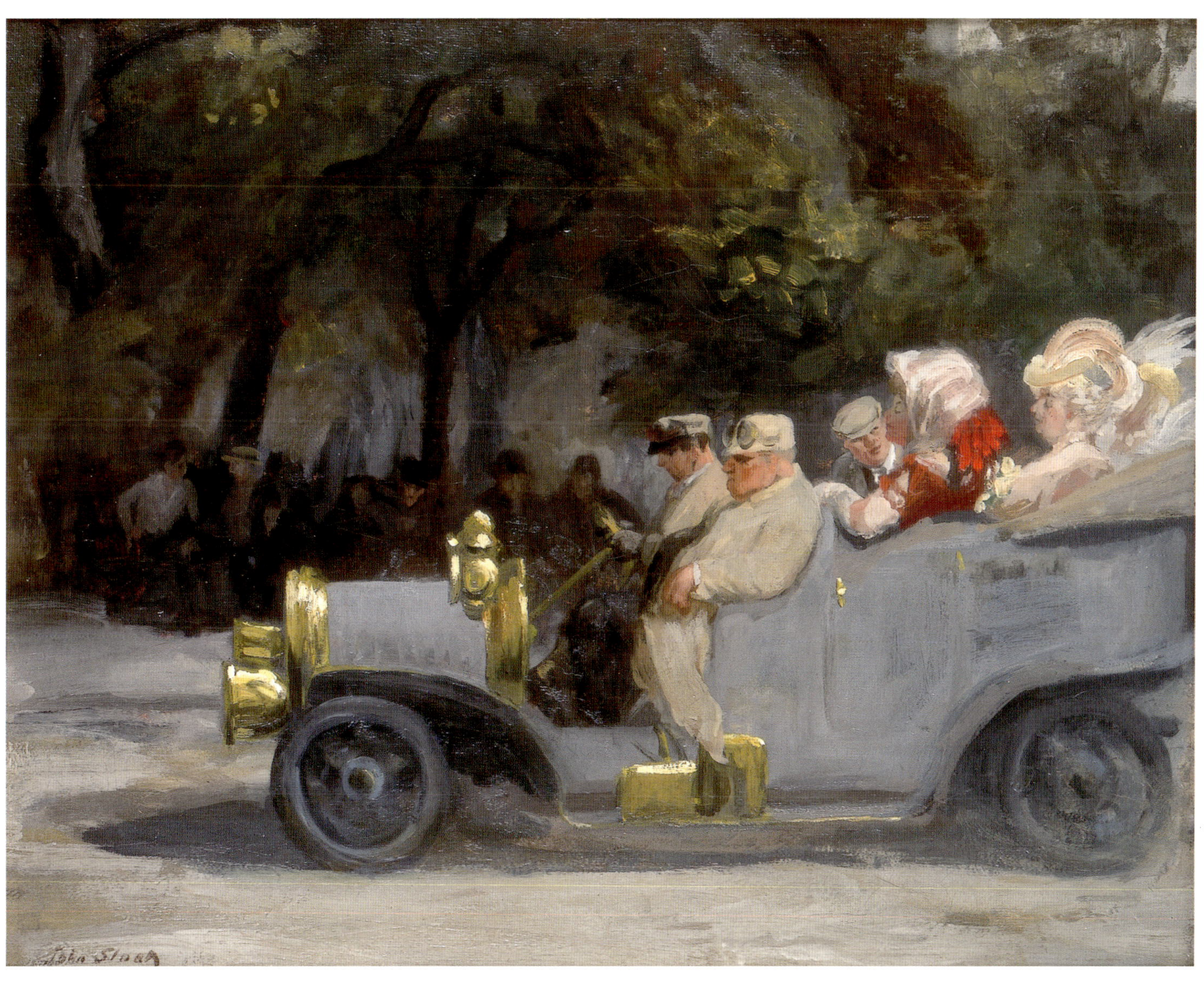

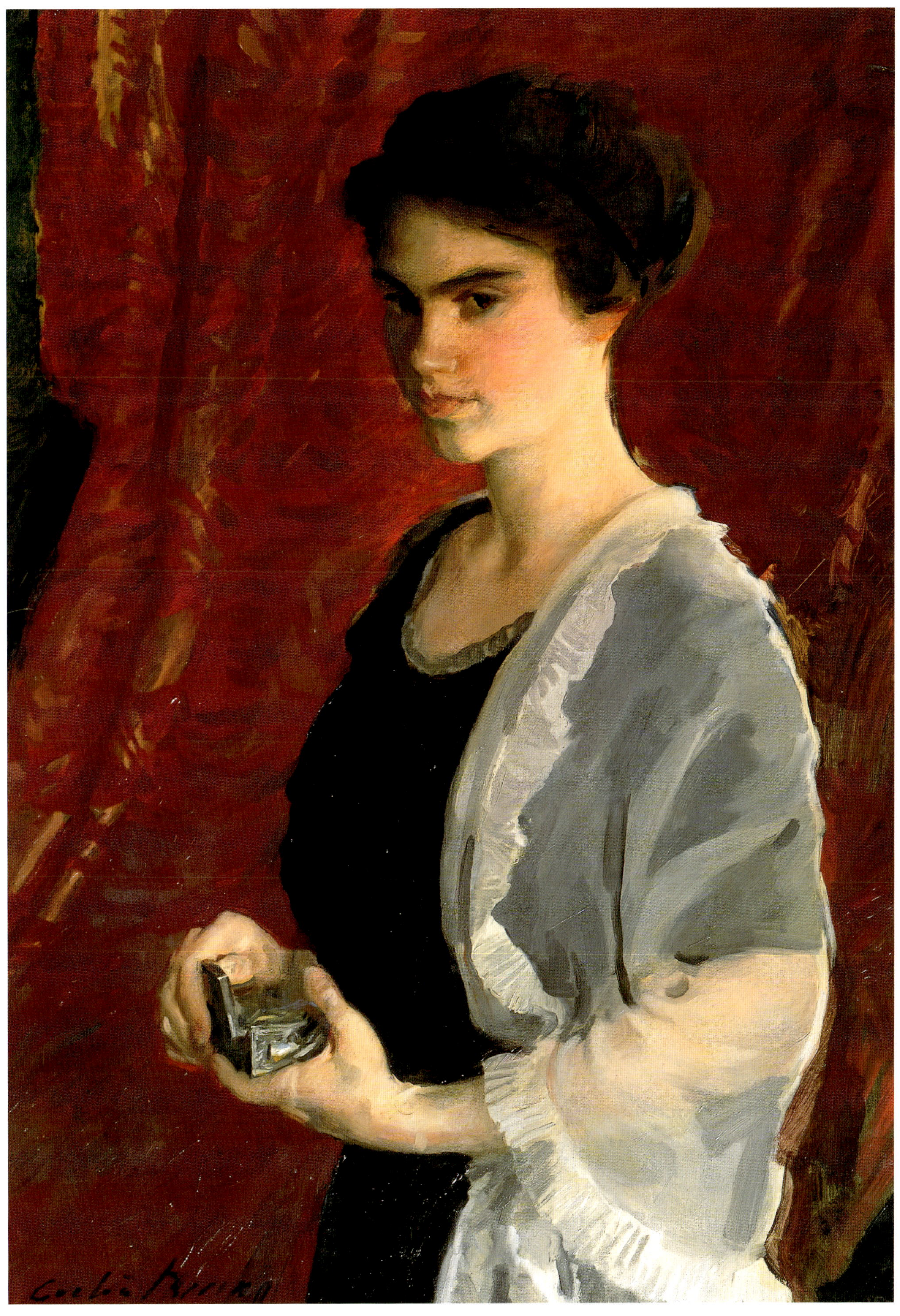

PLATE 36
John Singer Sargent (1856–1925)
EXHIBITOR 1891–1926
MEDAL 1903
*San Vagilio: A Boat with Golden Sail,* 1913
Oil on canvas, 22 x 28 inches
Private Collection

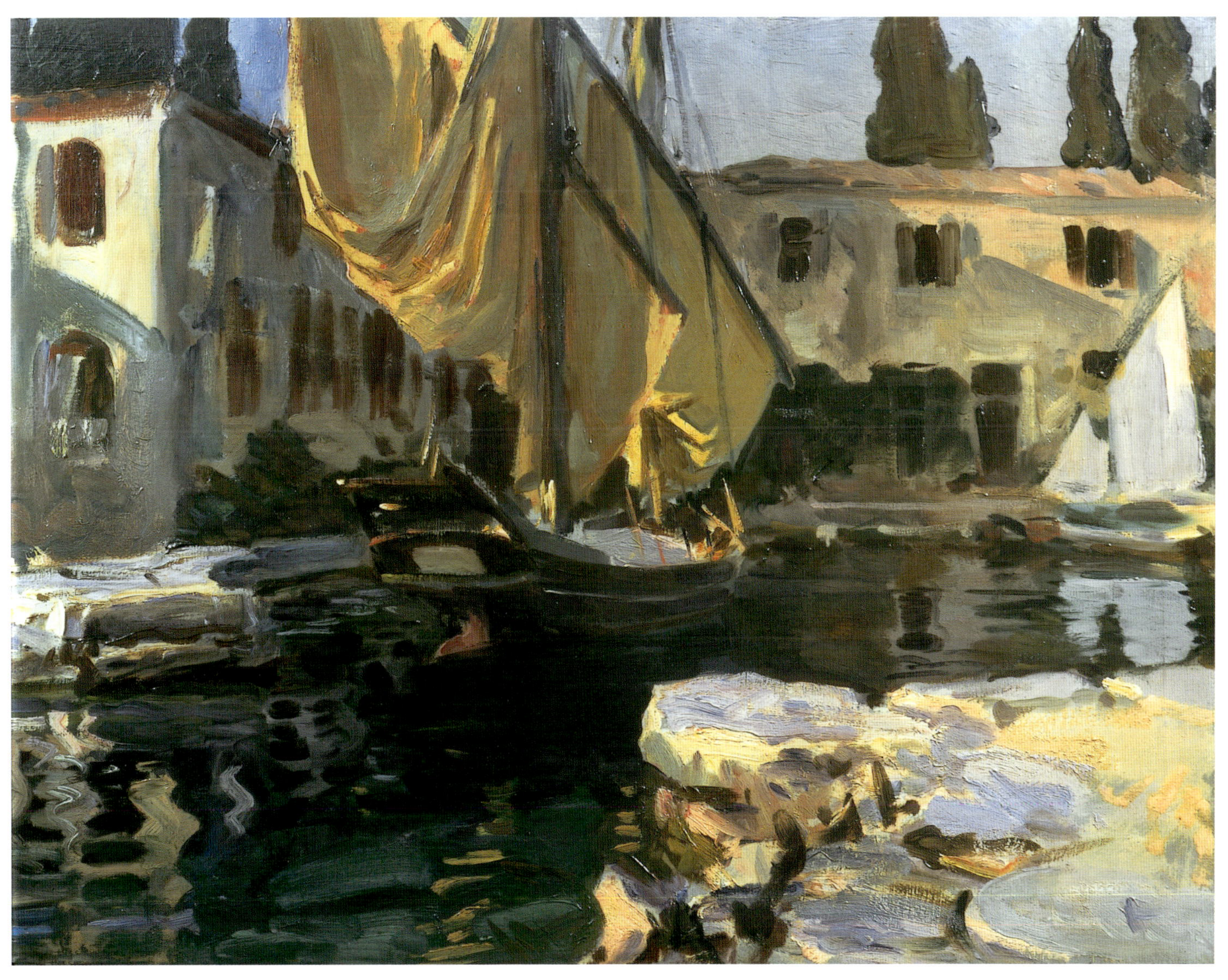

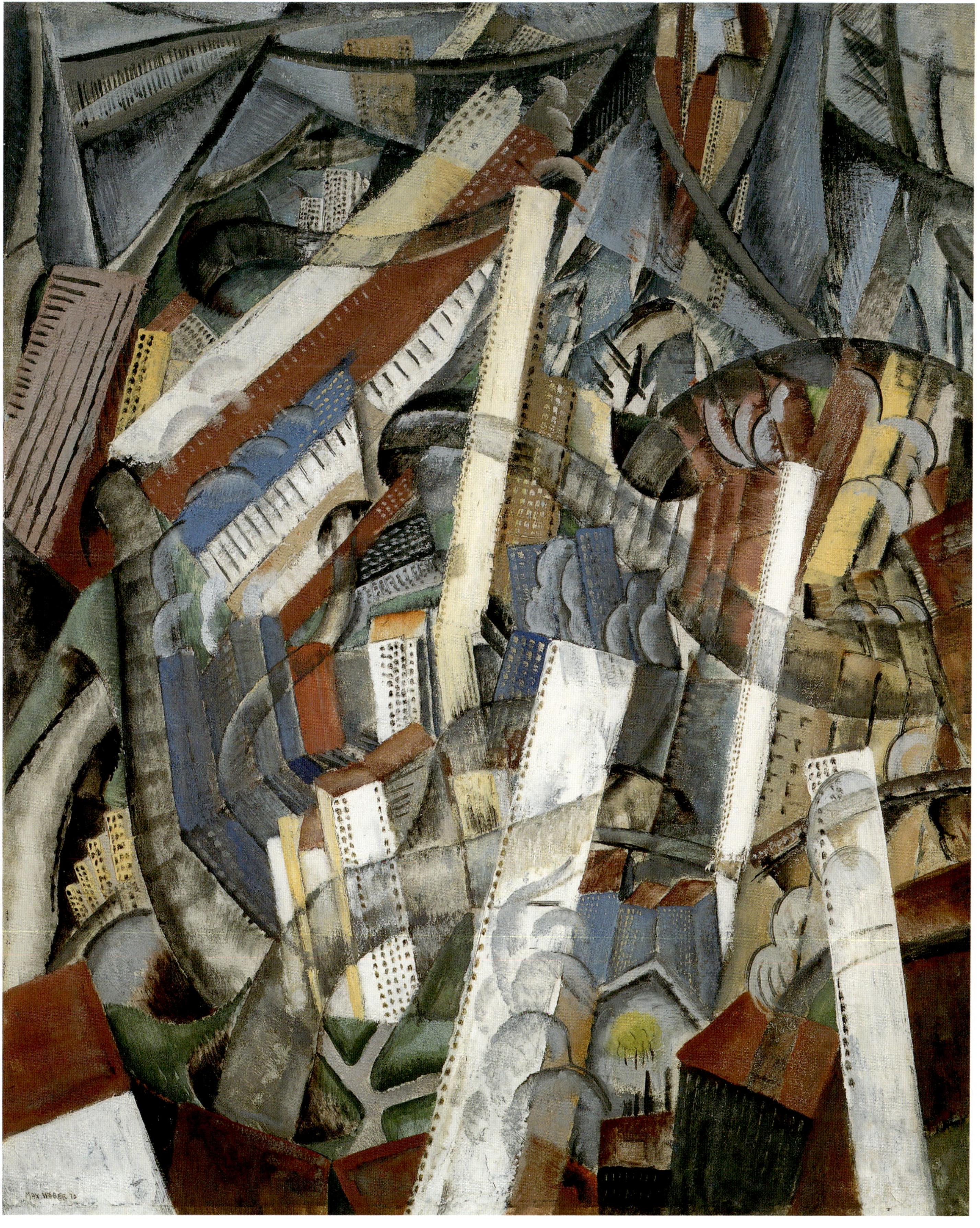

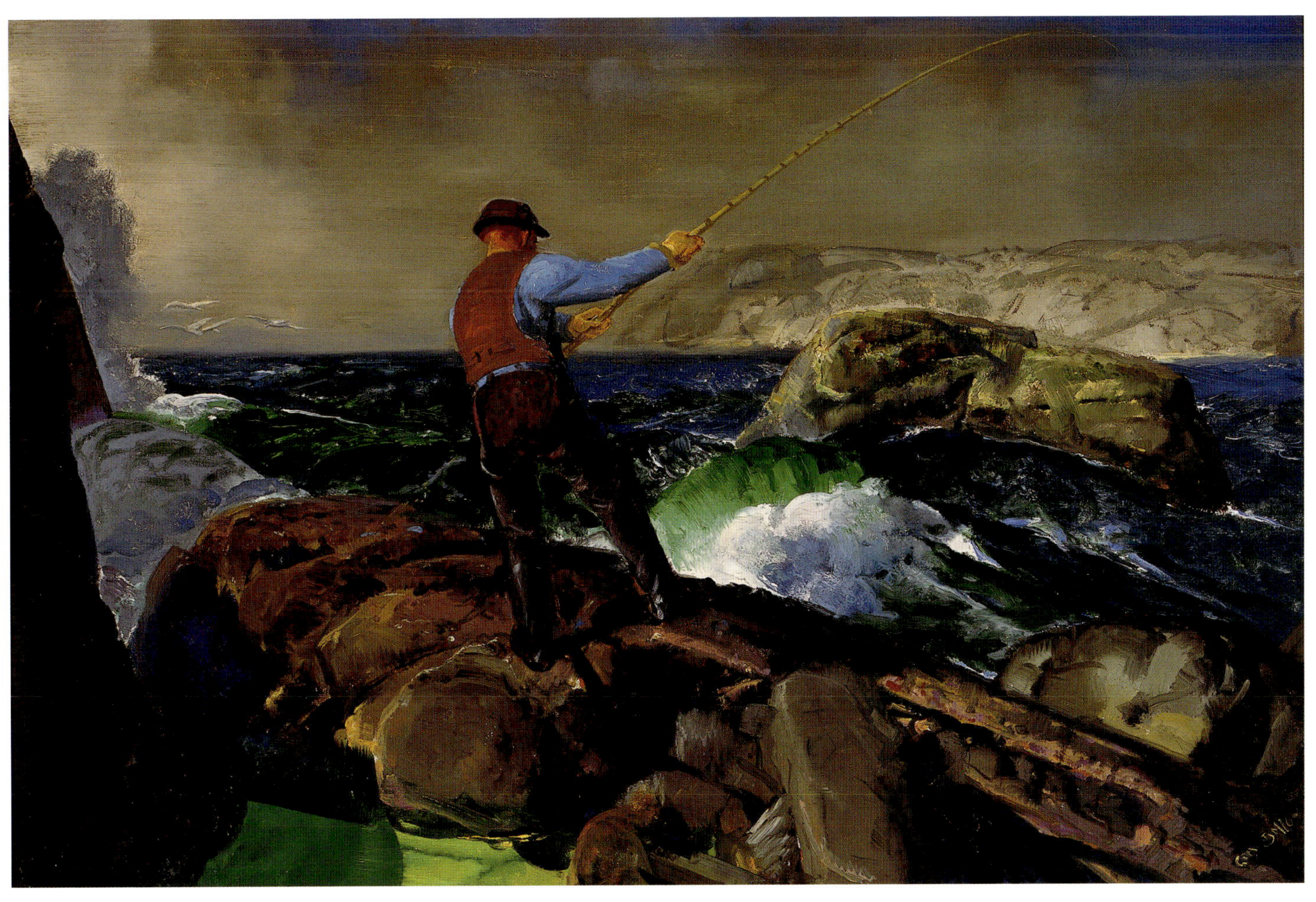

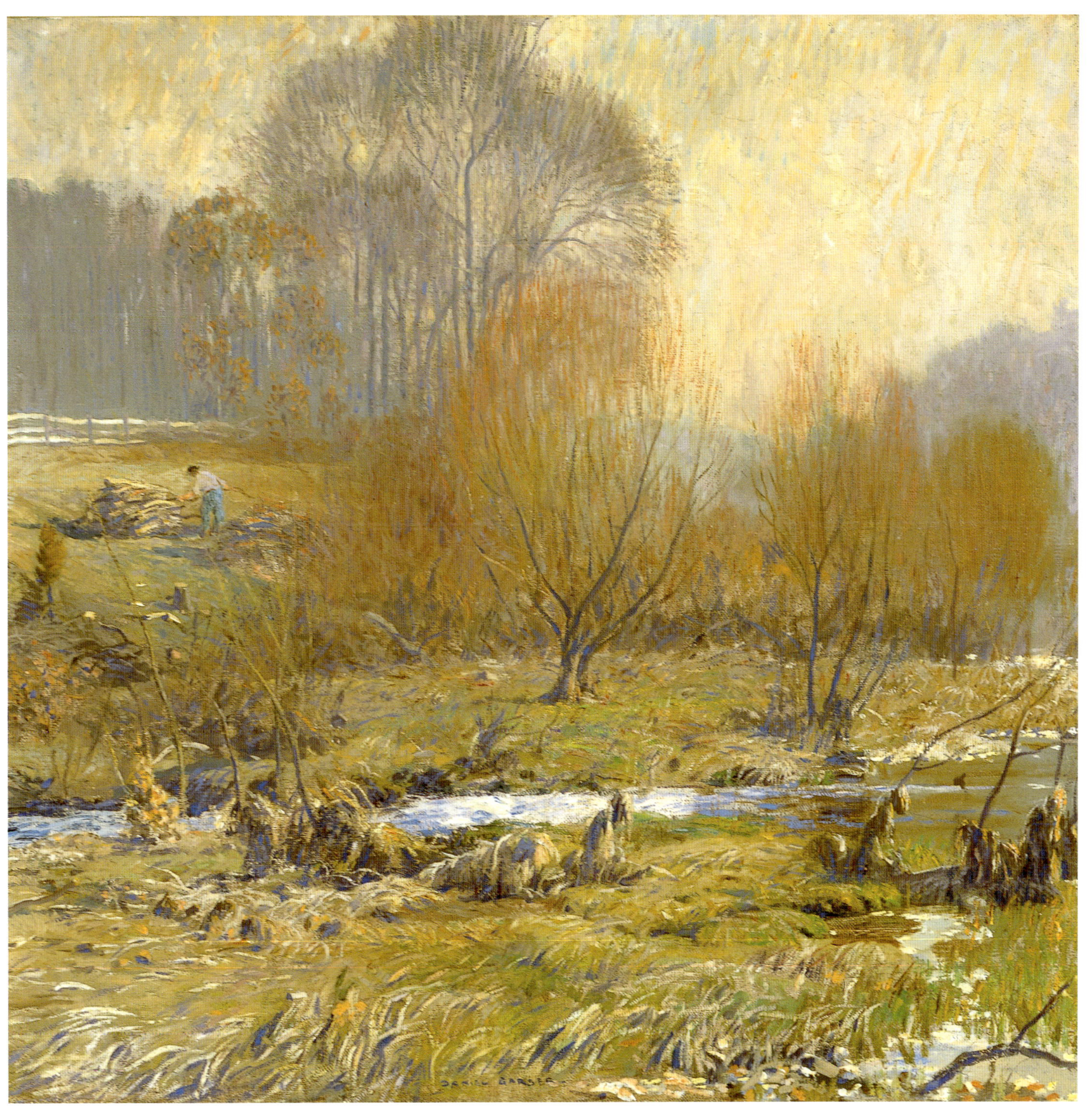

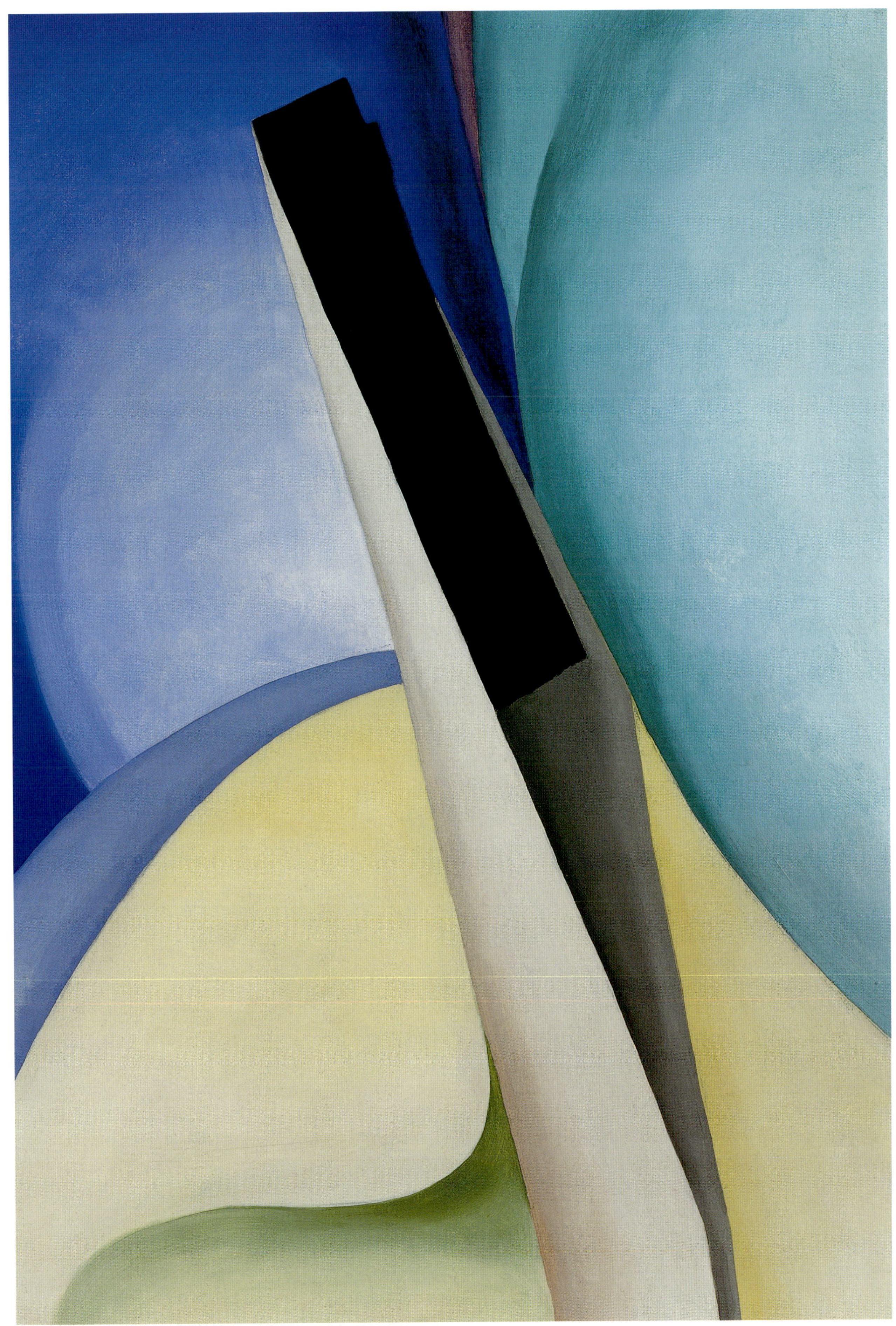

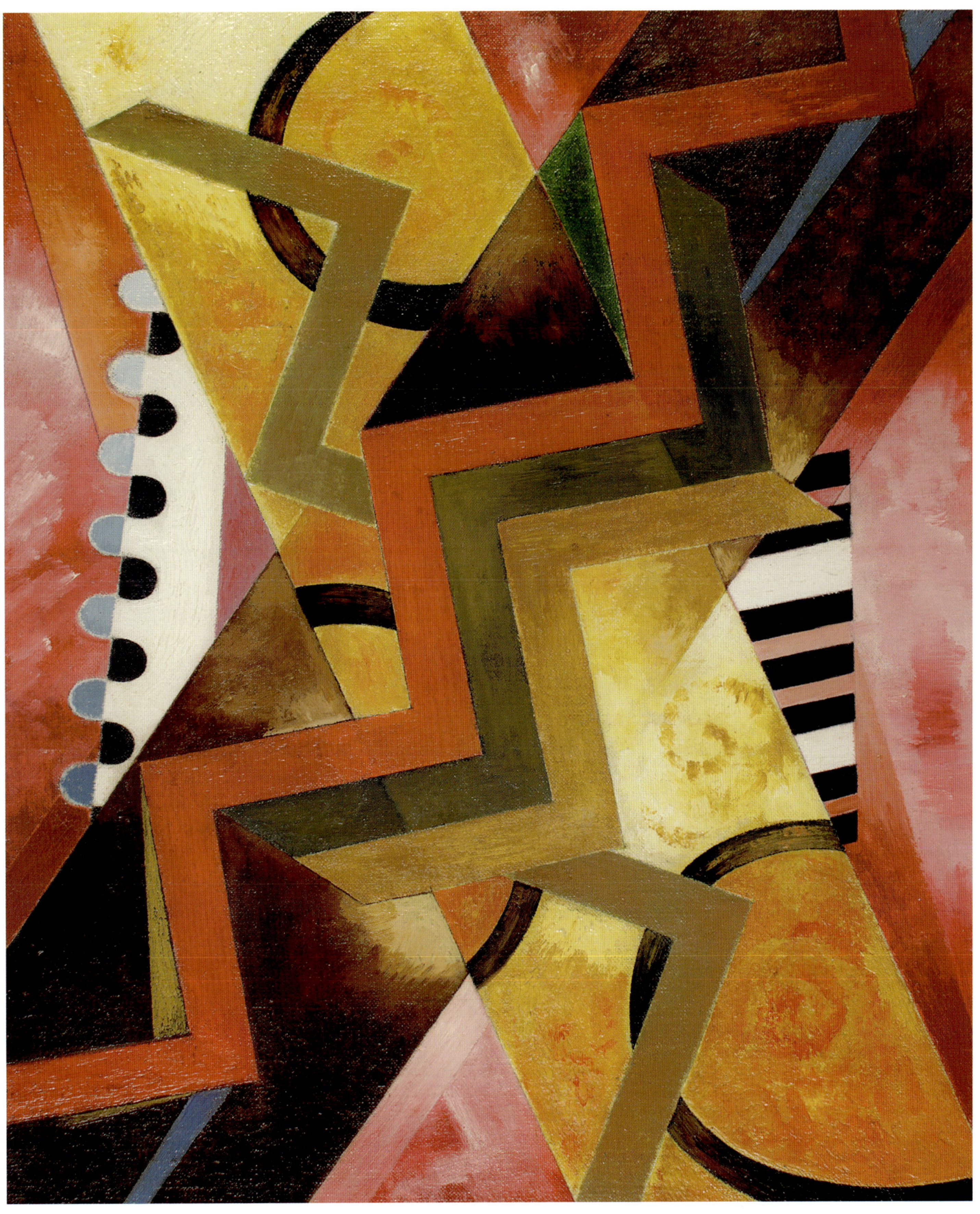

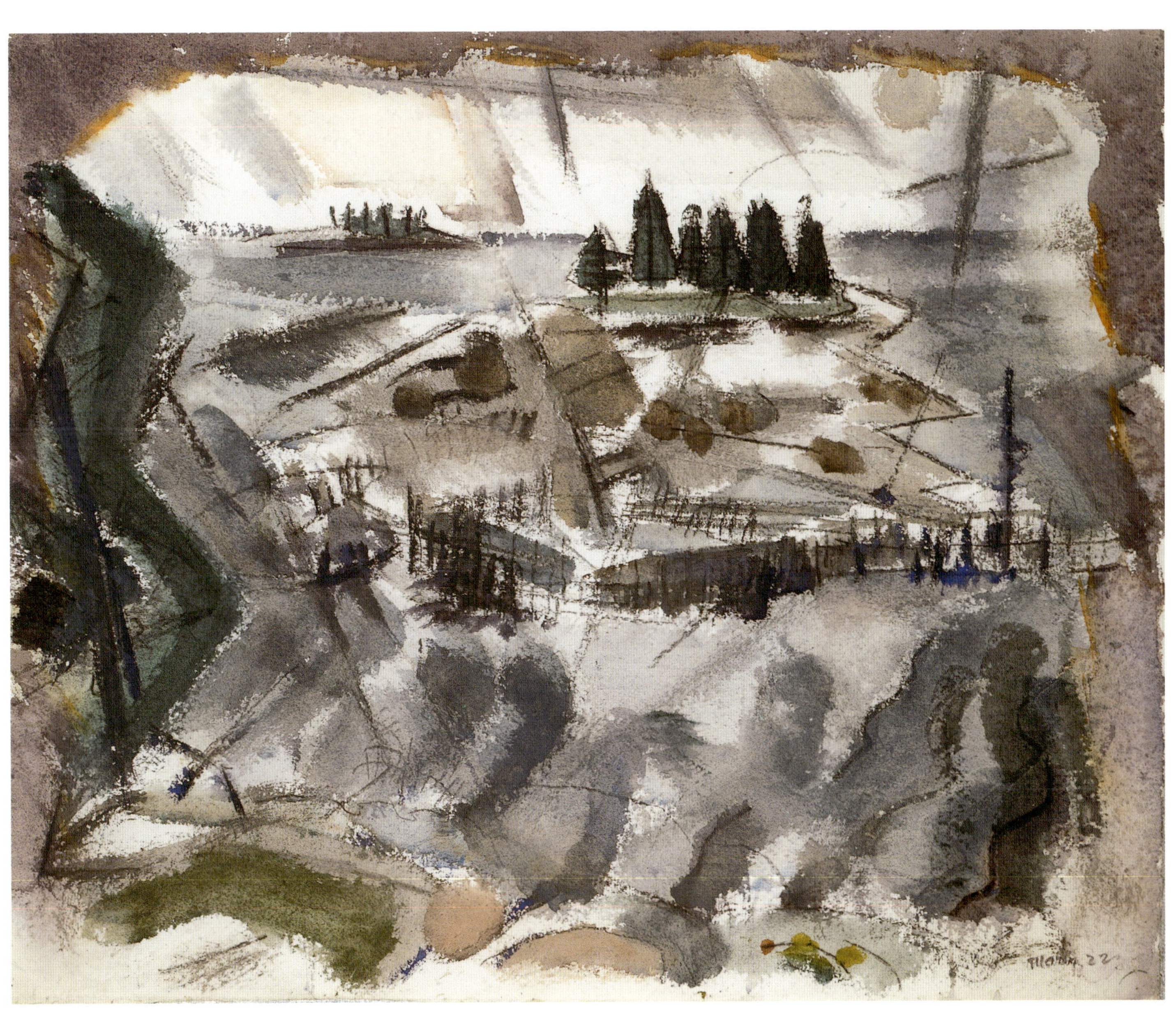

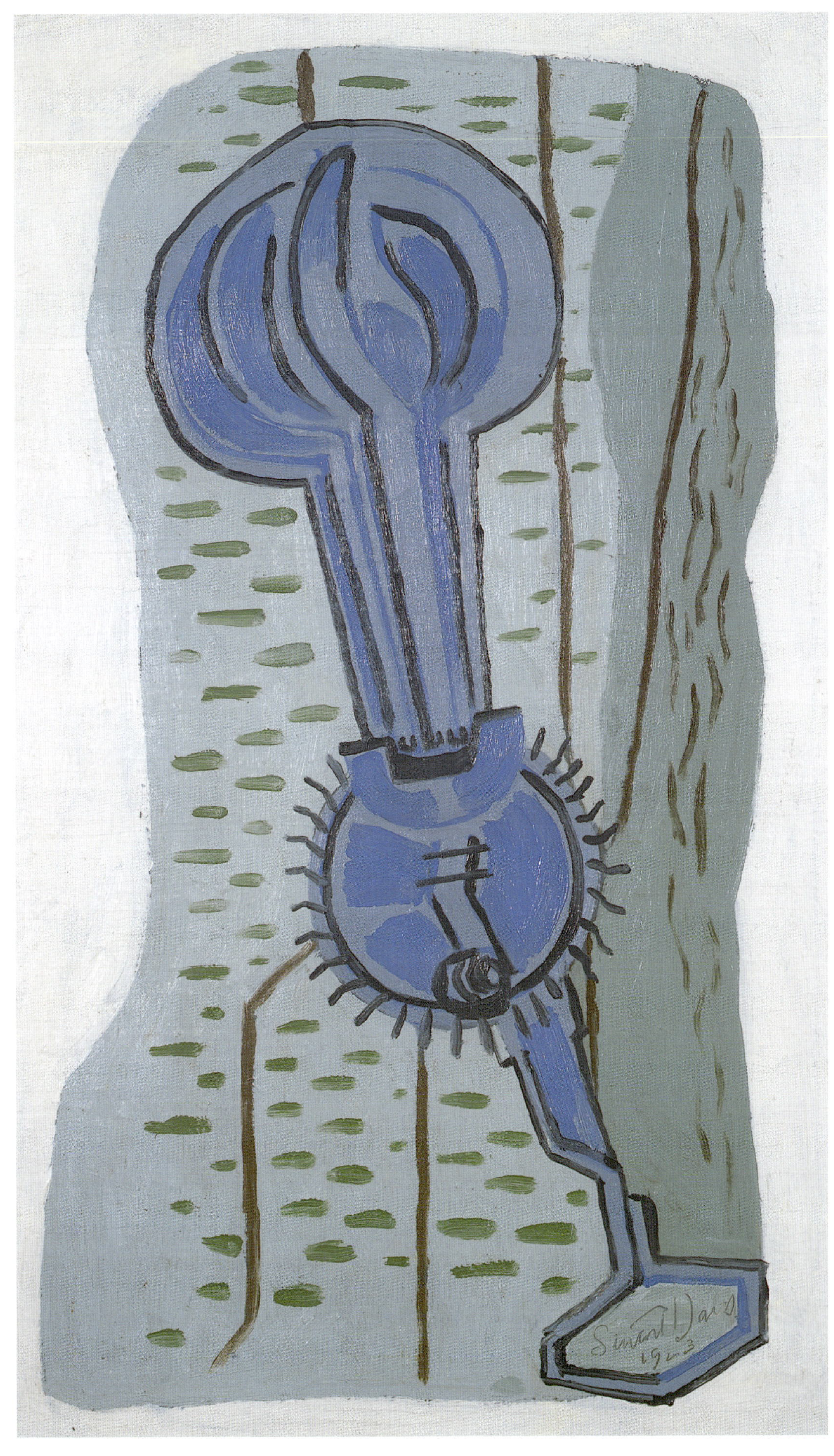


Stuart Davis
1923

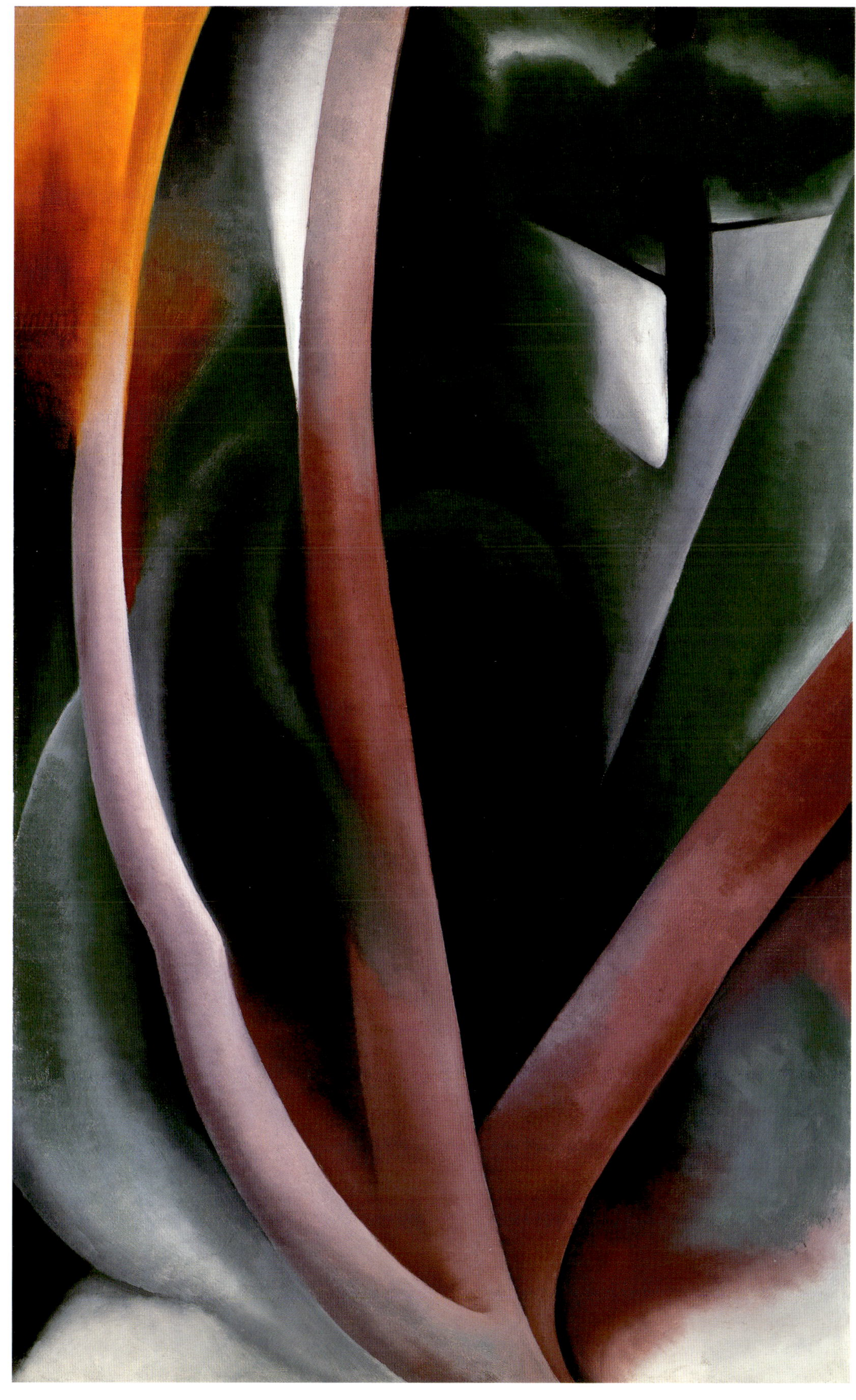

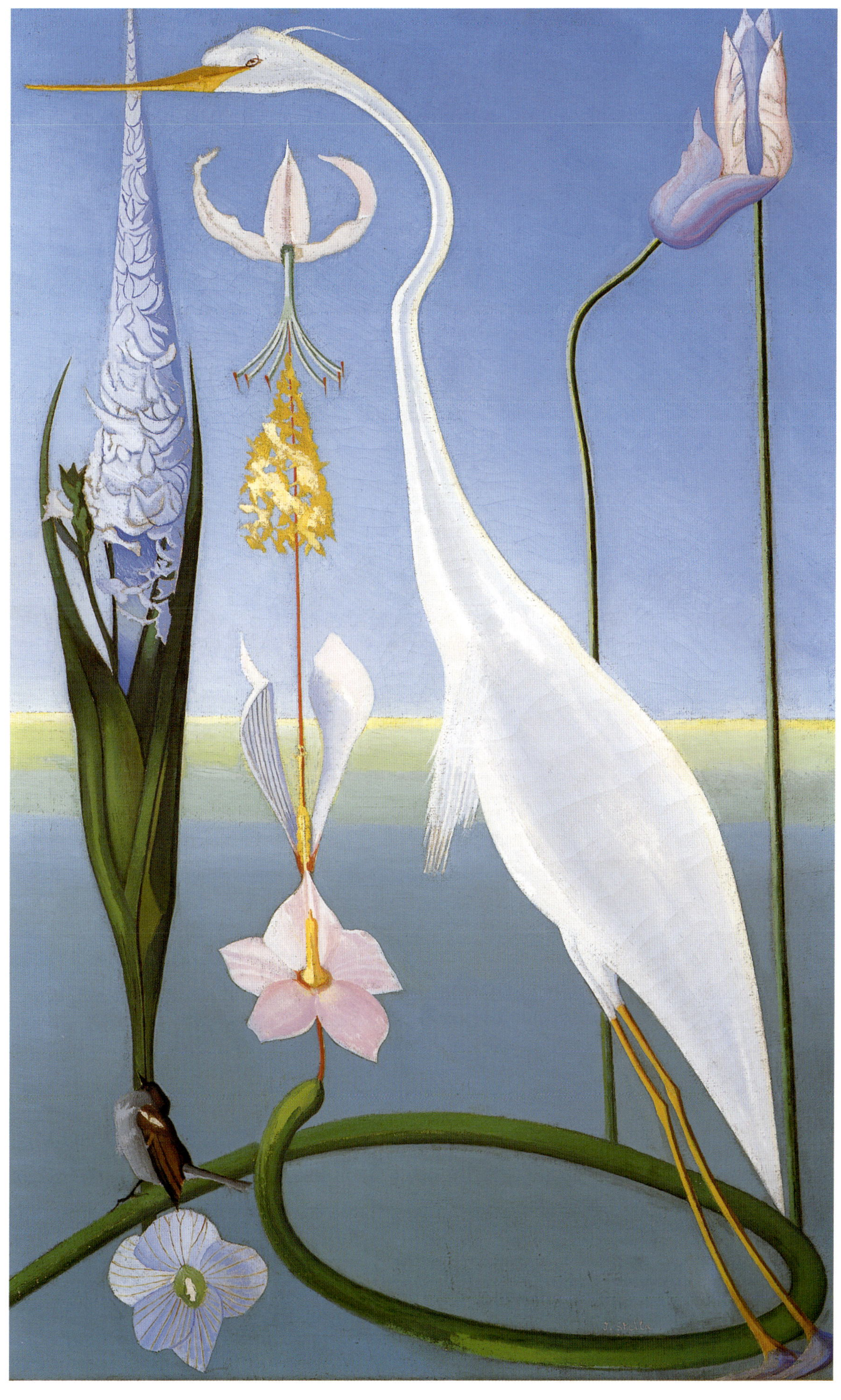

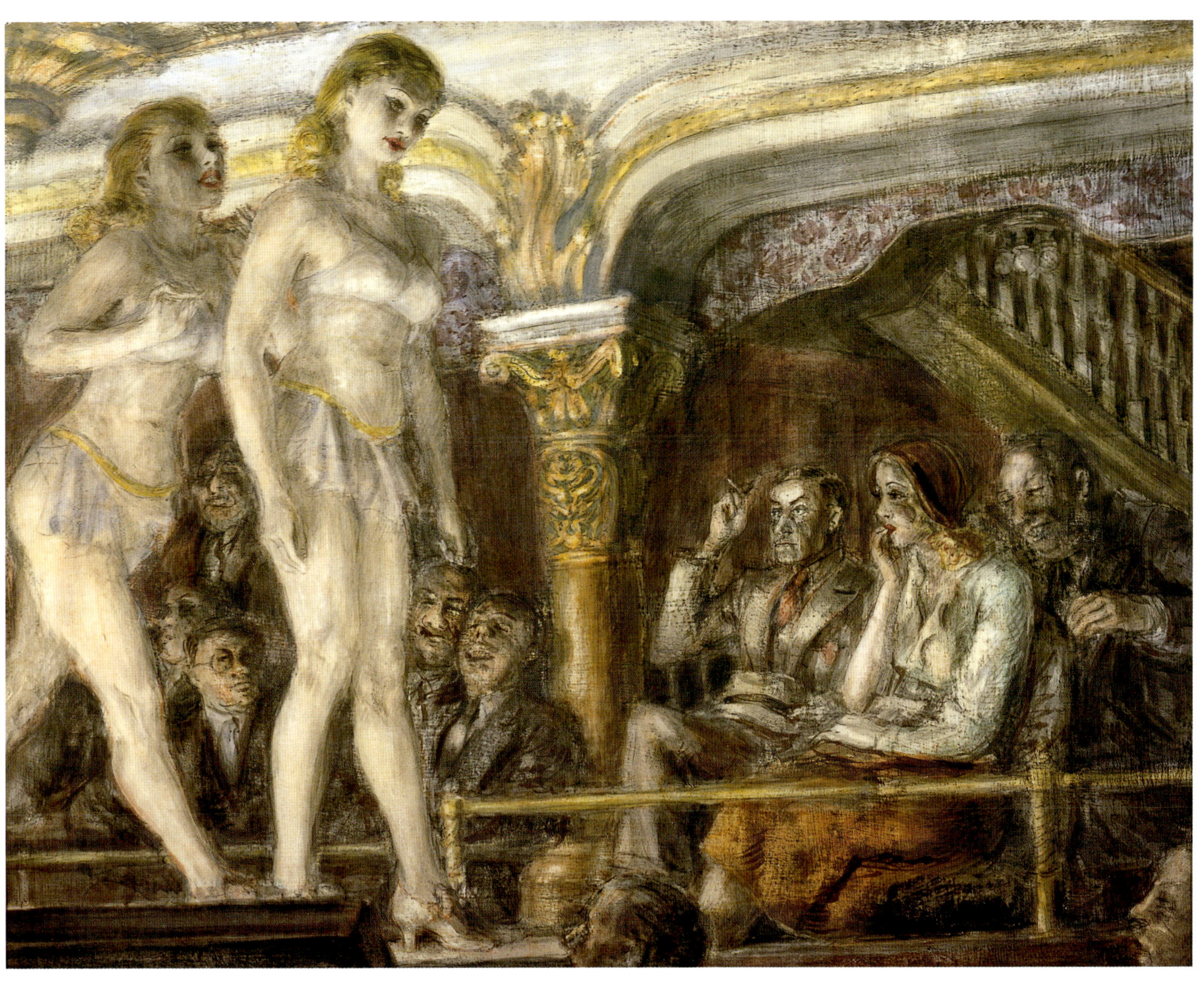

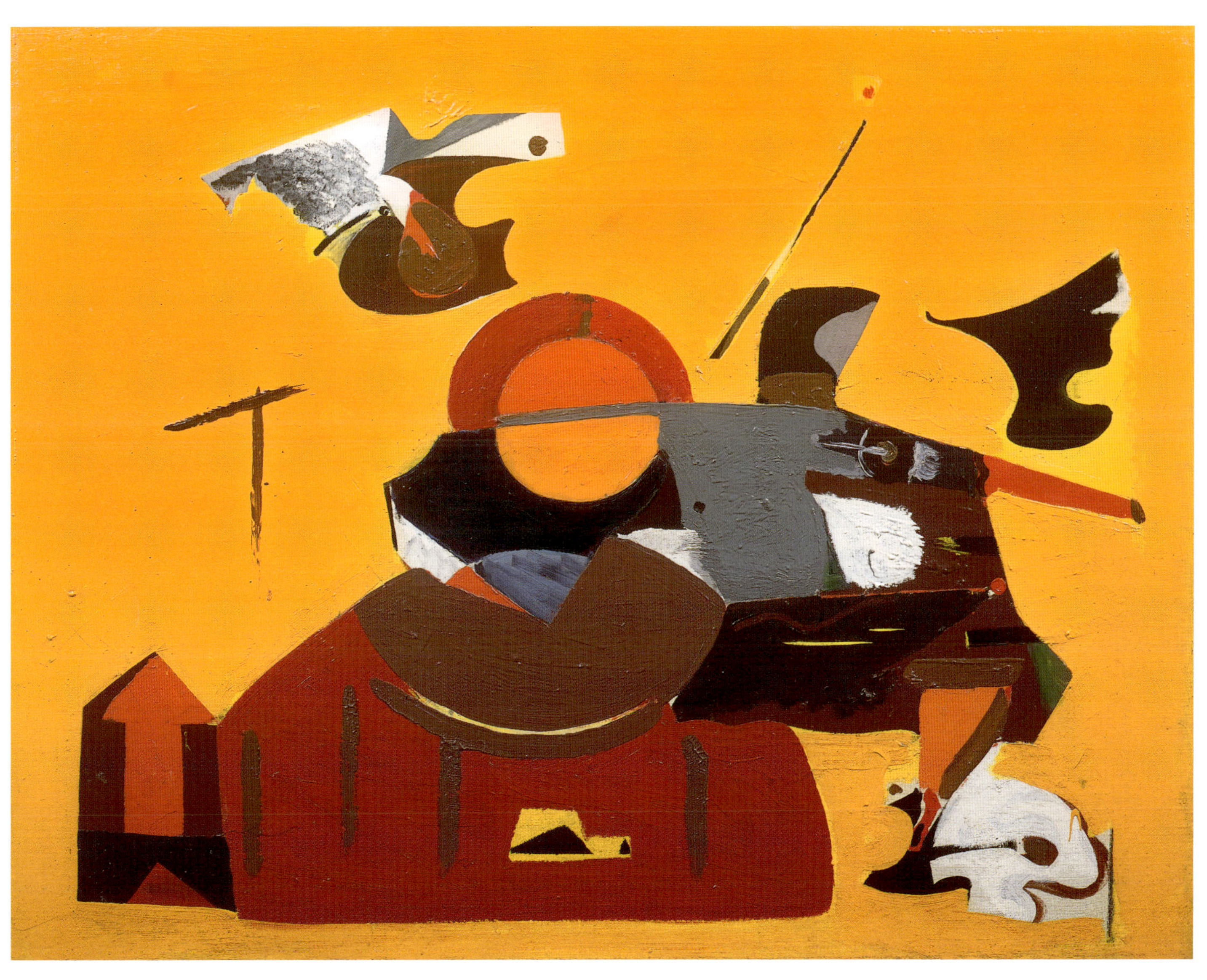

**PLATE 48**
Jacob Lawrence (1917–2000)
EXHIBITOR 1948–67
MEDAL 1997
*Christmas in Harlem,* 1937
Tempera on paper, 25 x 27 ½ inches
Collection of Rachel Skolnick and Joshua Skolnick

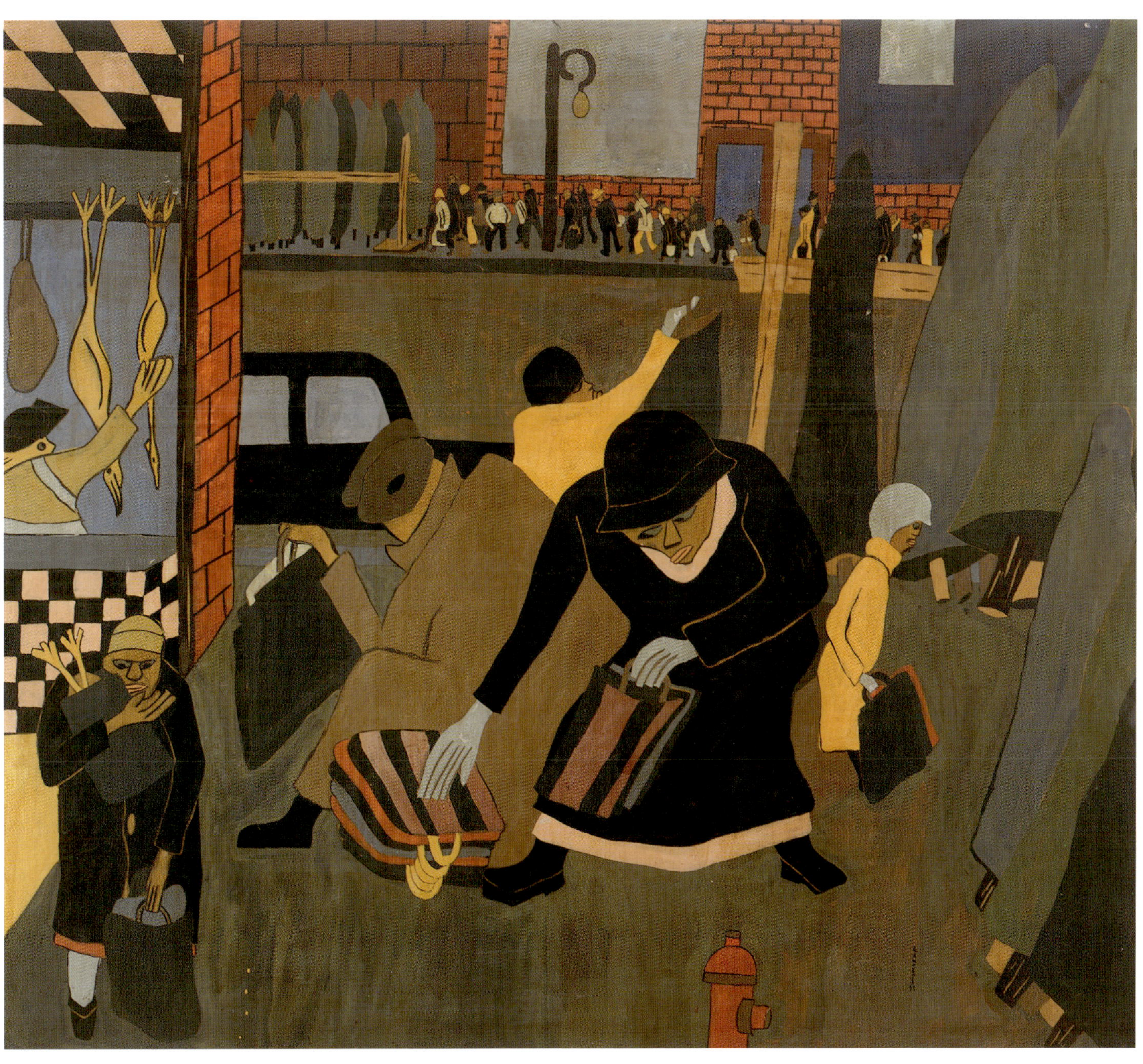

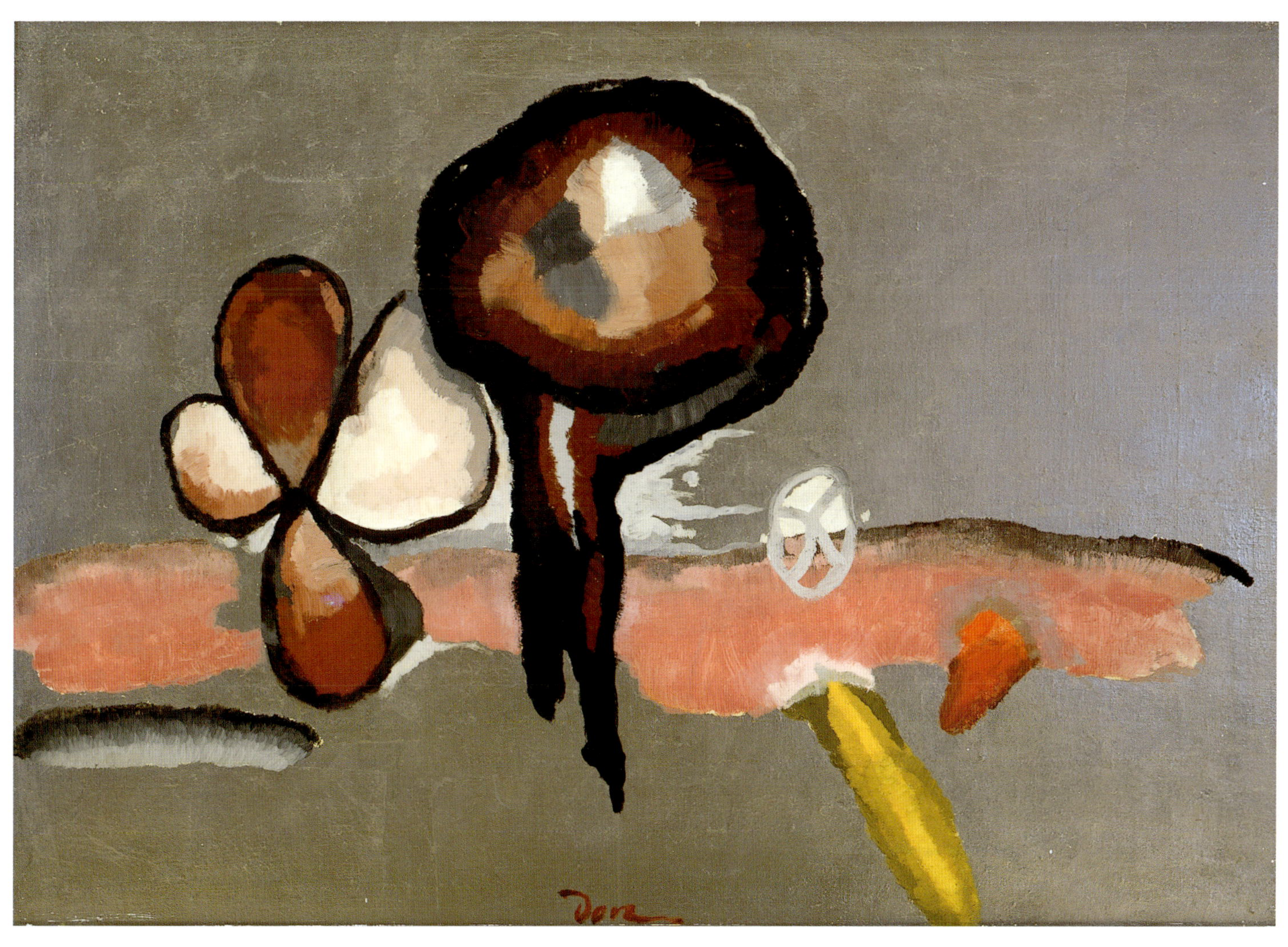

**PLATE 50**
Paul Cadmus (1904–1999)
EXHIBITOR 1938–58, 1967–69
*Hinky Dinky Parley Voo,* 1939
Oil and tempera on linen on panel, 36 x 36 inches
Collection of Linda Lichtenberg Kaplan

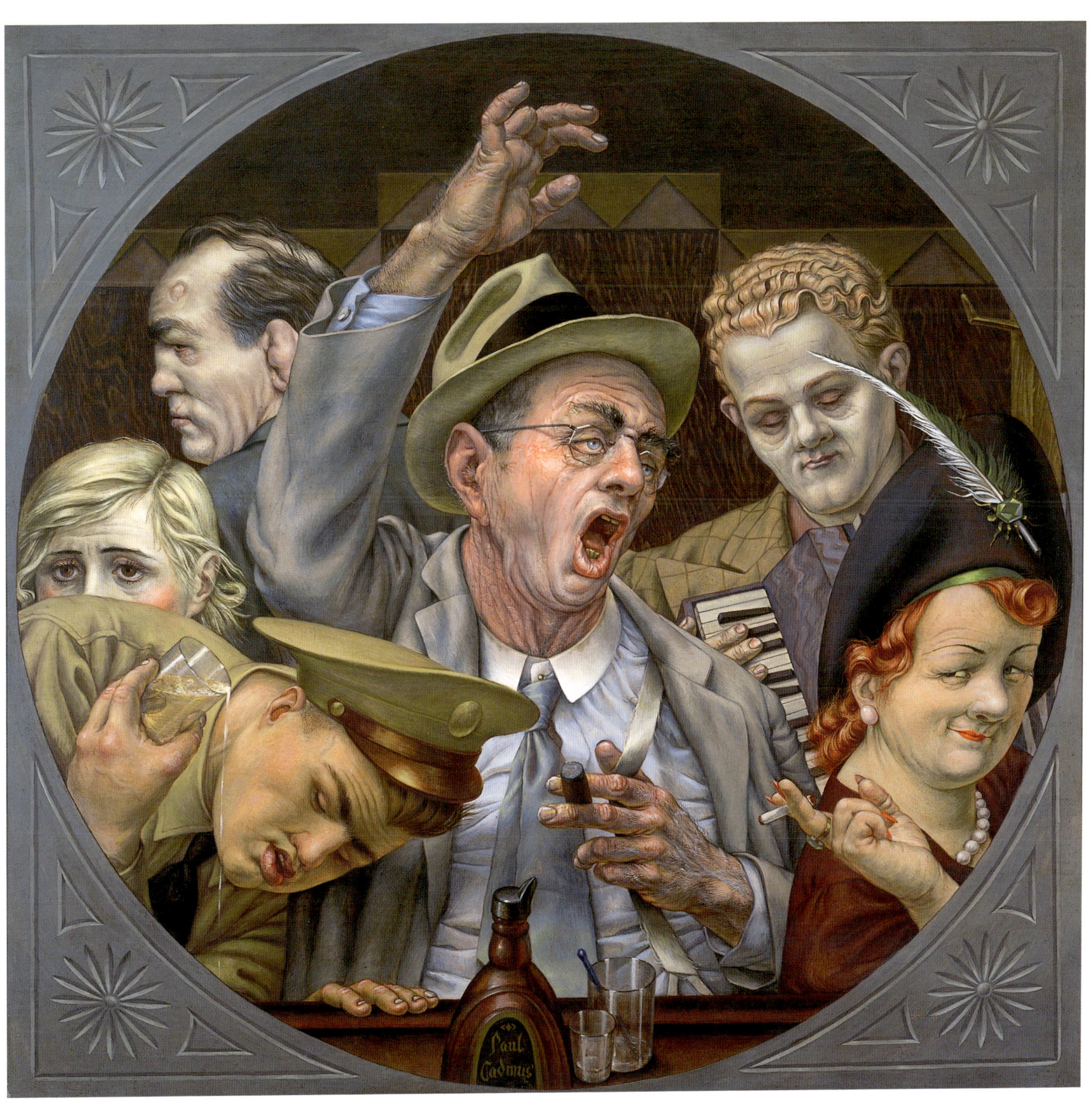

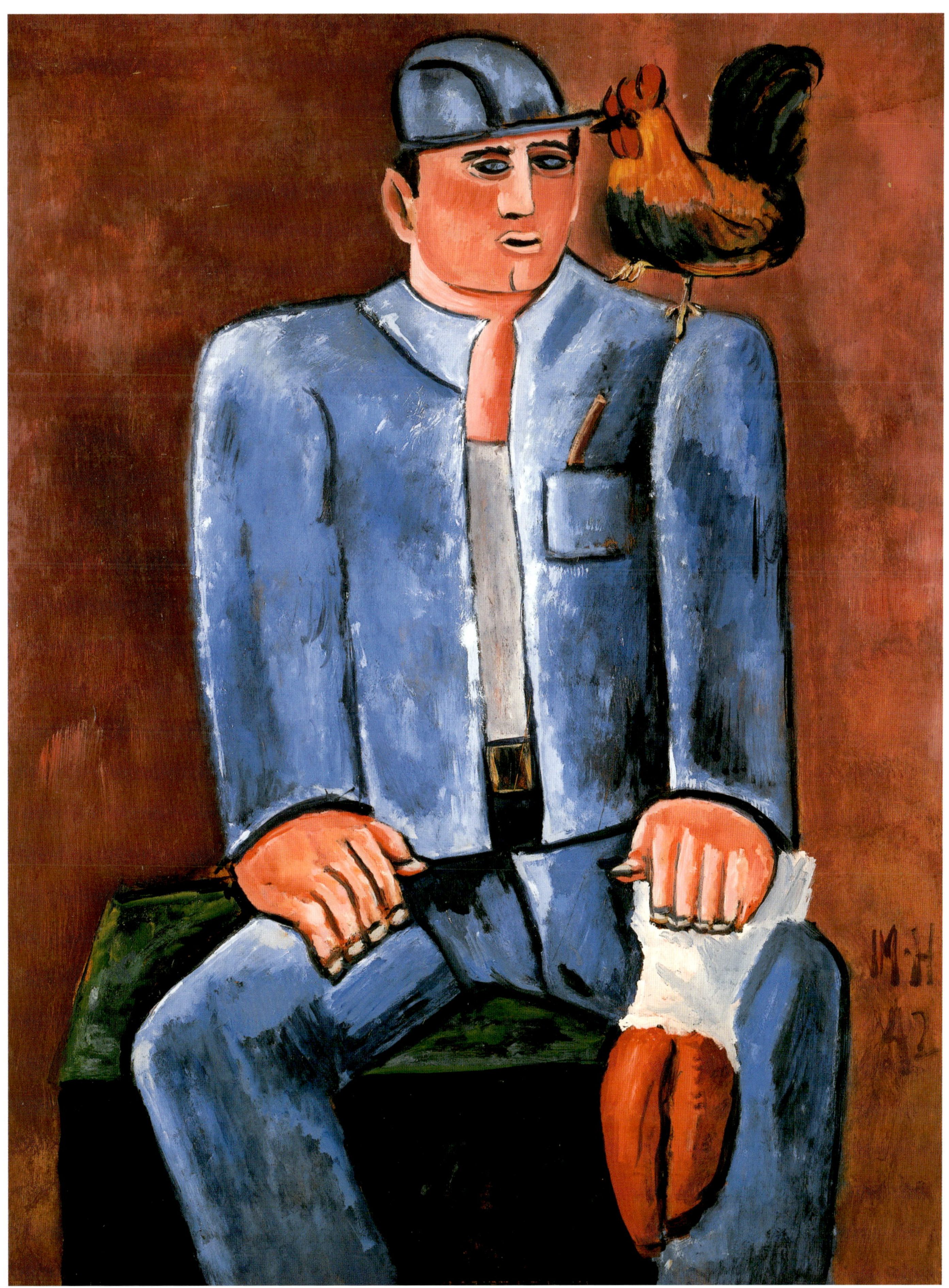

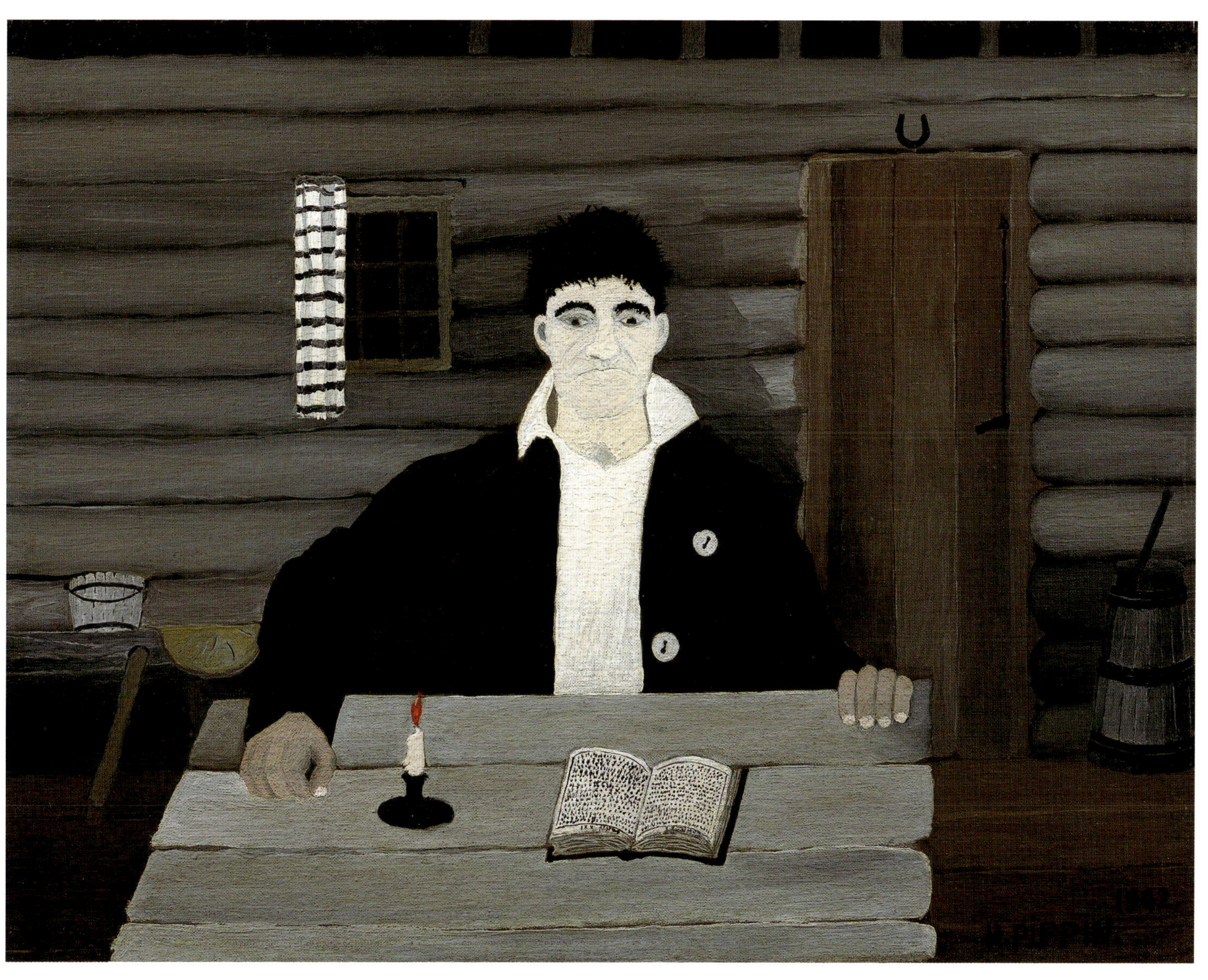

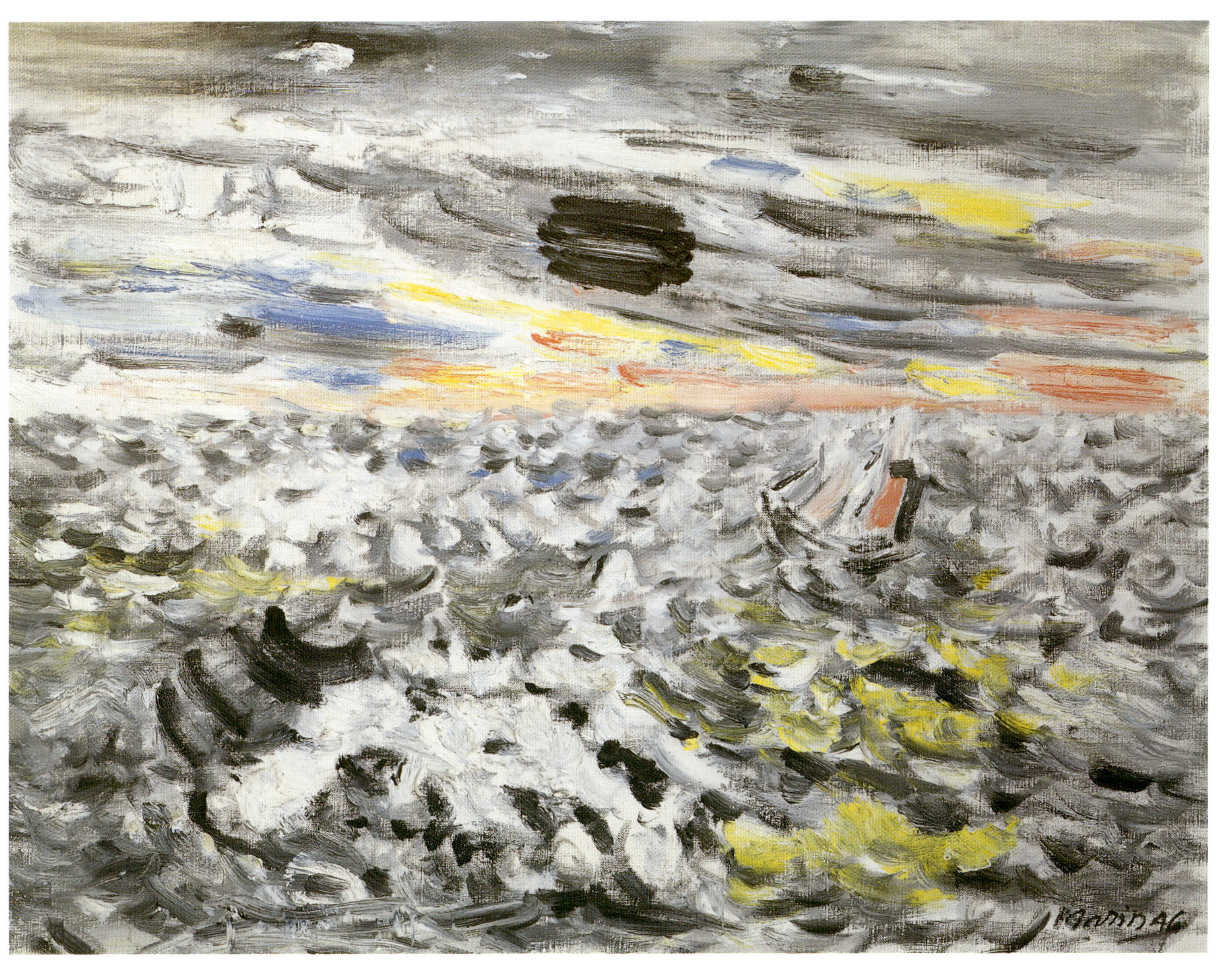

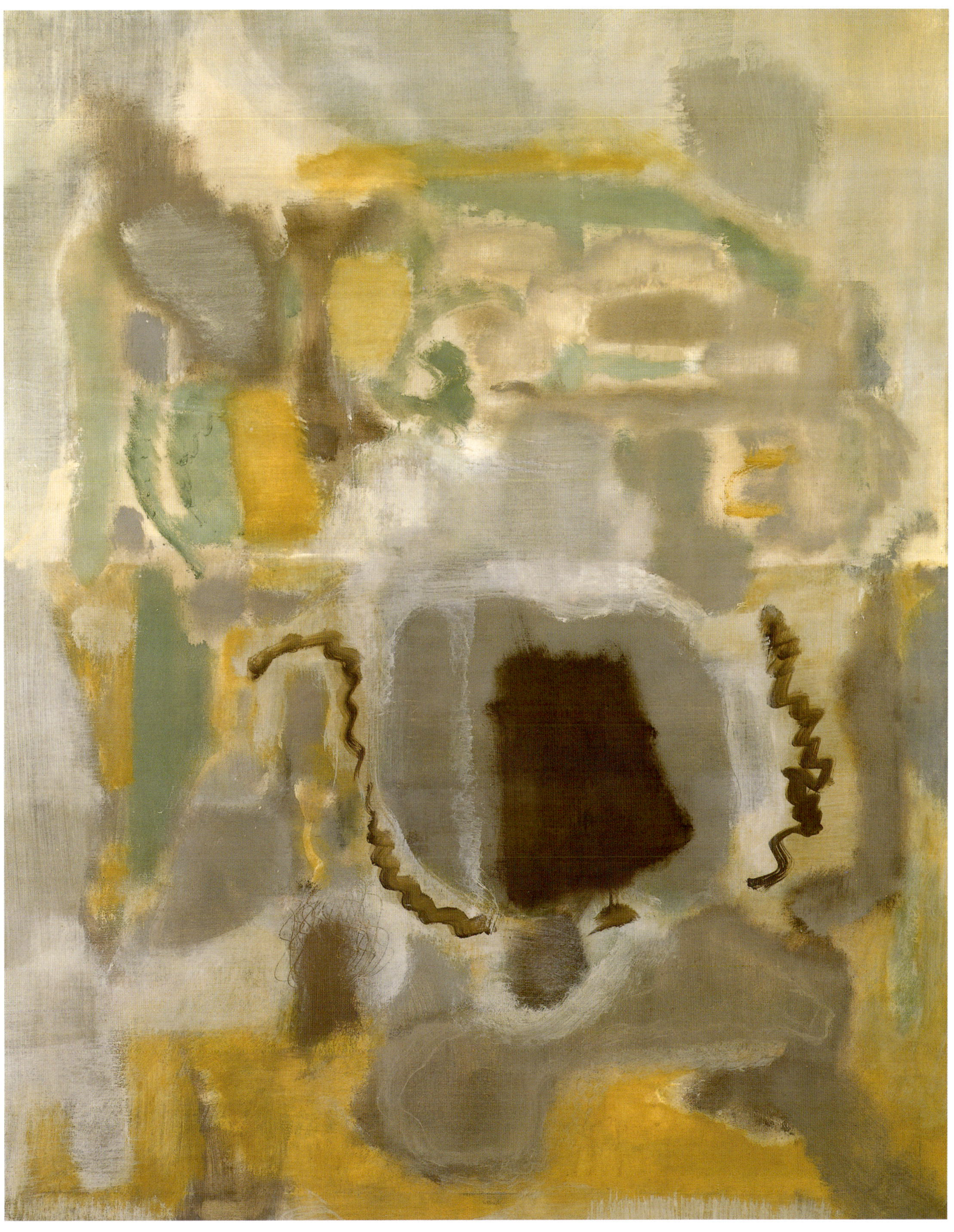

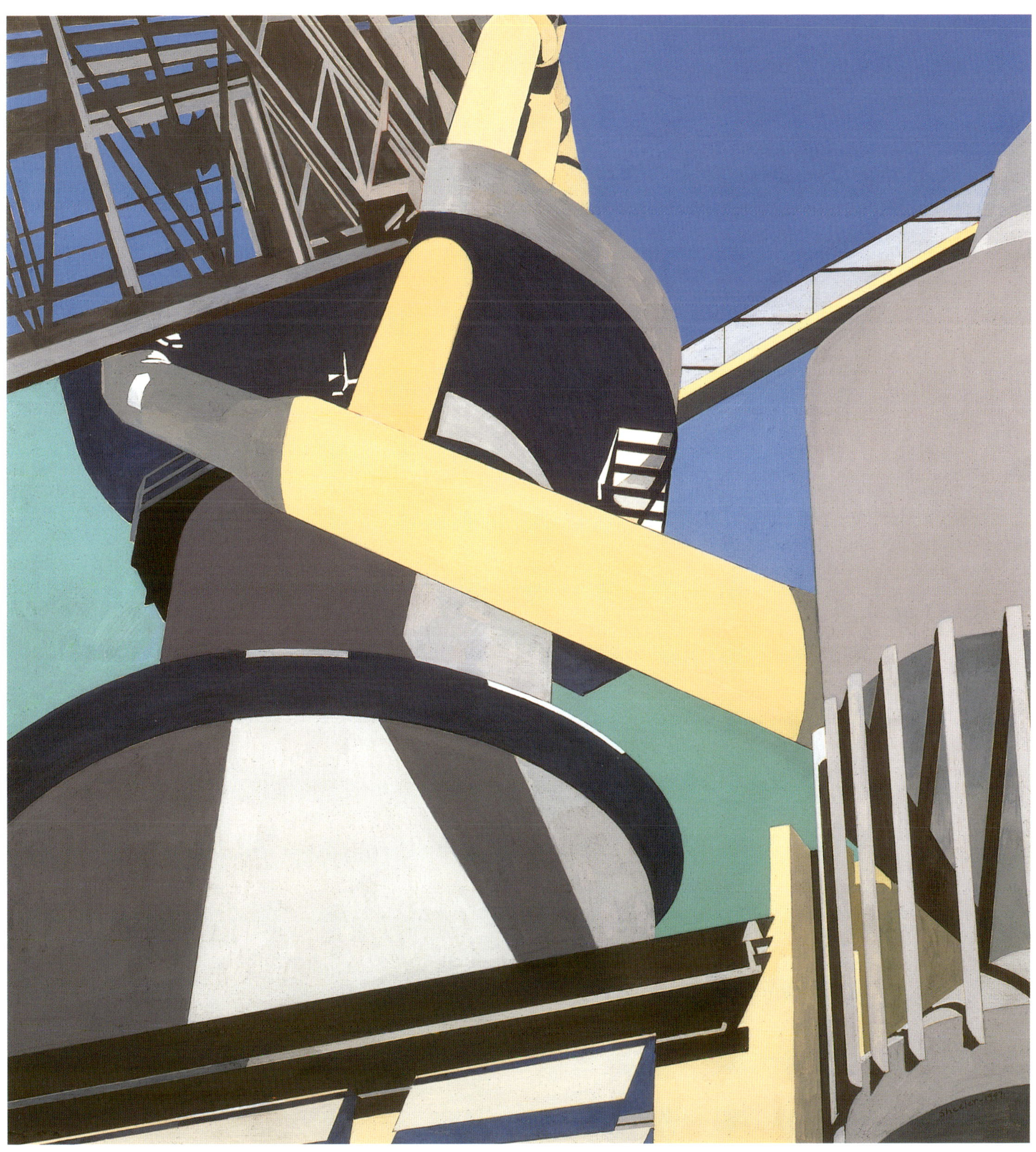

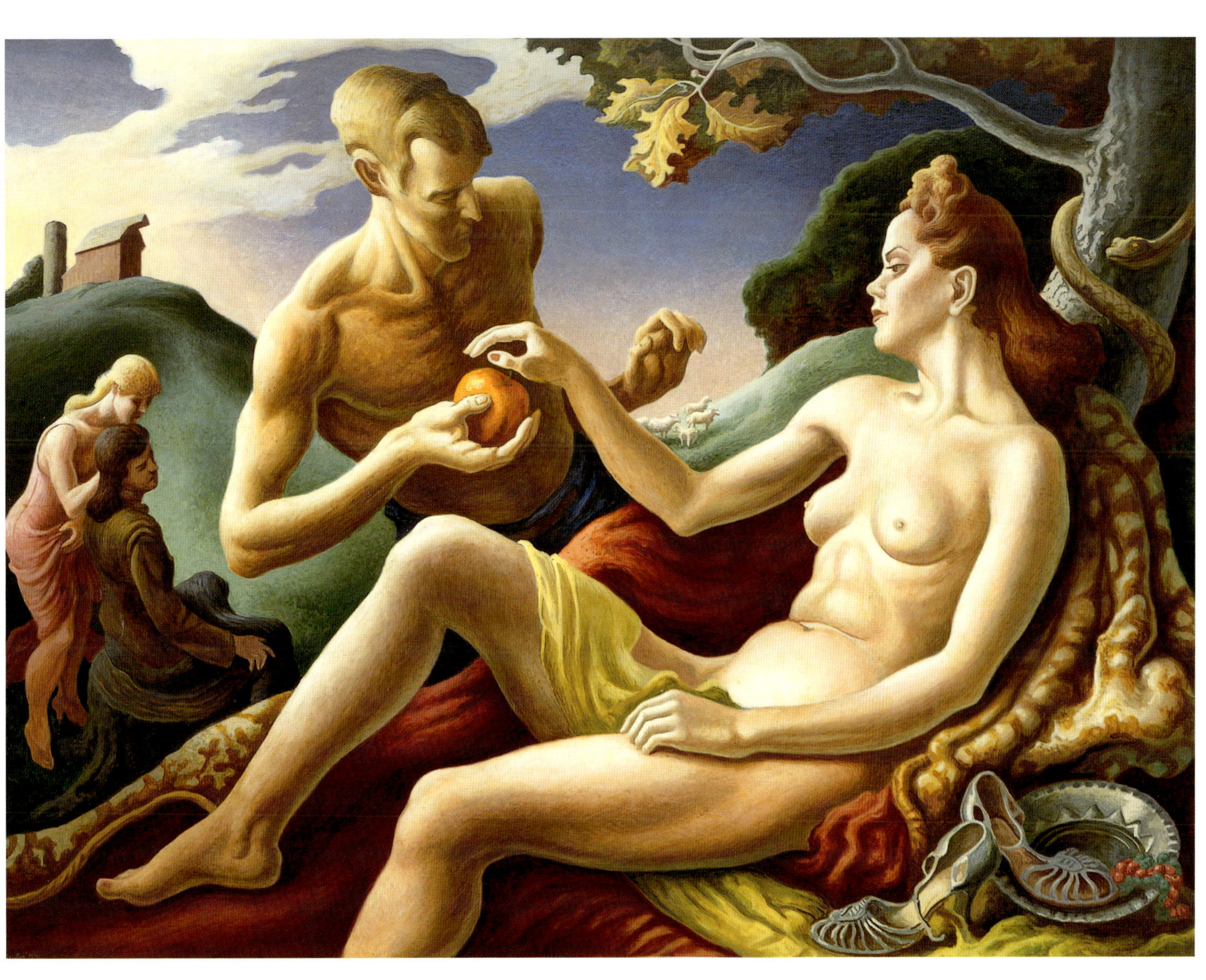

PLATE 57
Hans Hofmann (1880–1966)
*The Red Serpent,* 1949
Oil on canvas, 52 x 70 inches
Collection of Luther W. Brady

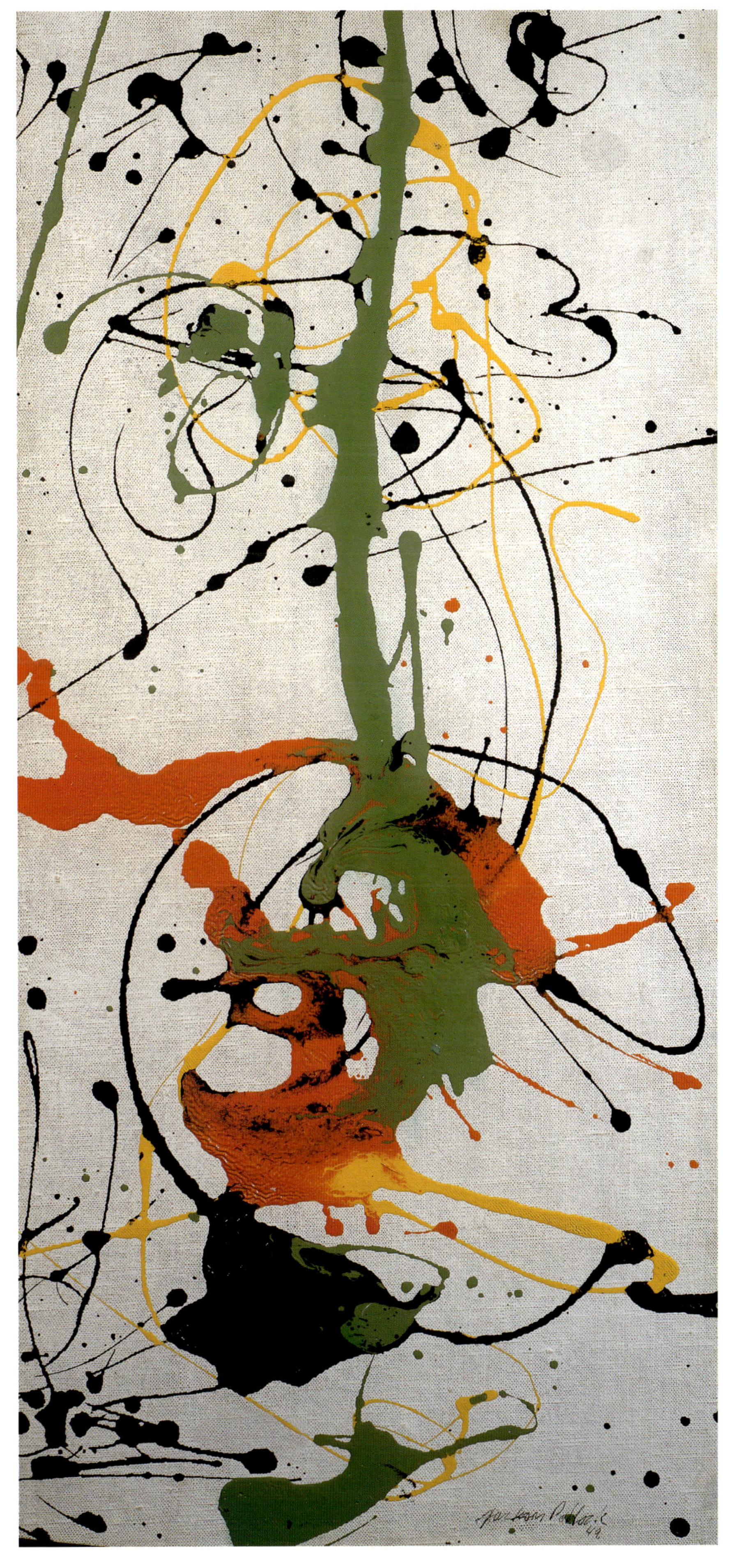

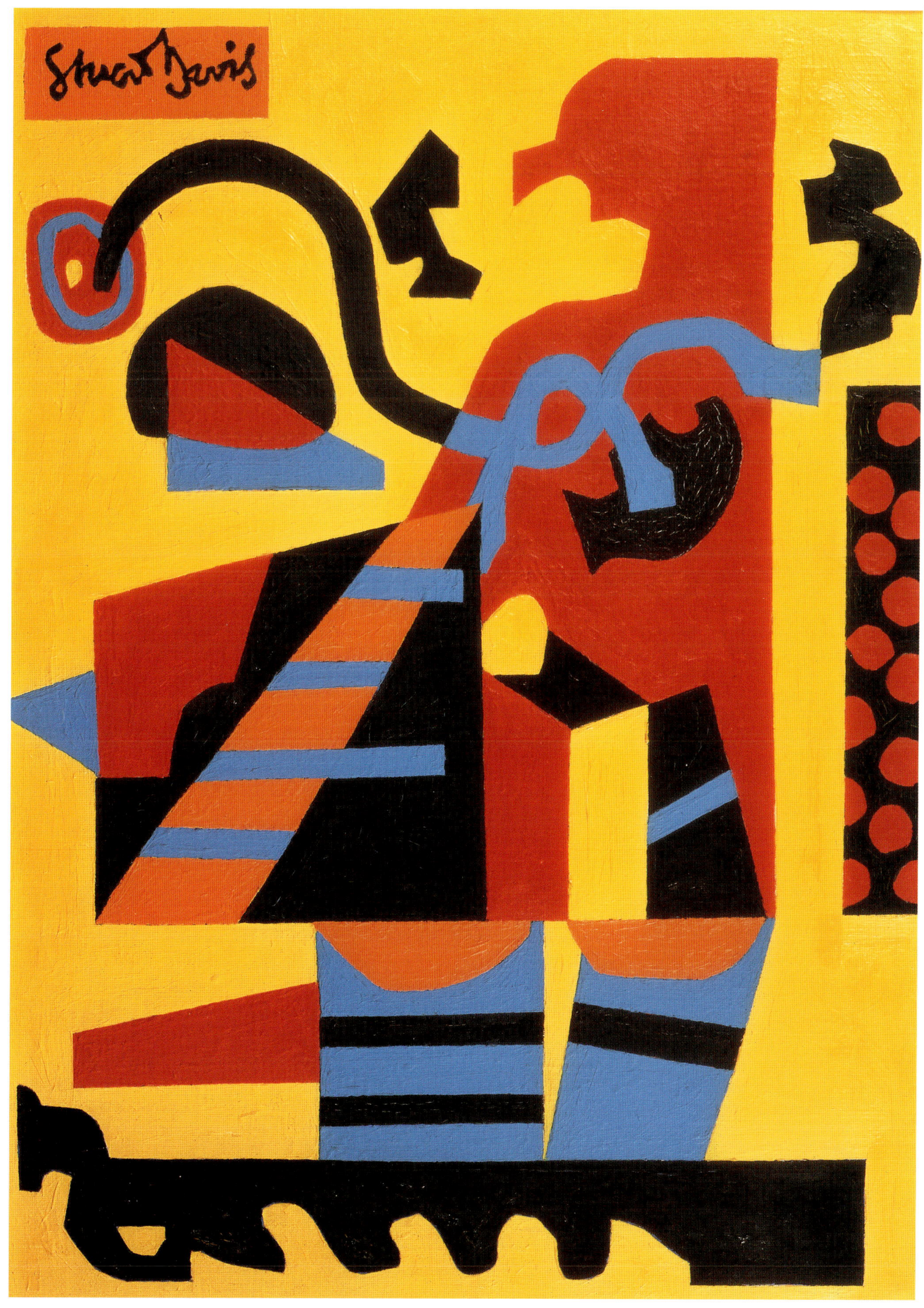
Stuart Davis

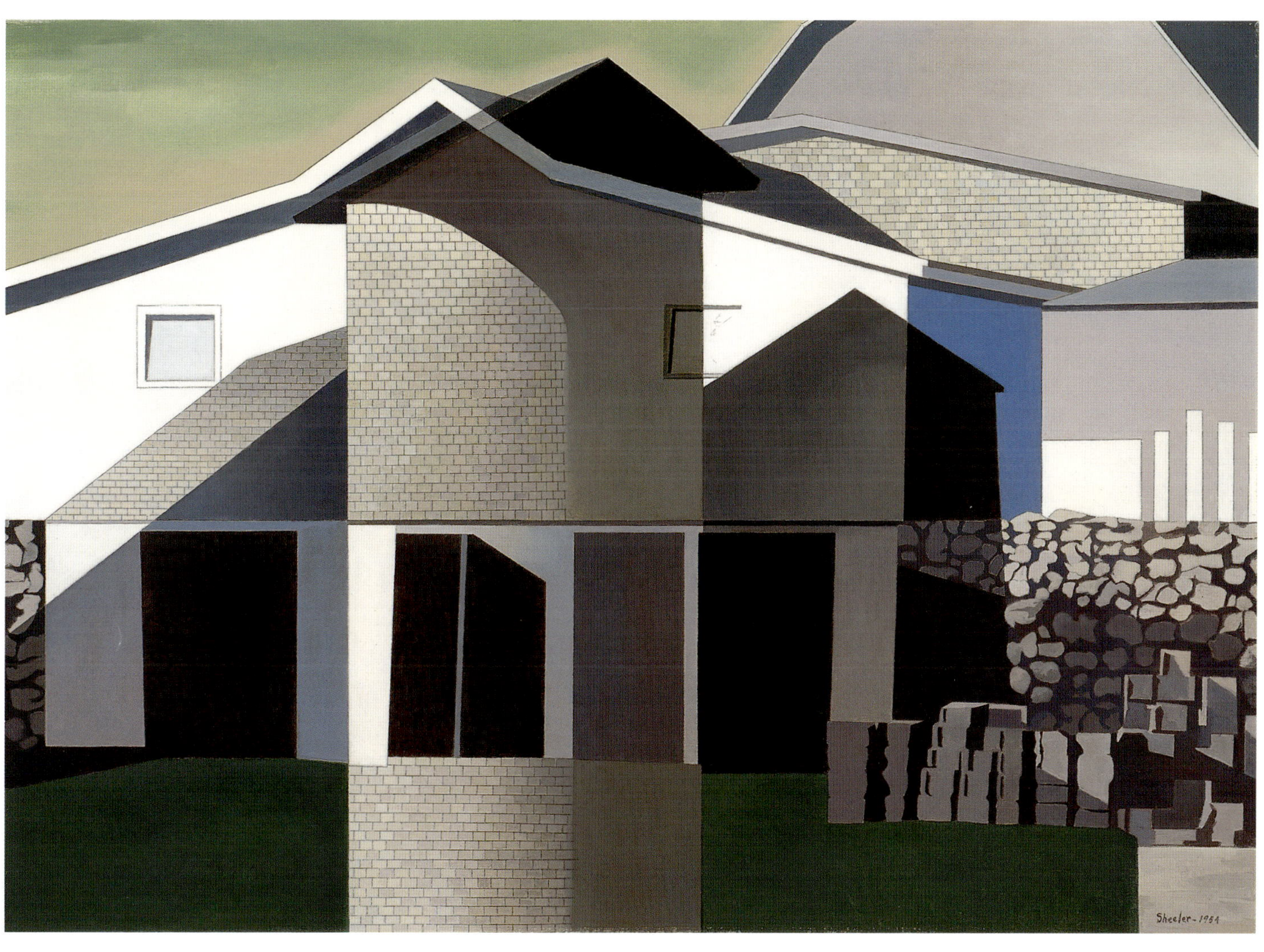

Sheeler-1959

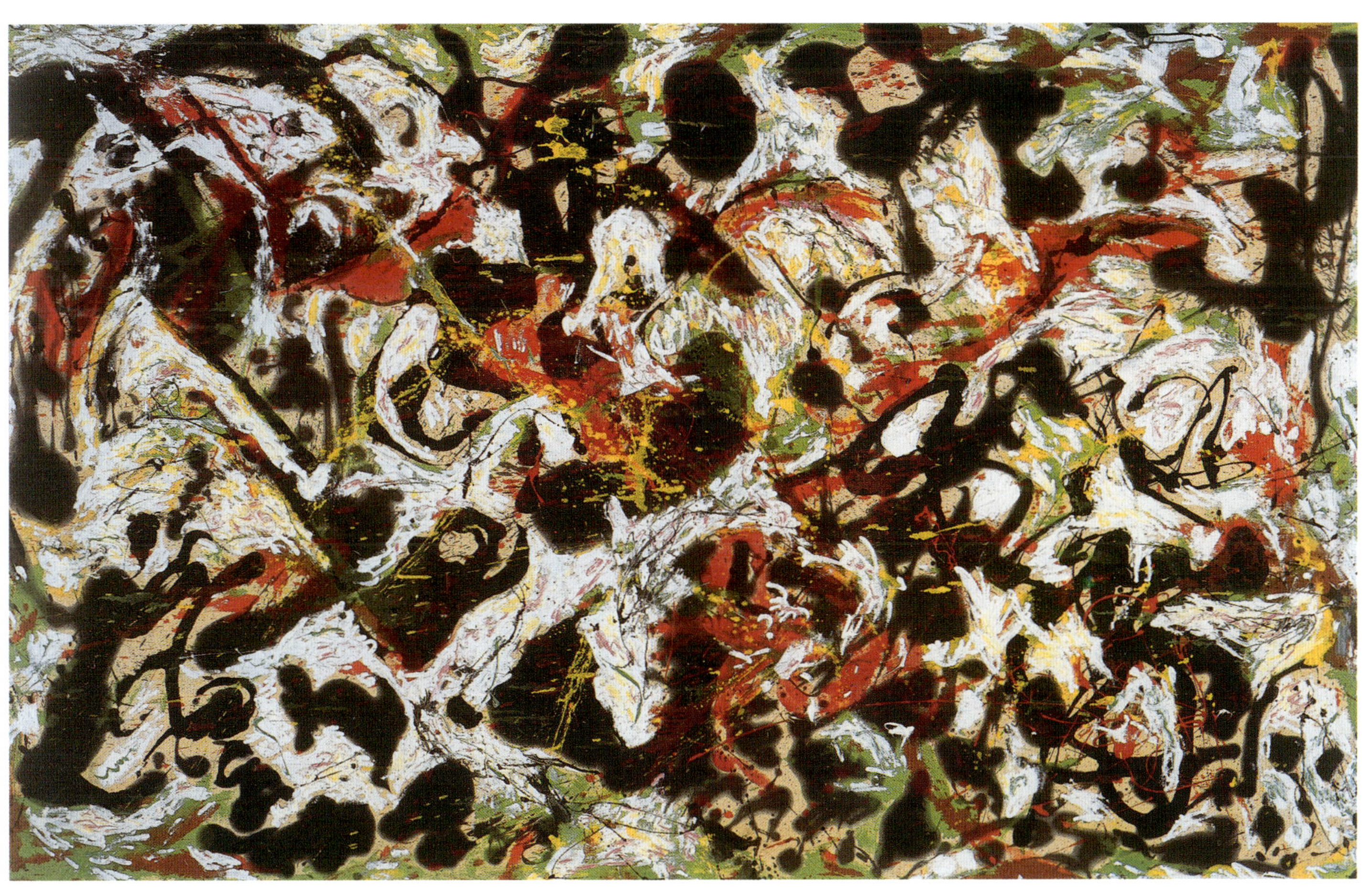

**PLATE 62**
Robert Motherwell (1915–1991)
EXHIBITOR 1946–68
MEDAL 1979
*In Ochre with Gestural Black,* 1956
Oil and commercial paint on canvas, 74 x 89 inches
Anonymous Loan

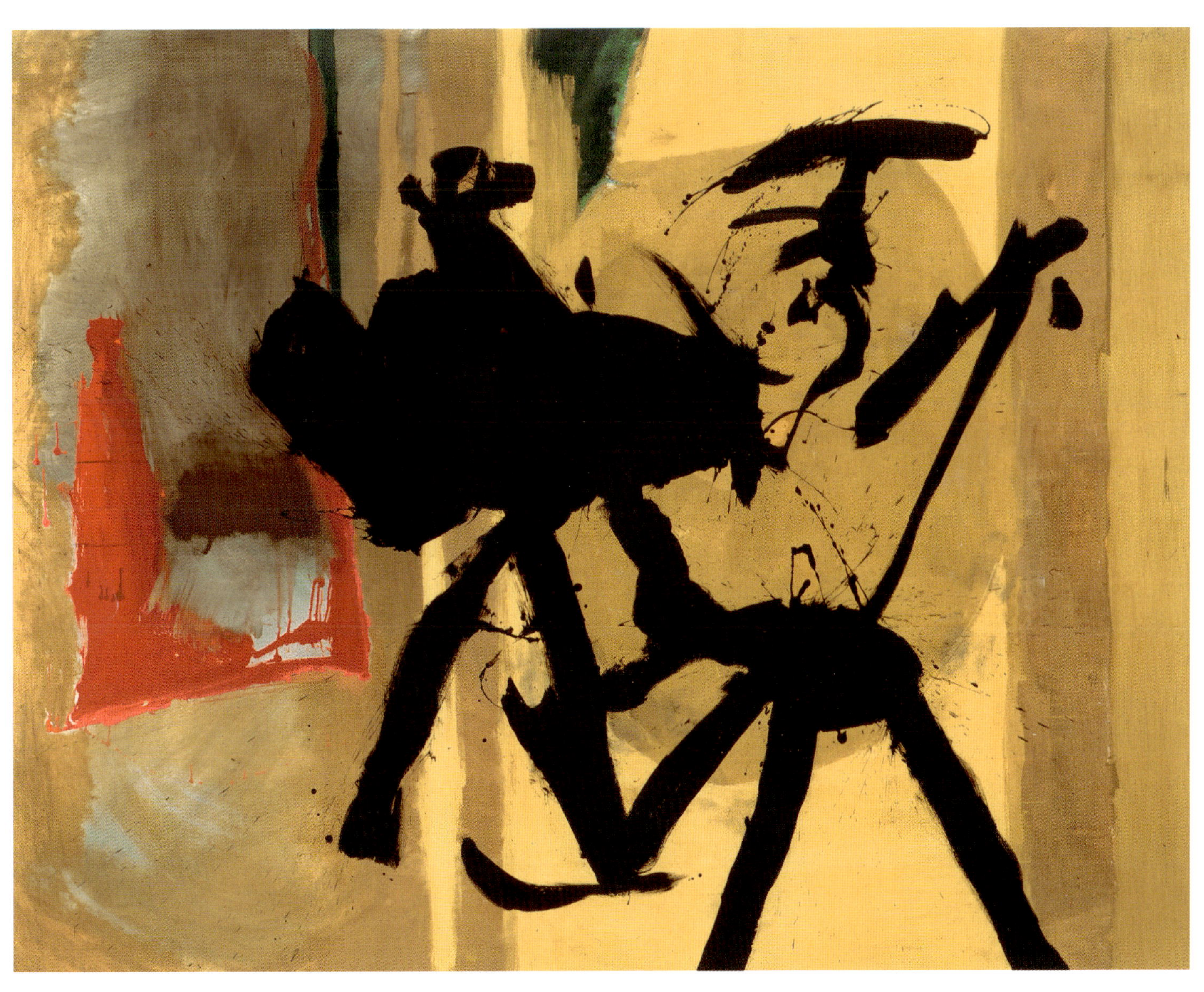

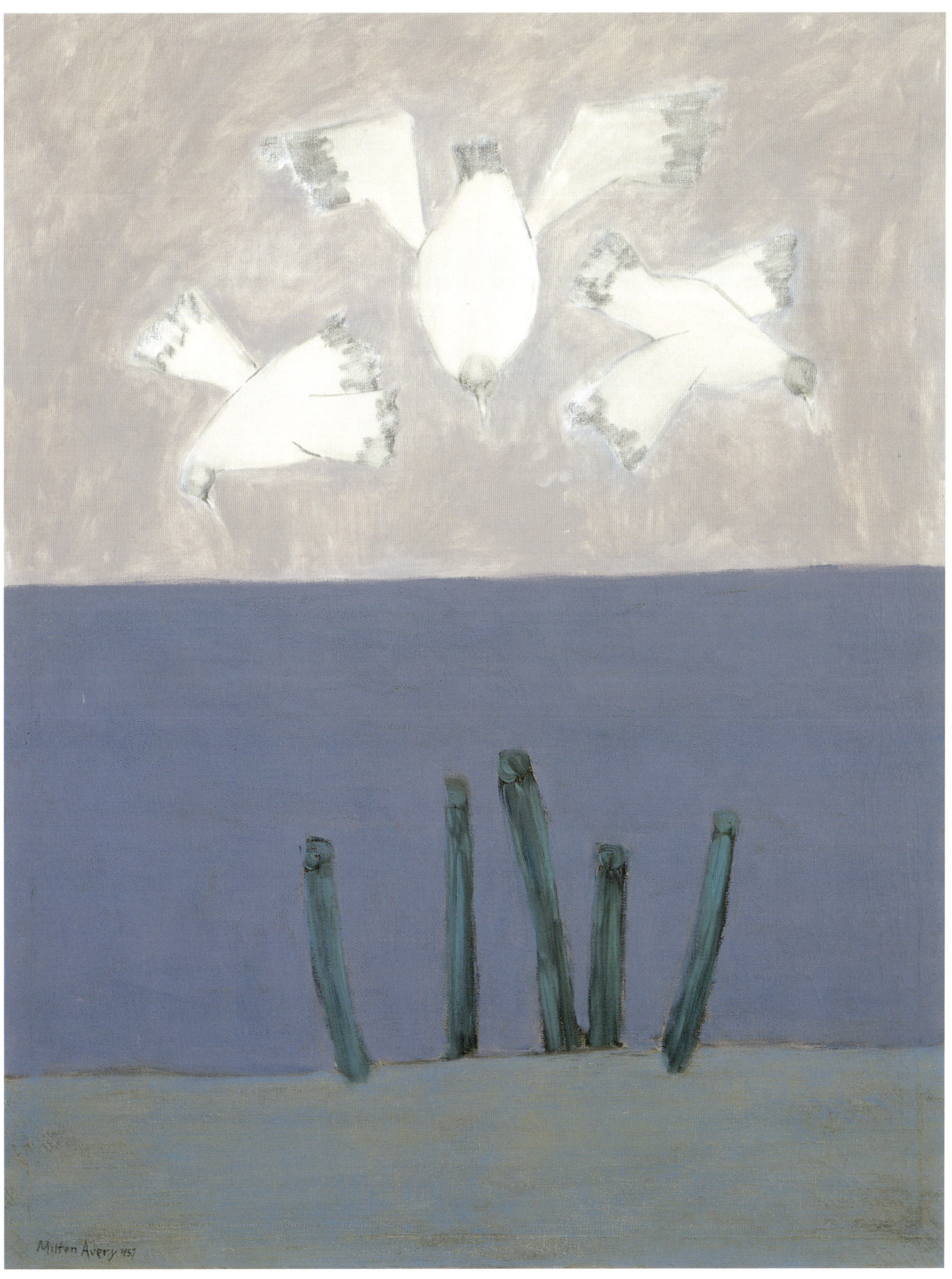


Milton Avery 1957

PLATE 64
Helen Frankenthaler (b. 1928)
EXHIBITOR 1964–68
MEDAL 2005
*Happiest New 1960,* ca. 1959
Mixed media on paper, 48 x 91 inches
Anonymous Loan

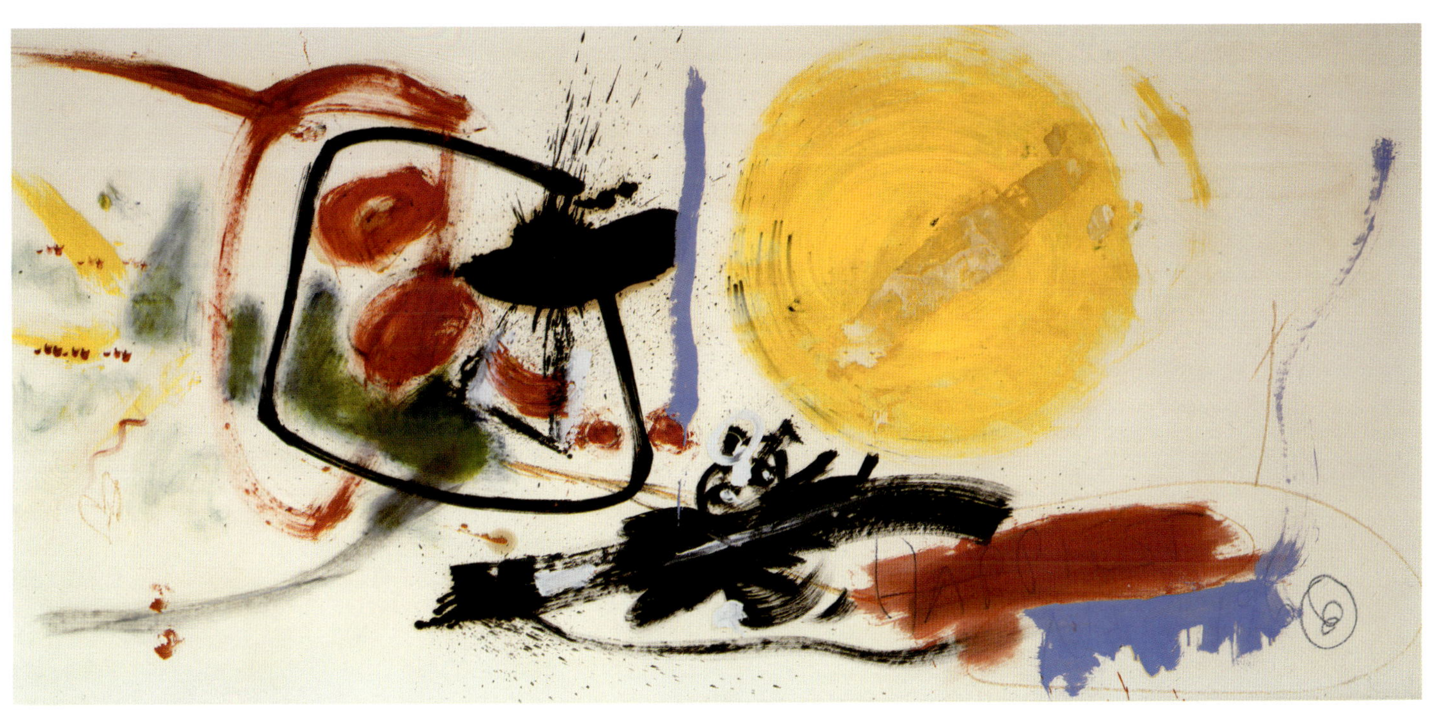

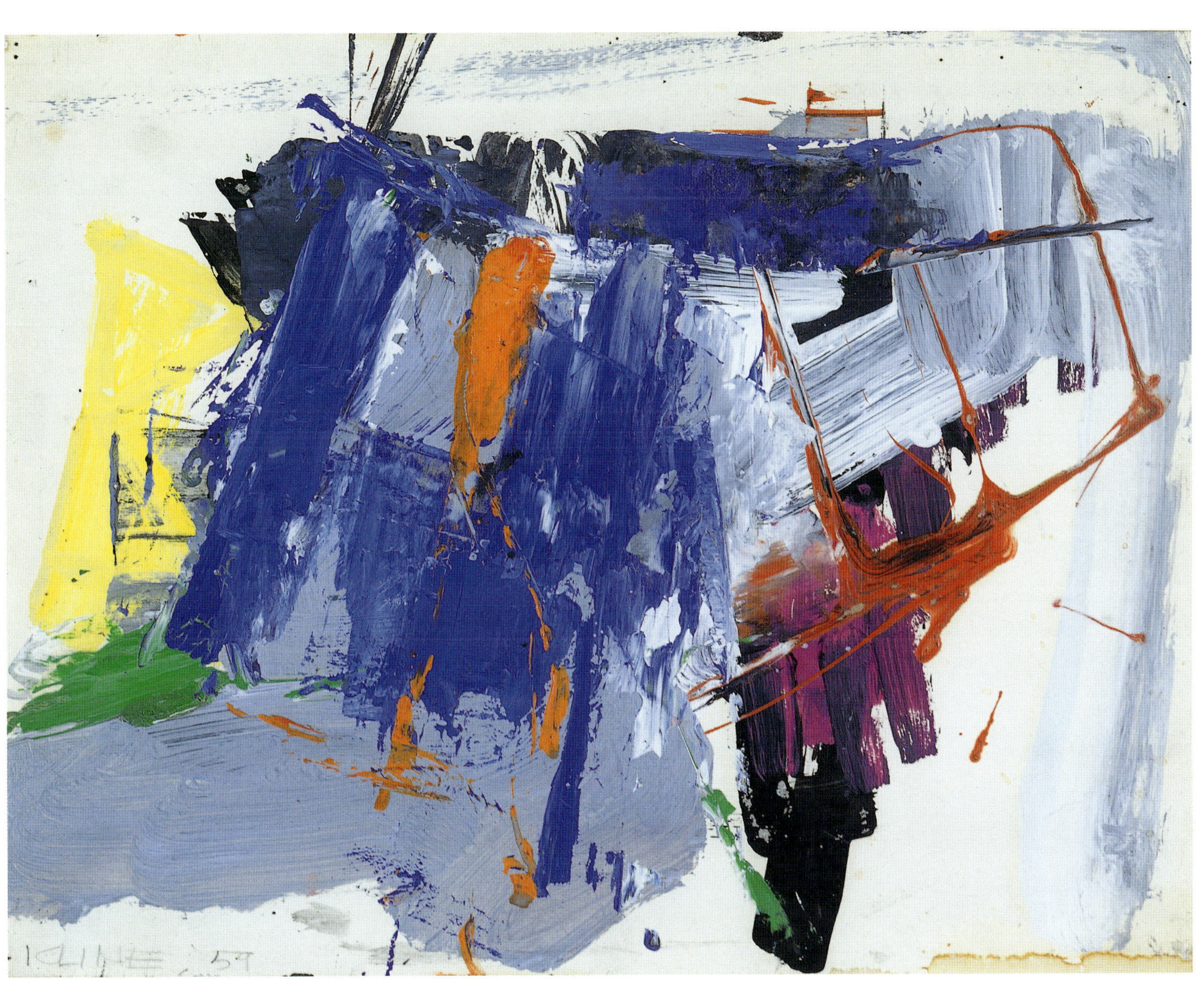

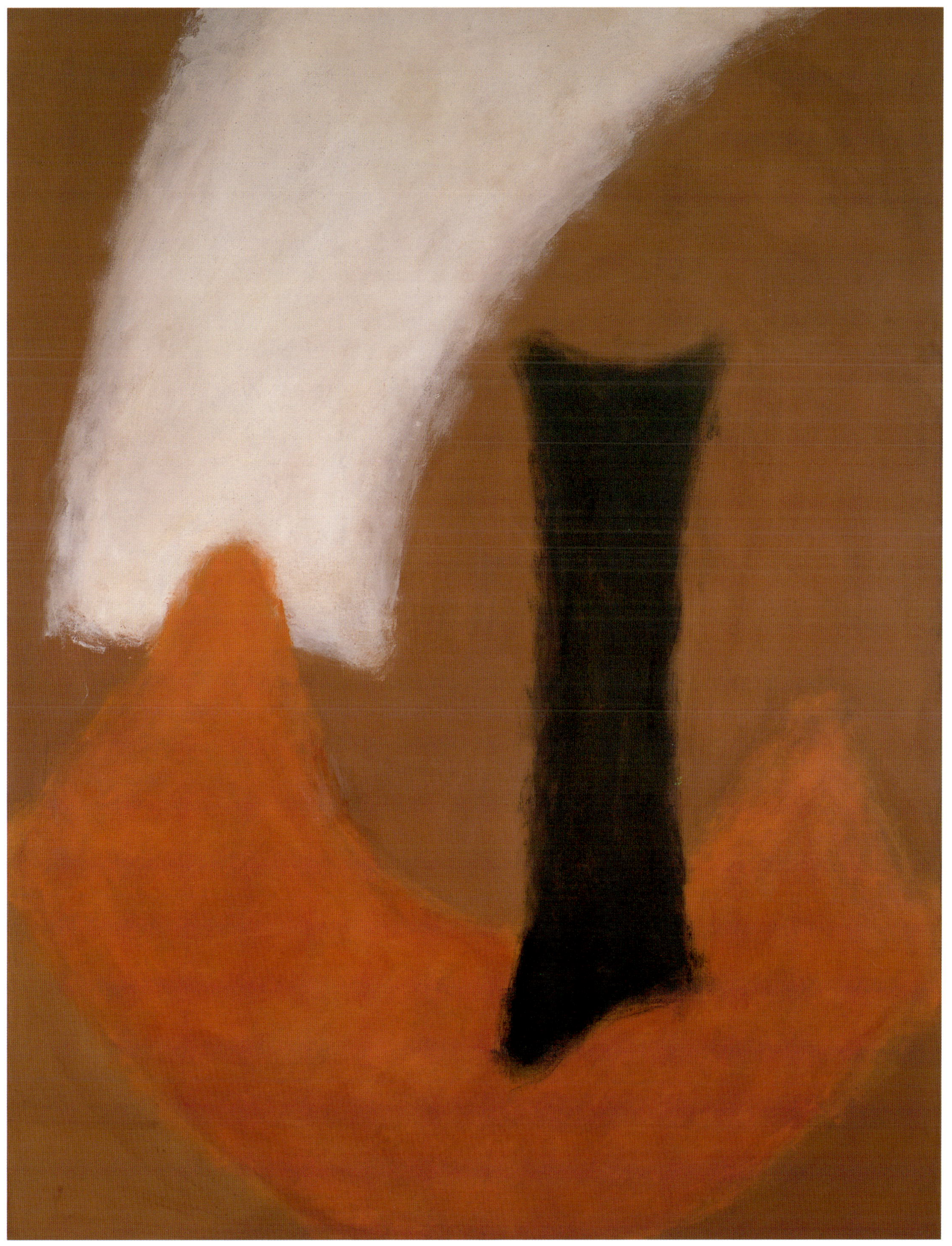

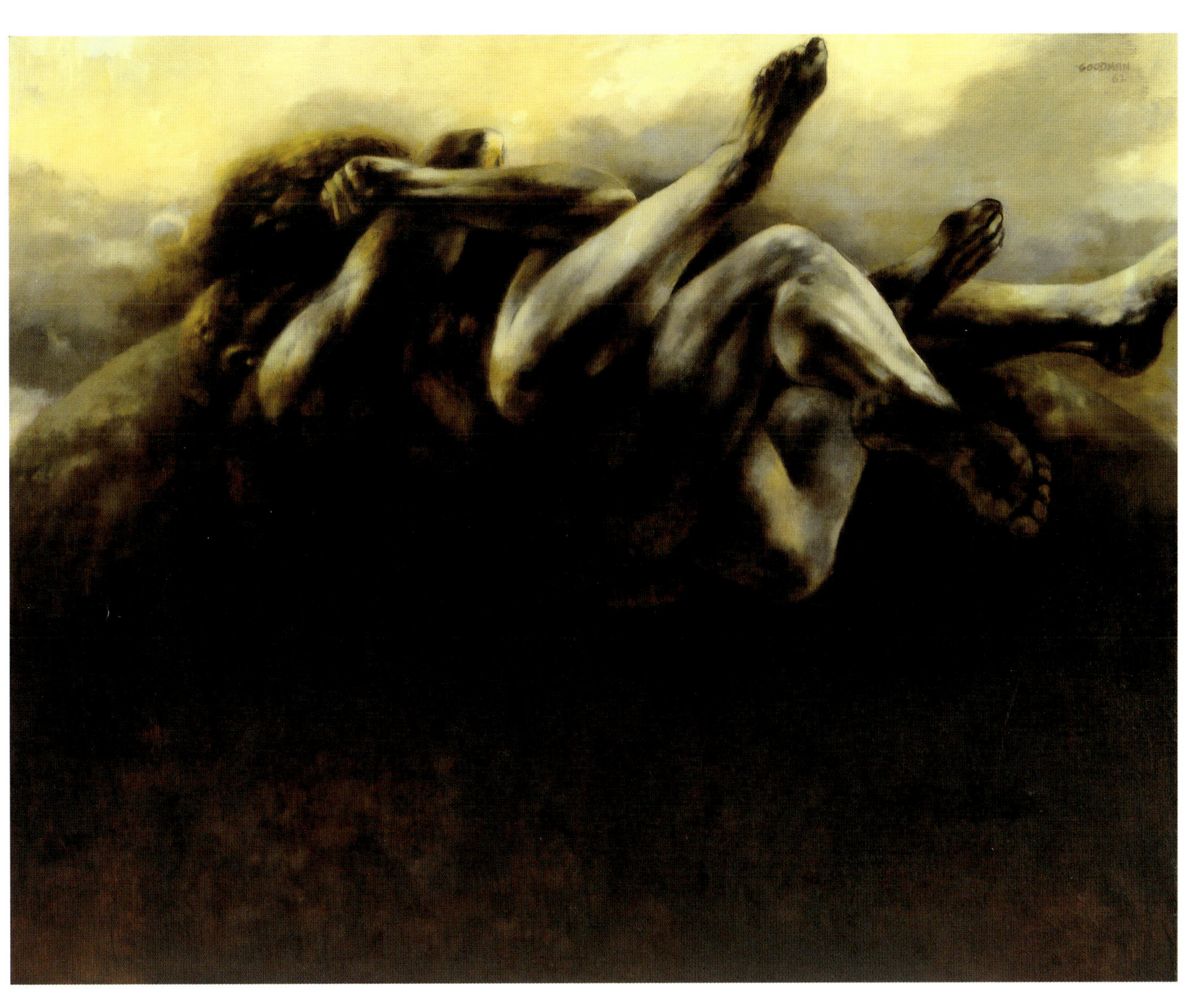

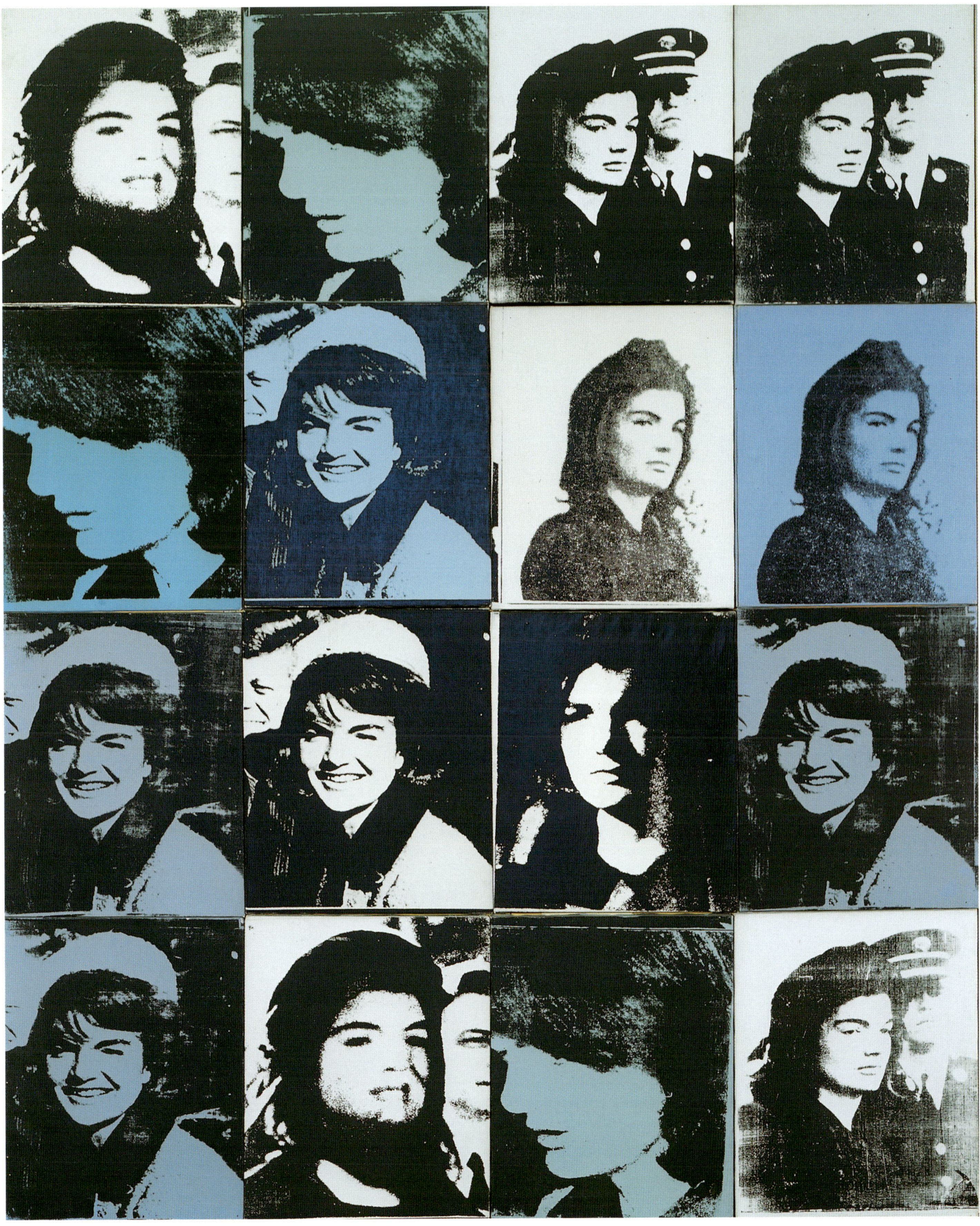

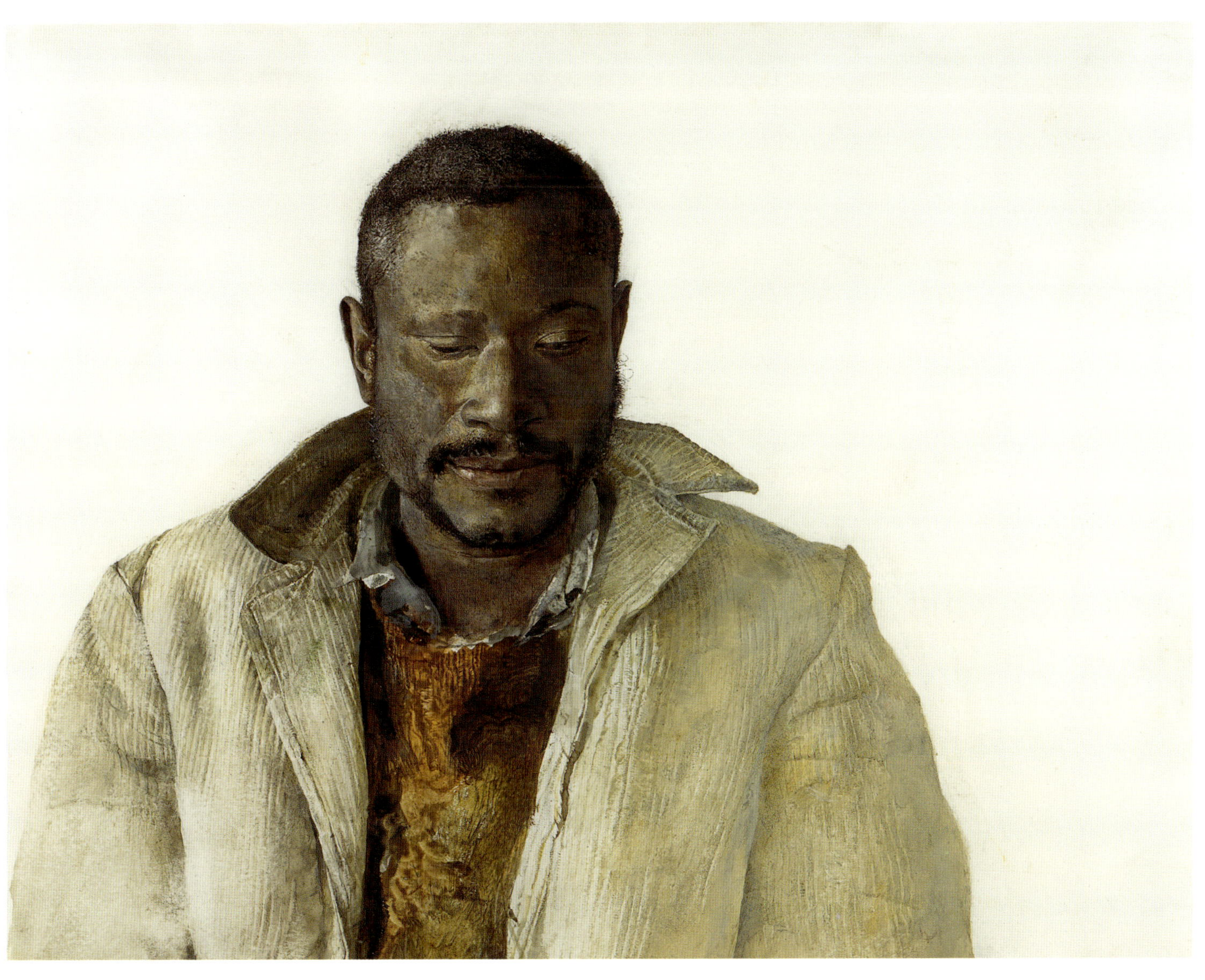

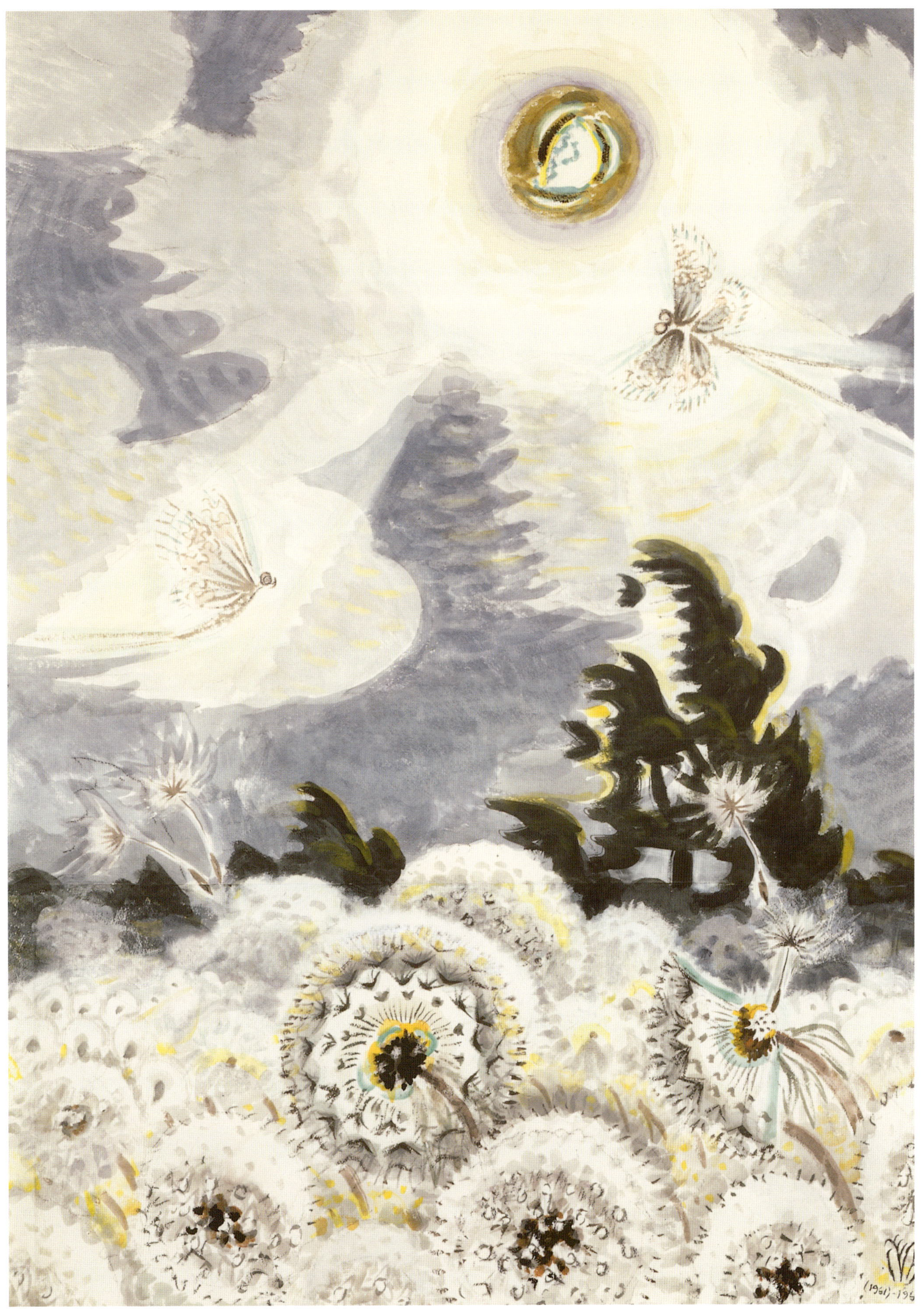

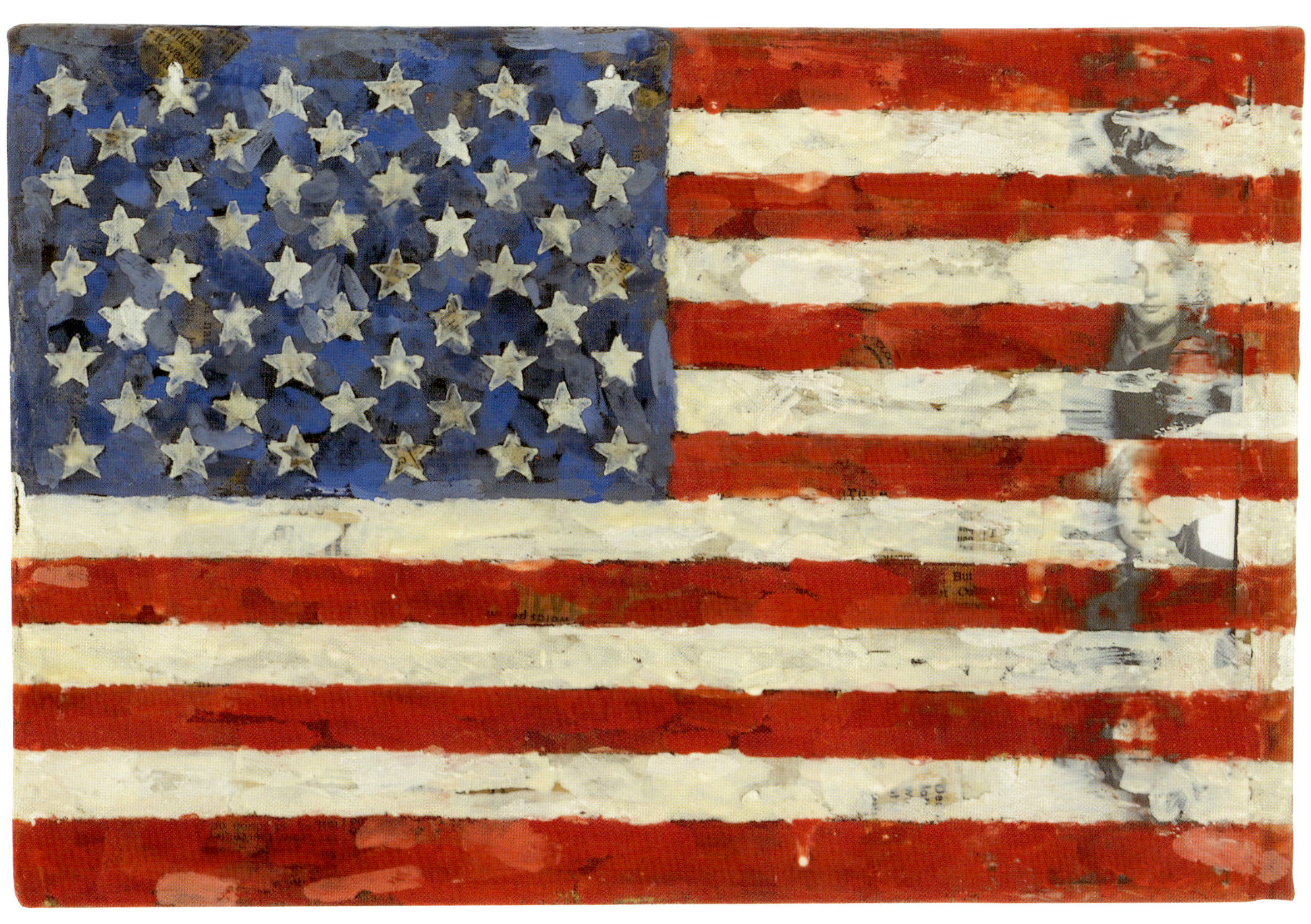

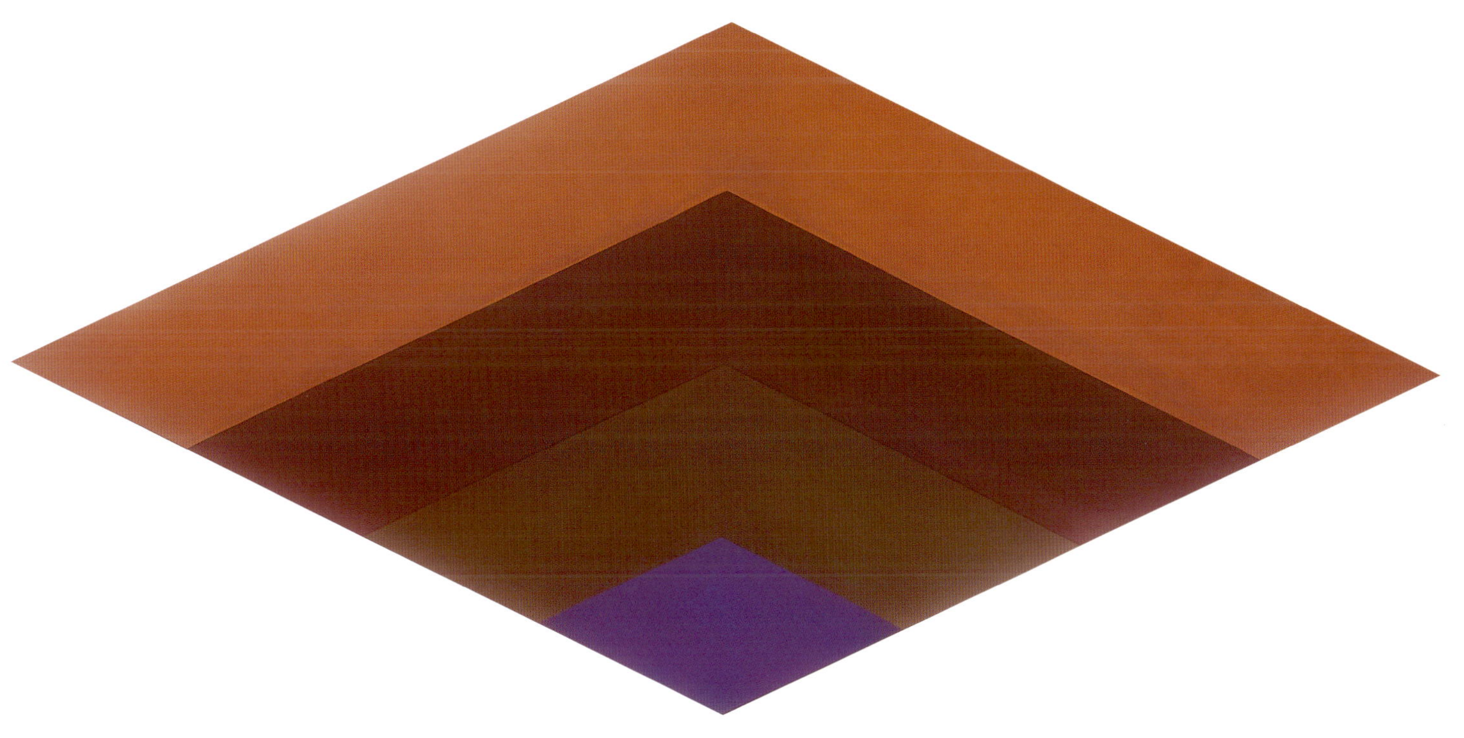

**PLATE 73**
Robert Rauschenberg (b. 1925)
EXHIBITOR 1967, 1969
*Drawing III for 700th Birthday of Dante (A) and (B), 1965*
Solvent transfer, collage, graphite and acrylic on paper,
(A) 14 ½ x 30 ½ inches
(B) 13 ½ x 30 inches
Anonymous Loan

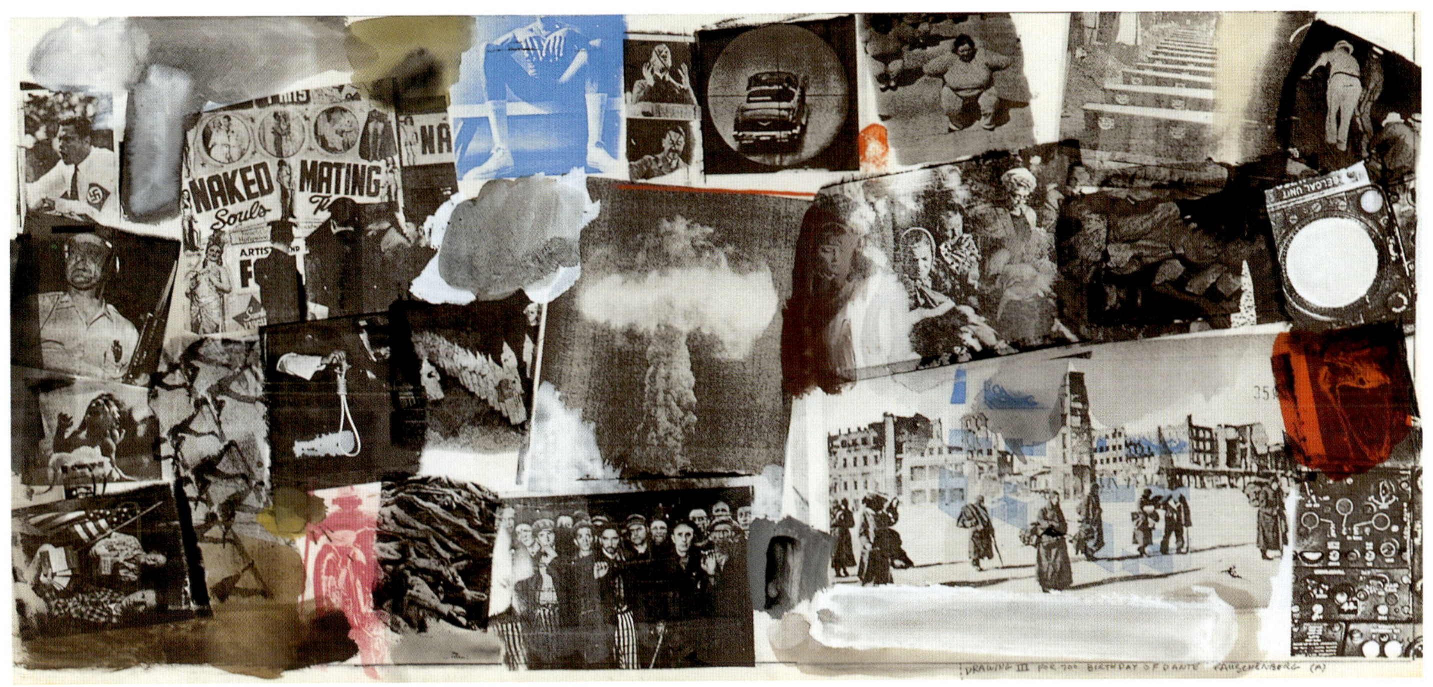

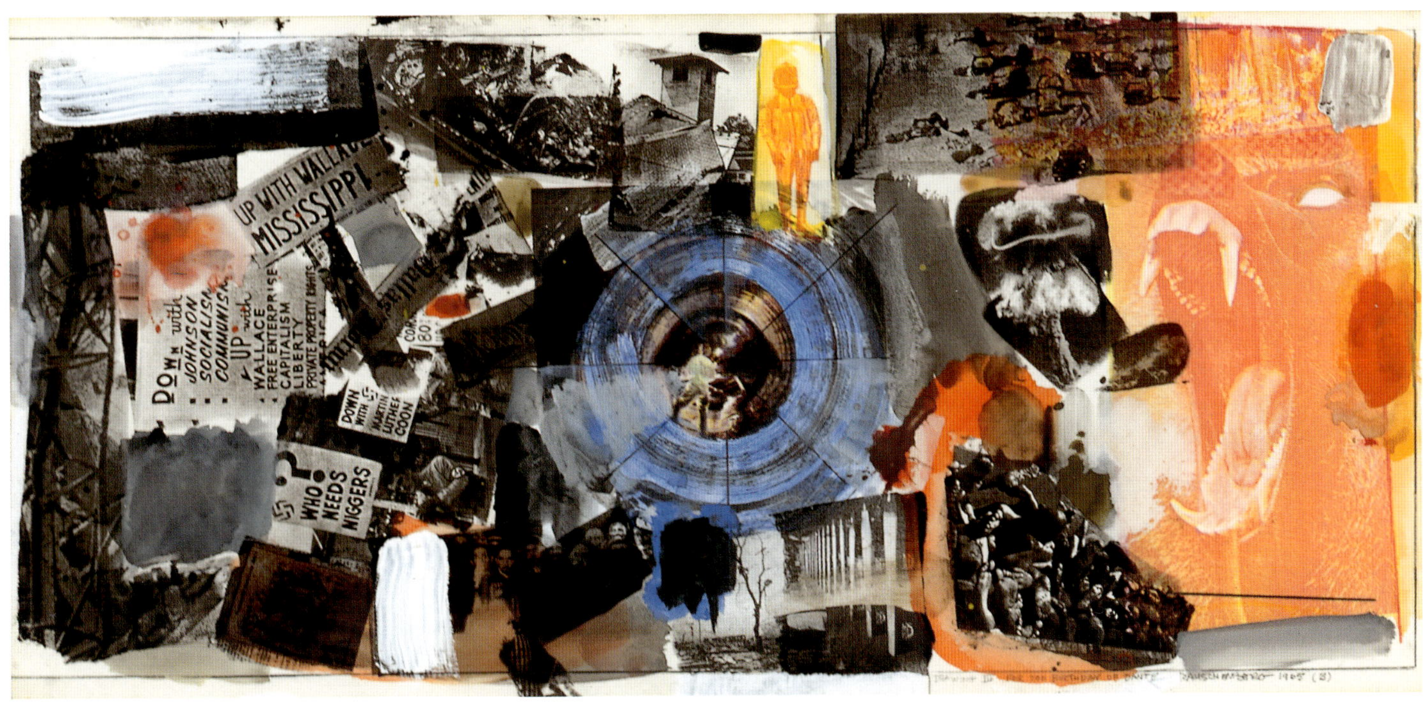

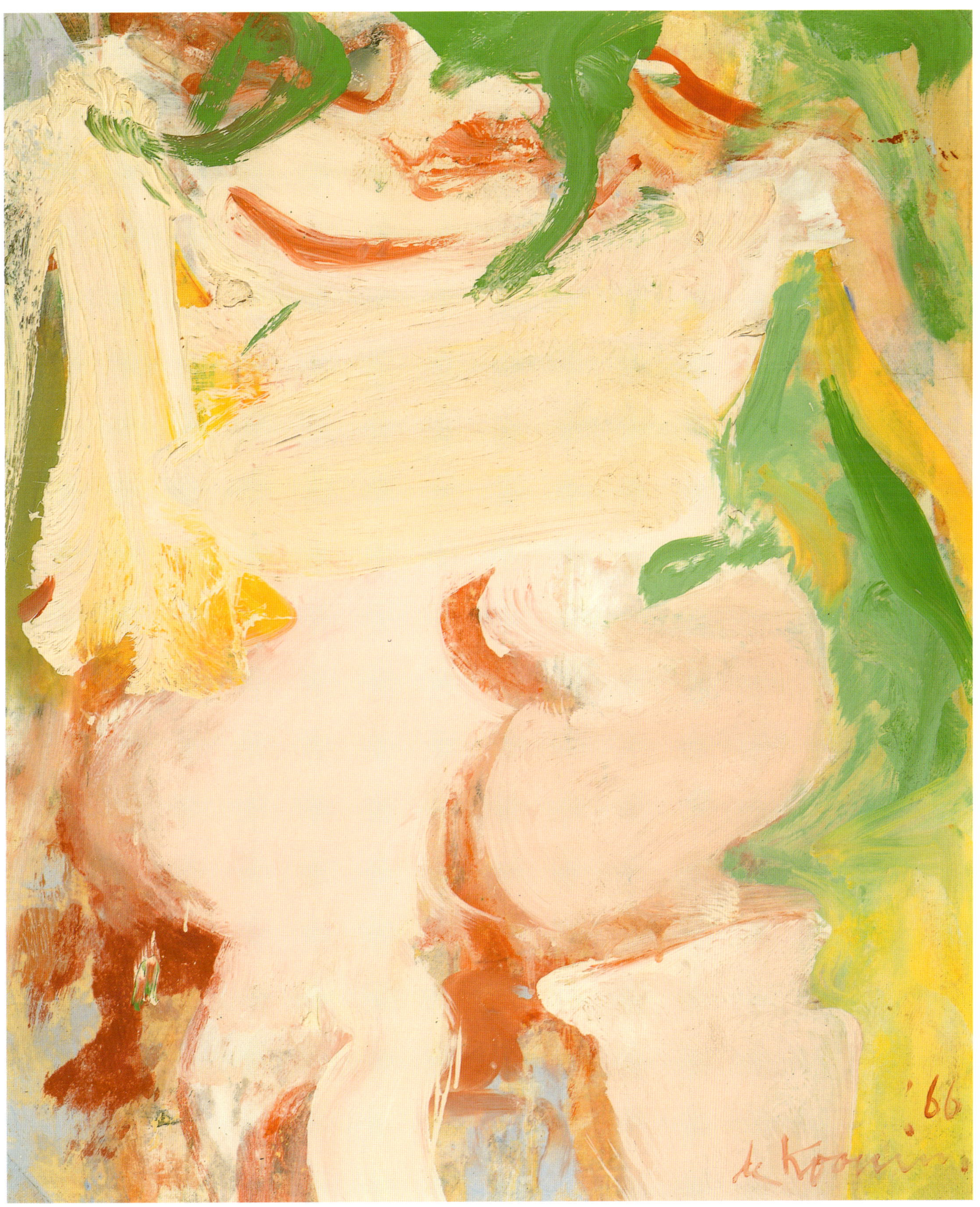

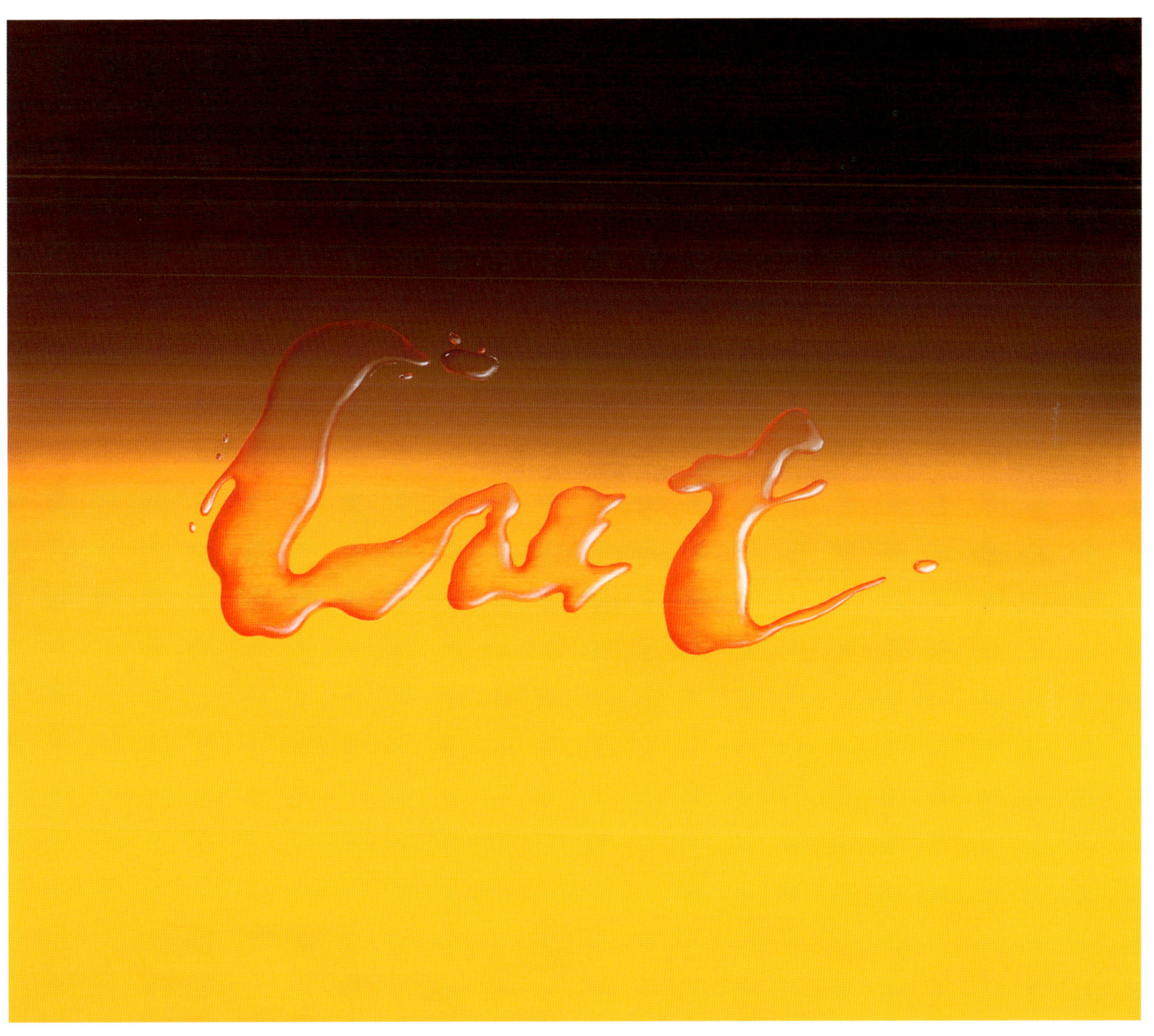
Cut.

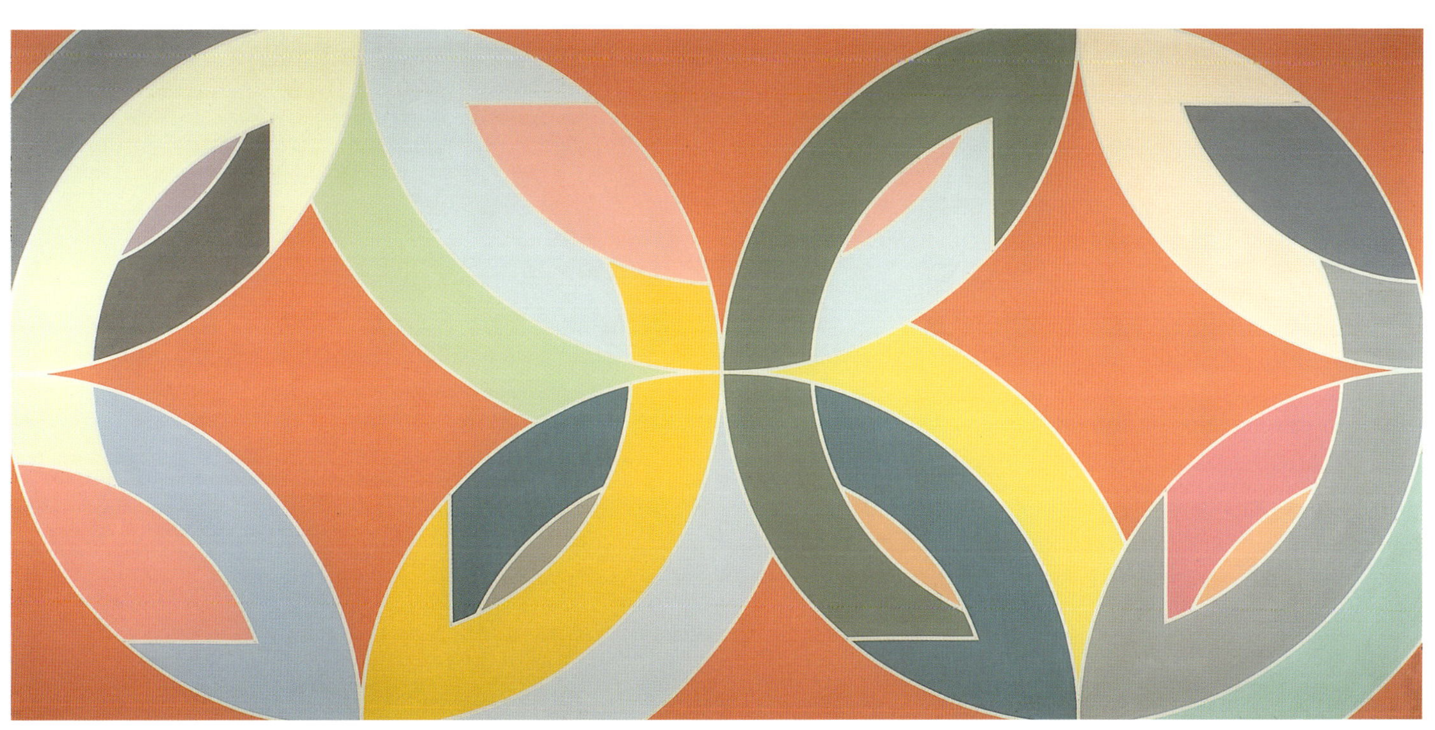

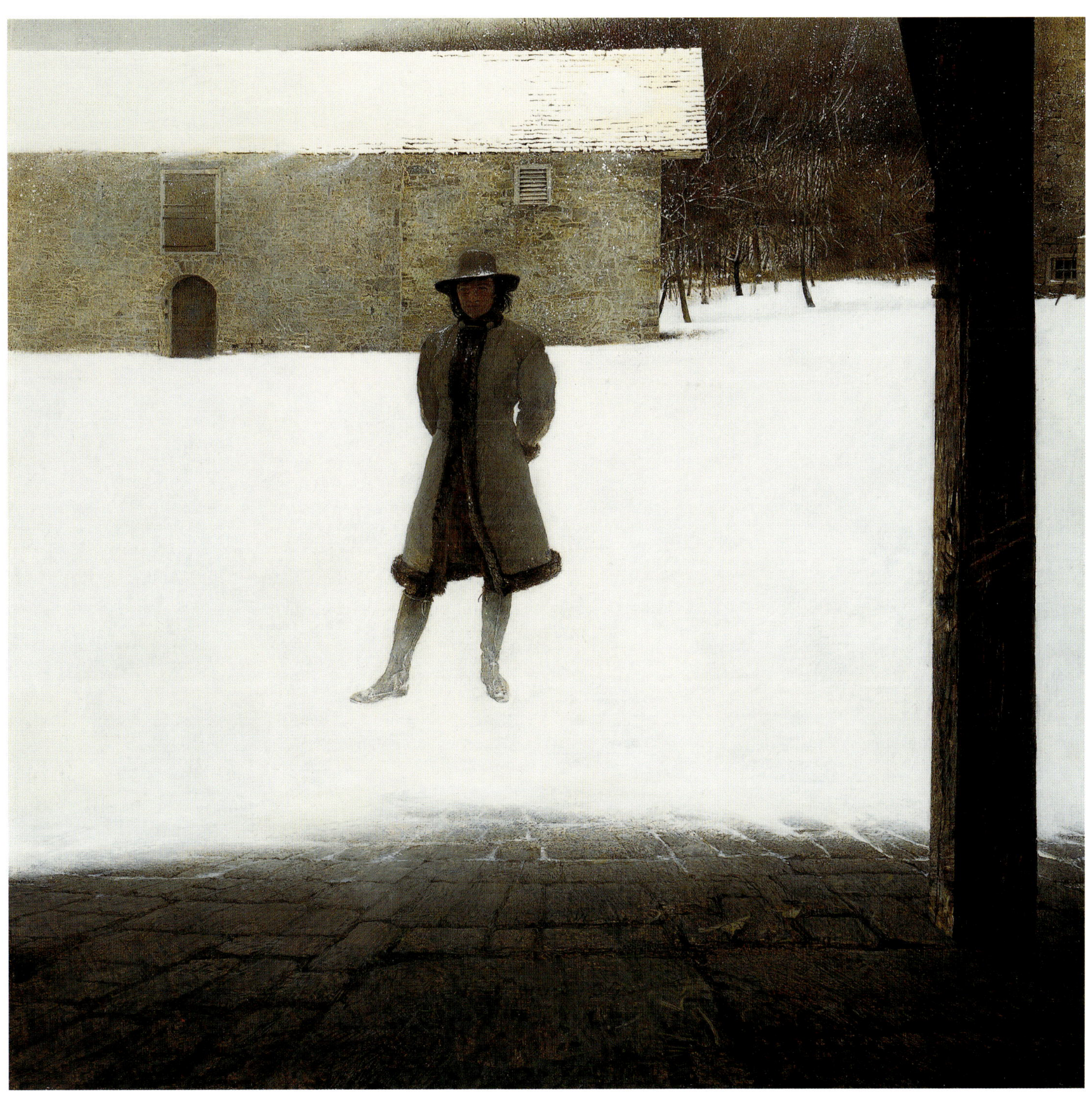

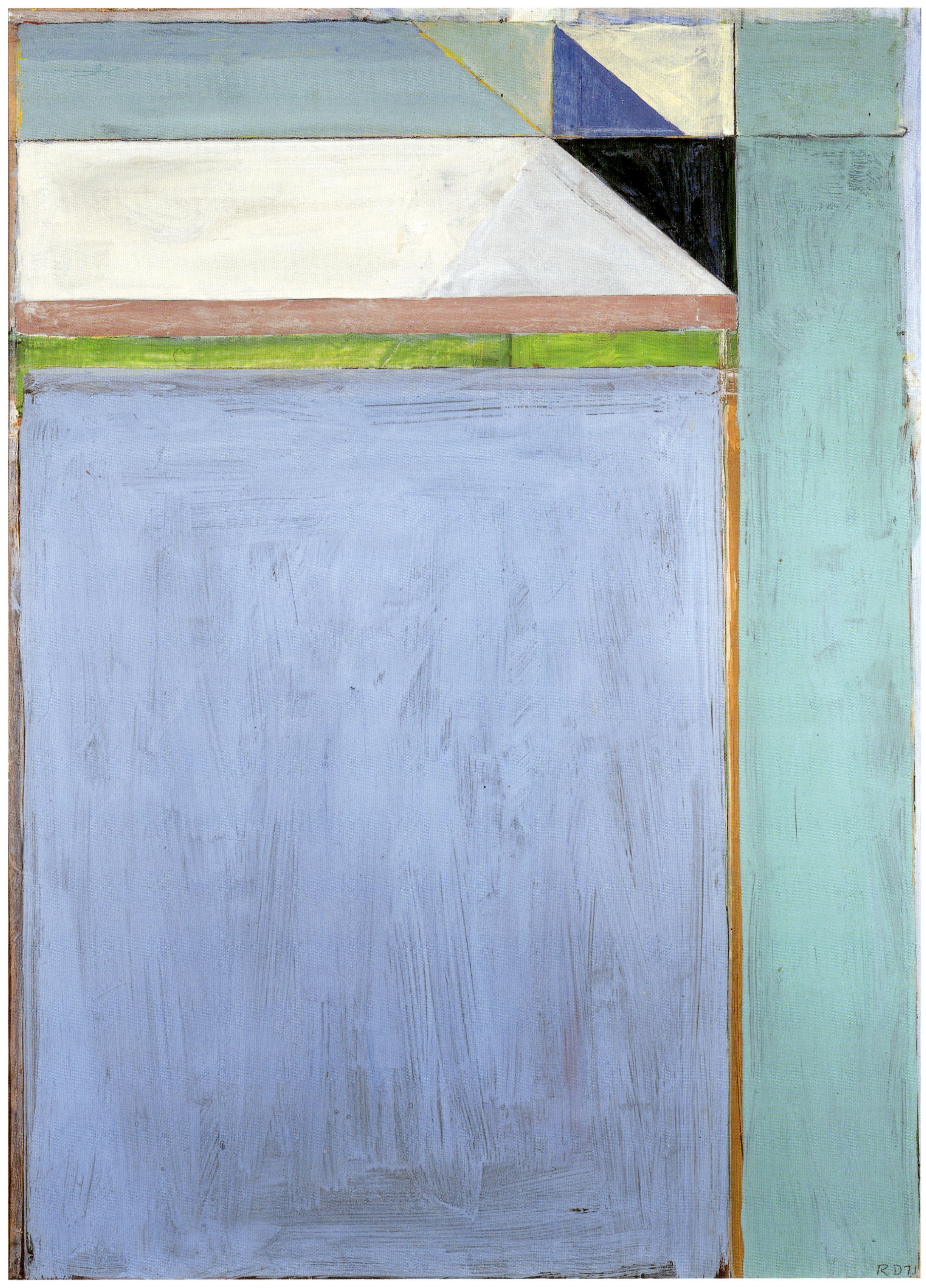

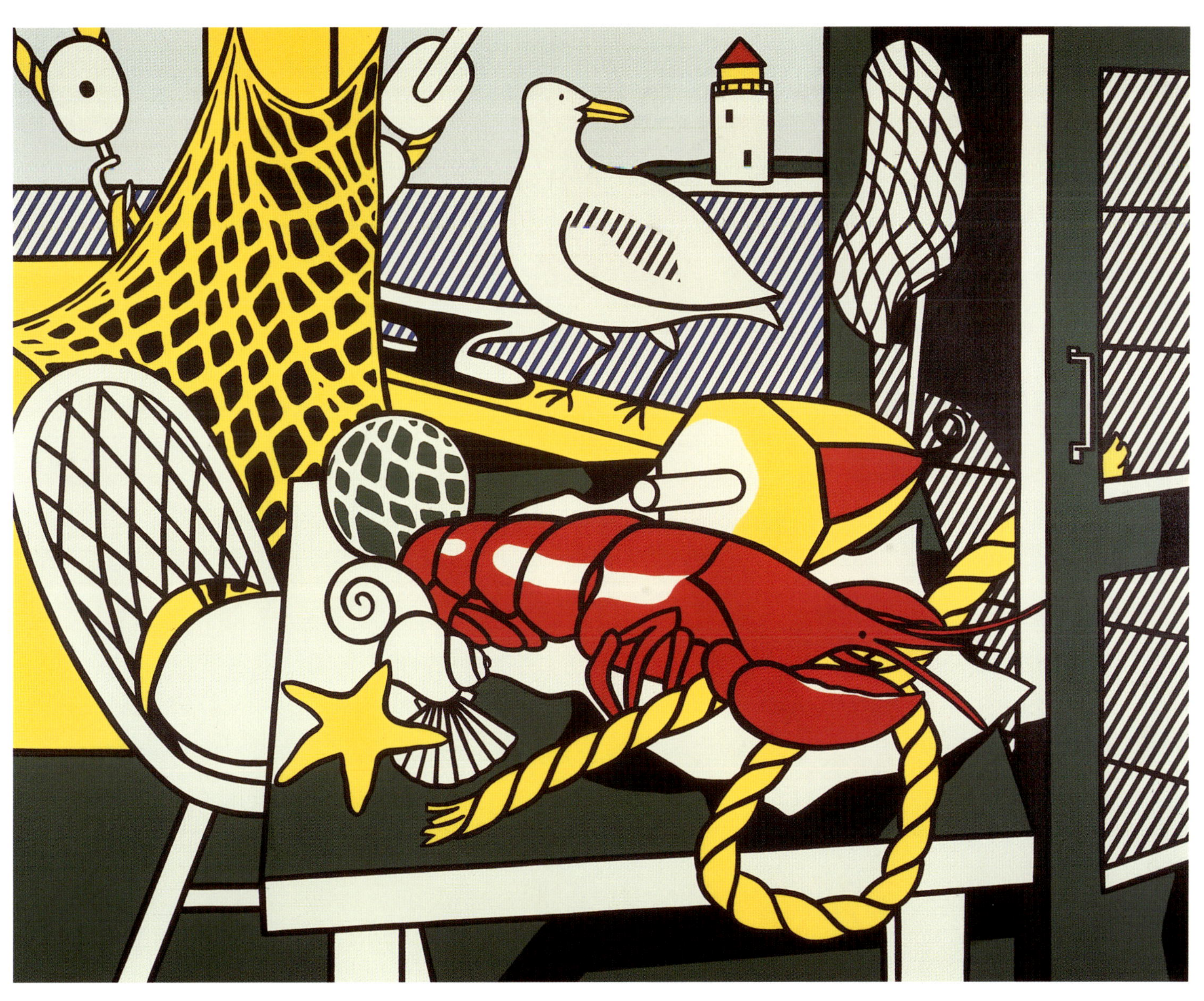

**PLATE 81**
Romare Bearden (1911–1988)
EXHIBITOR 1947, 1954
*Morning,* 1975
Collage on paper, 13 ½ x 17 ½ inches
Collection of David and Thelma Driskell

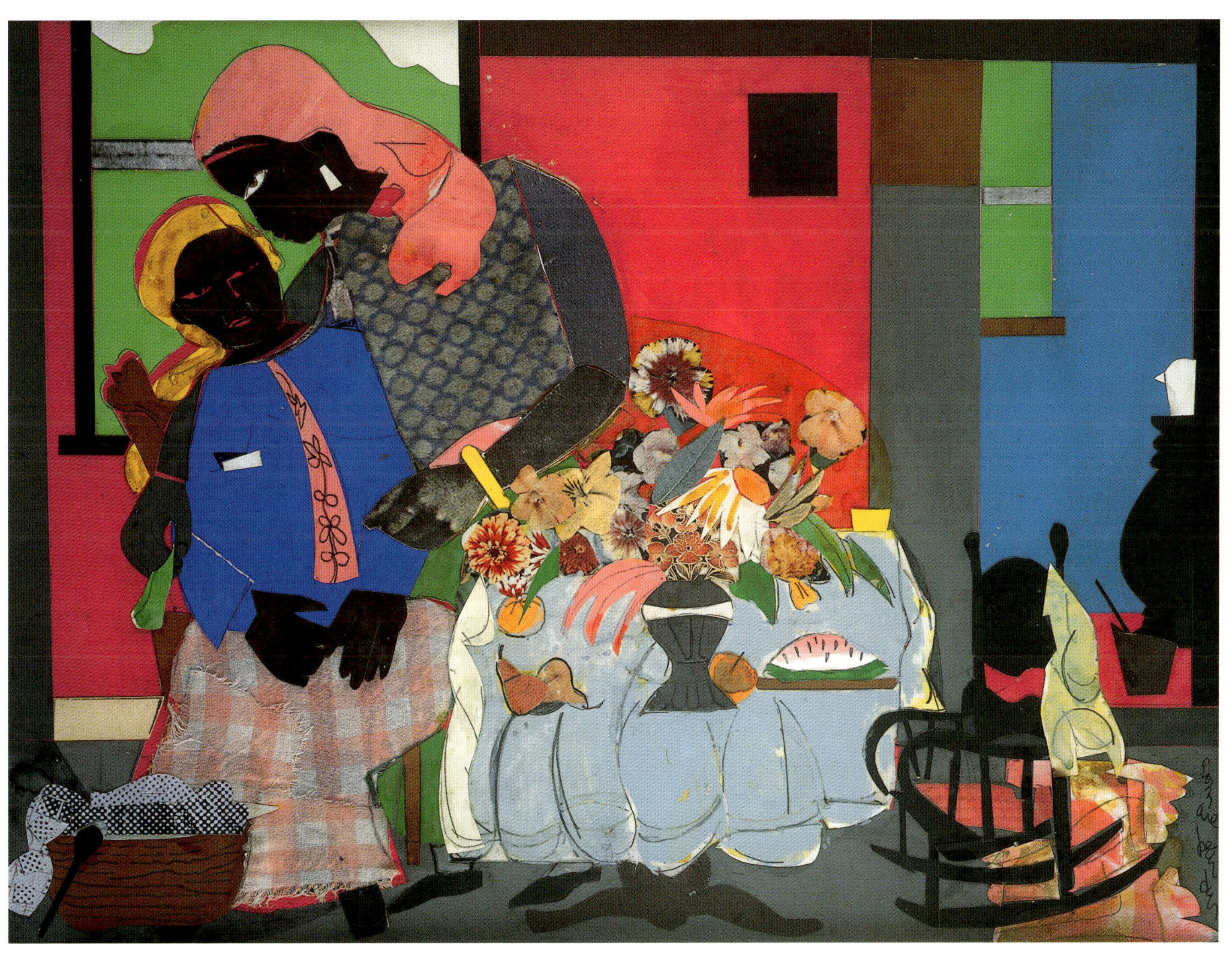

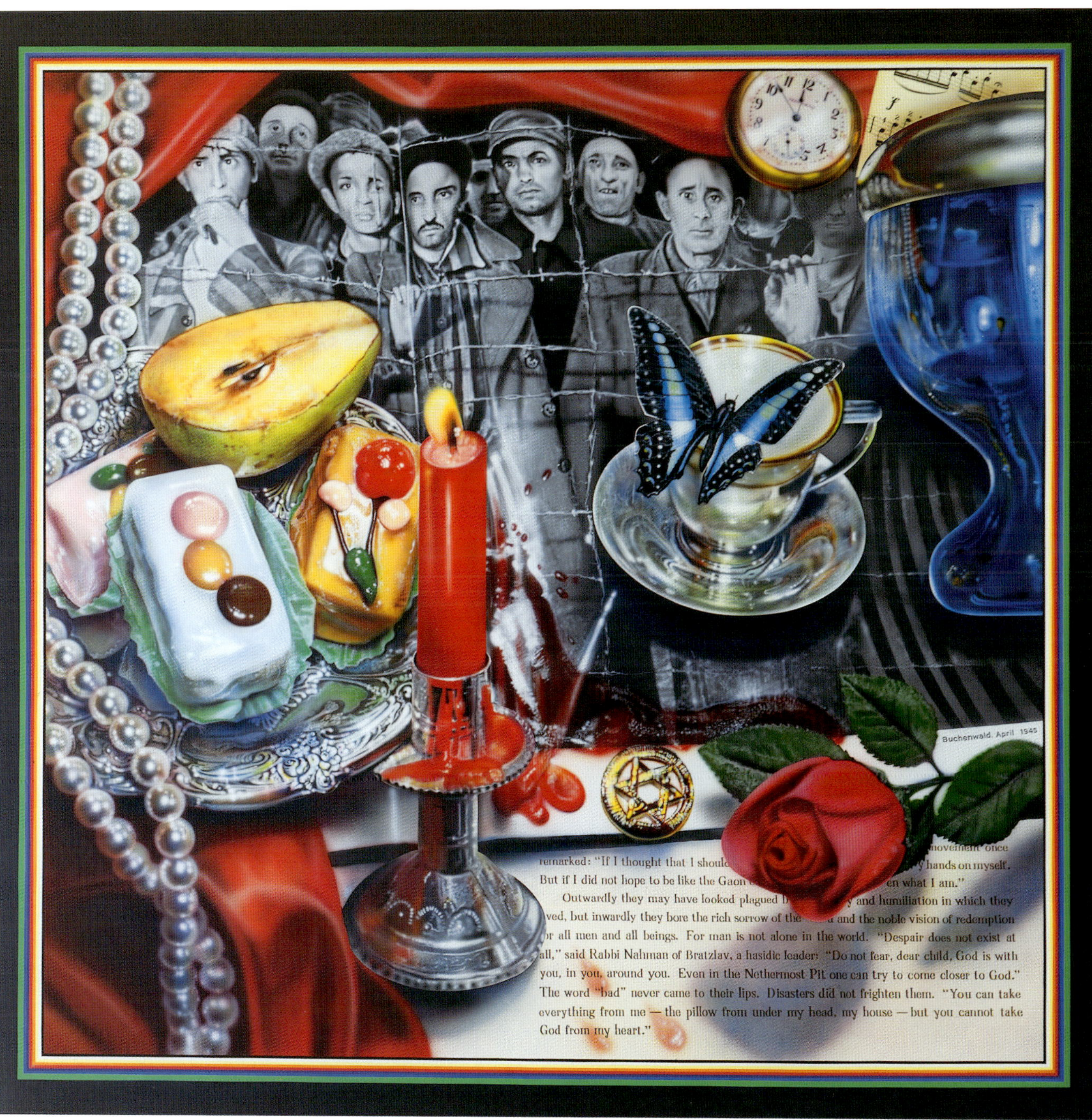

Buchenwald, April 1945
movement once remarked: "If I thought that I should ... hands on myself. But if I did not hope to be like the Gaon ... en what I am."
Outwardly they may have looked plagued b... y and humiliation in which they ... ved, but inwardly they bore the rich sorrow of the ... and the noble vision of redemption ... r all men and all beings. For man is not alone in the world. "Despair does not exist at all," said Rabbi Nahman of Bratzlav, a hasidic leader: "Do not fear, dear child, God is with you, in you, around you. Even in the Nethermost Pit one can try to come closer to God." The word "bad" never came to their lips. Disasters did not frighten them. "You can take everything from me — the pillow from under my head, my house — but you cannot take God from my heart."

PLATE 83
Philip Guston (1913–1980)
EXHIBITOR 1944–51
*Studio Celebration*, 1978
Oil on canvas, 52 x 60 inches
Collection of Mrs. Robert S. Lee

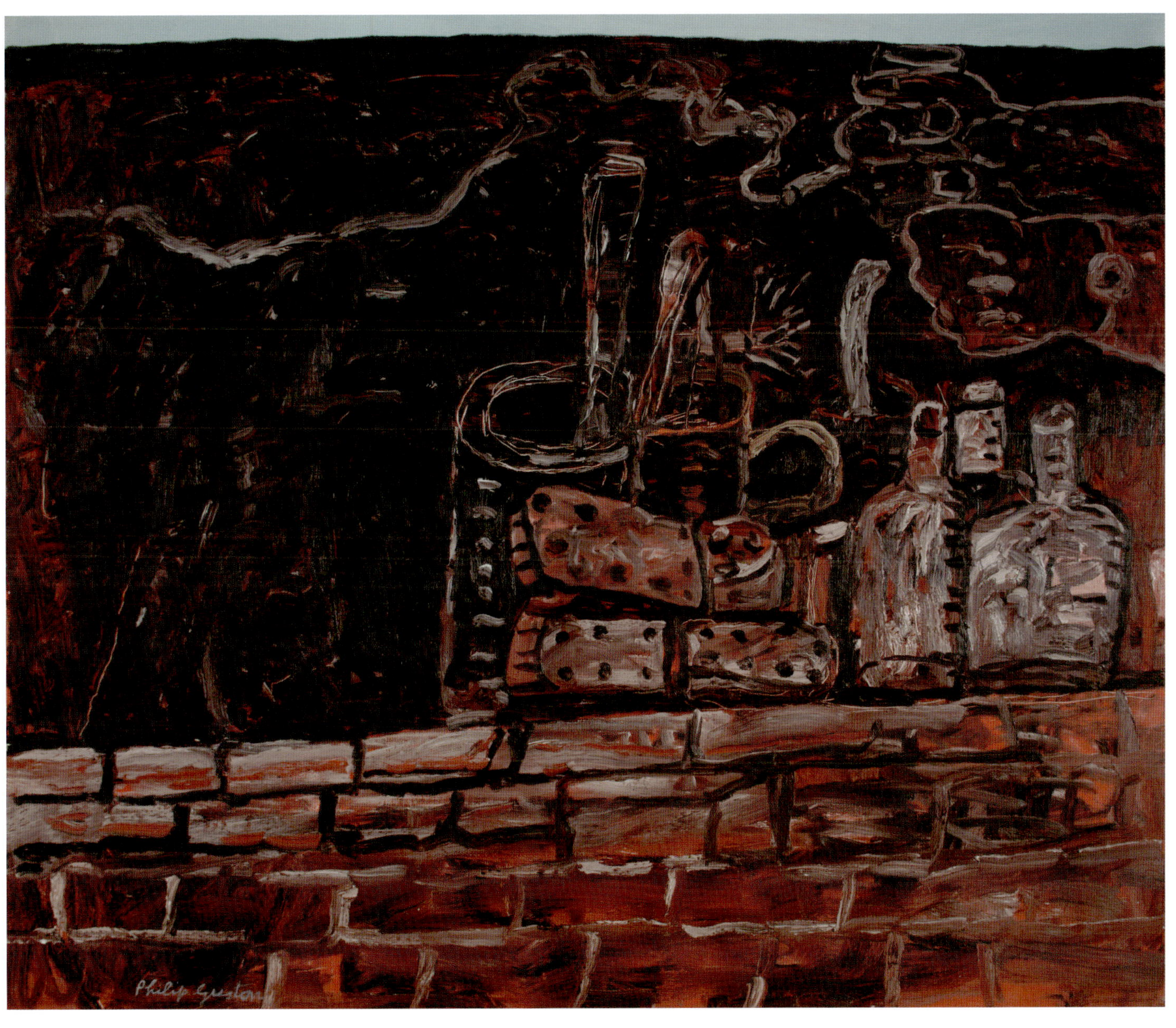

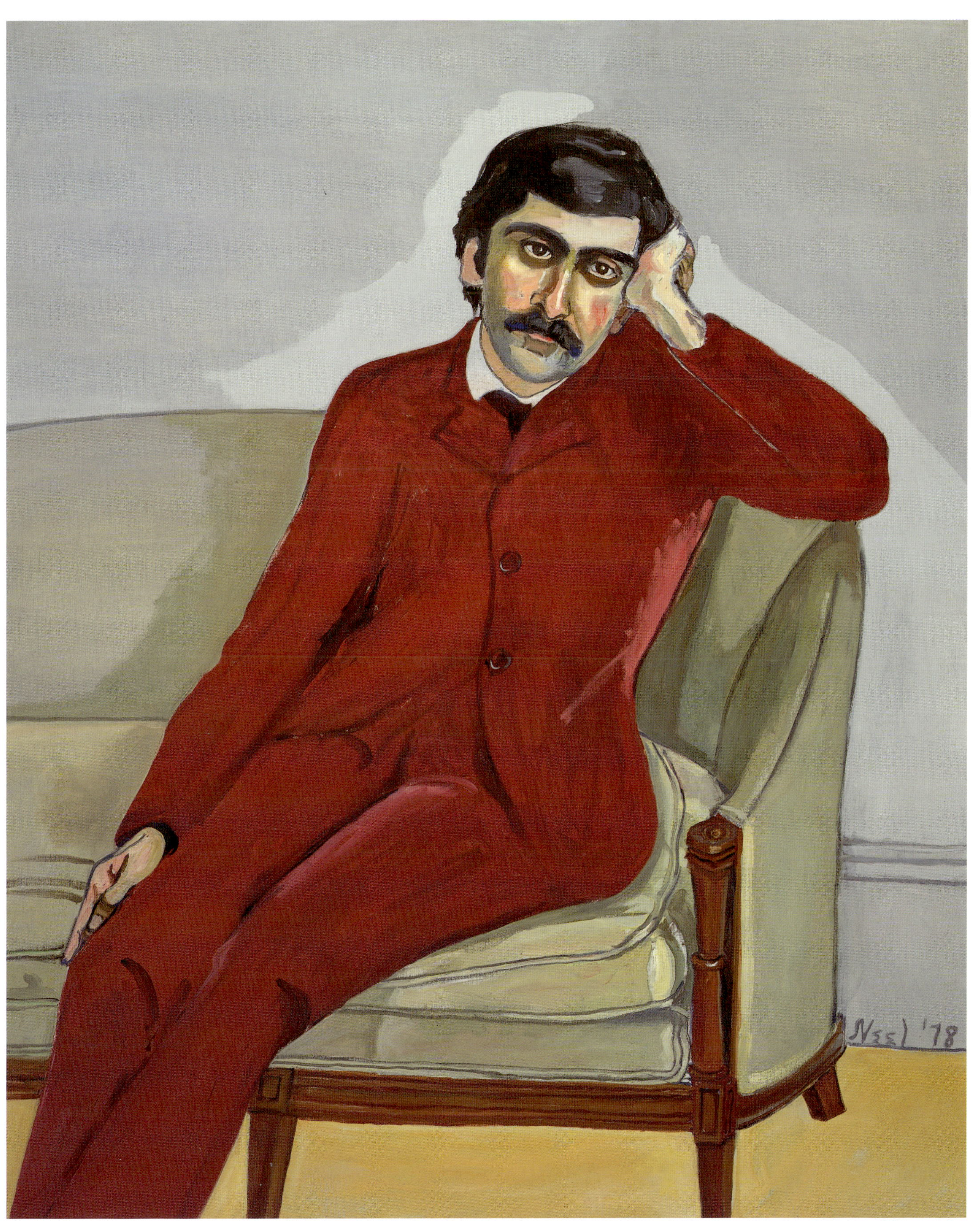

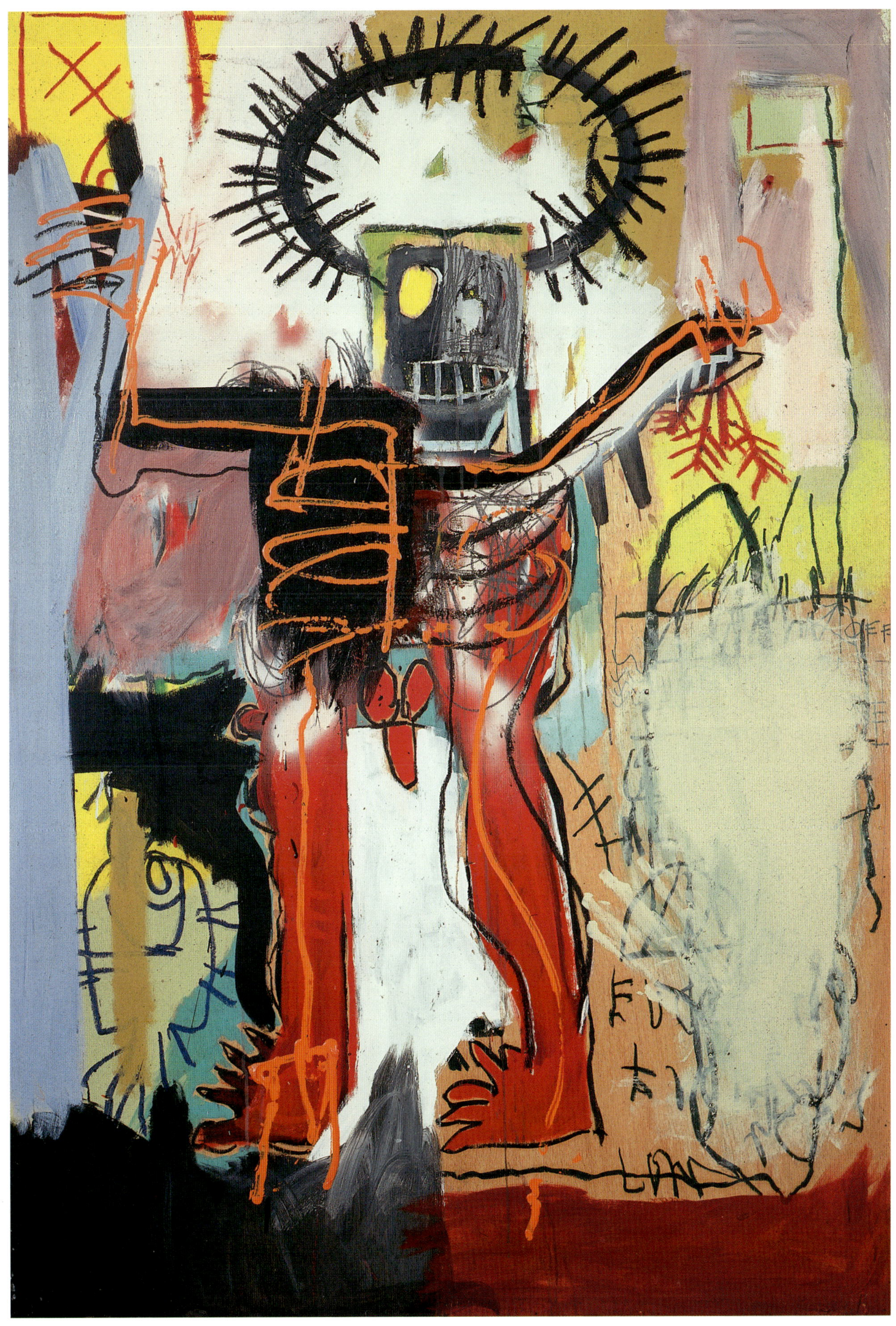

Ellsworth Kelly (b. 1923)
*Dark Blue Curve II,* 1982
Oil on canvas, 92 ⅝ x 105 inches
Collection of Mari and Peter Shaw

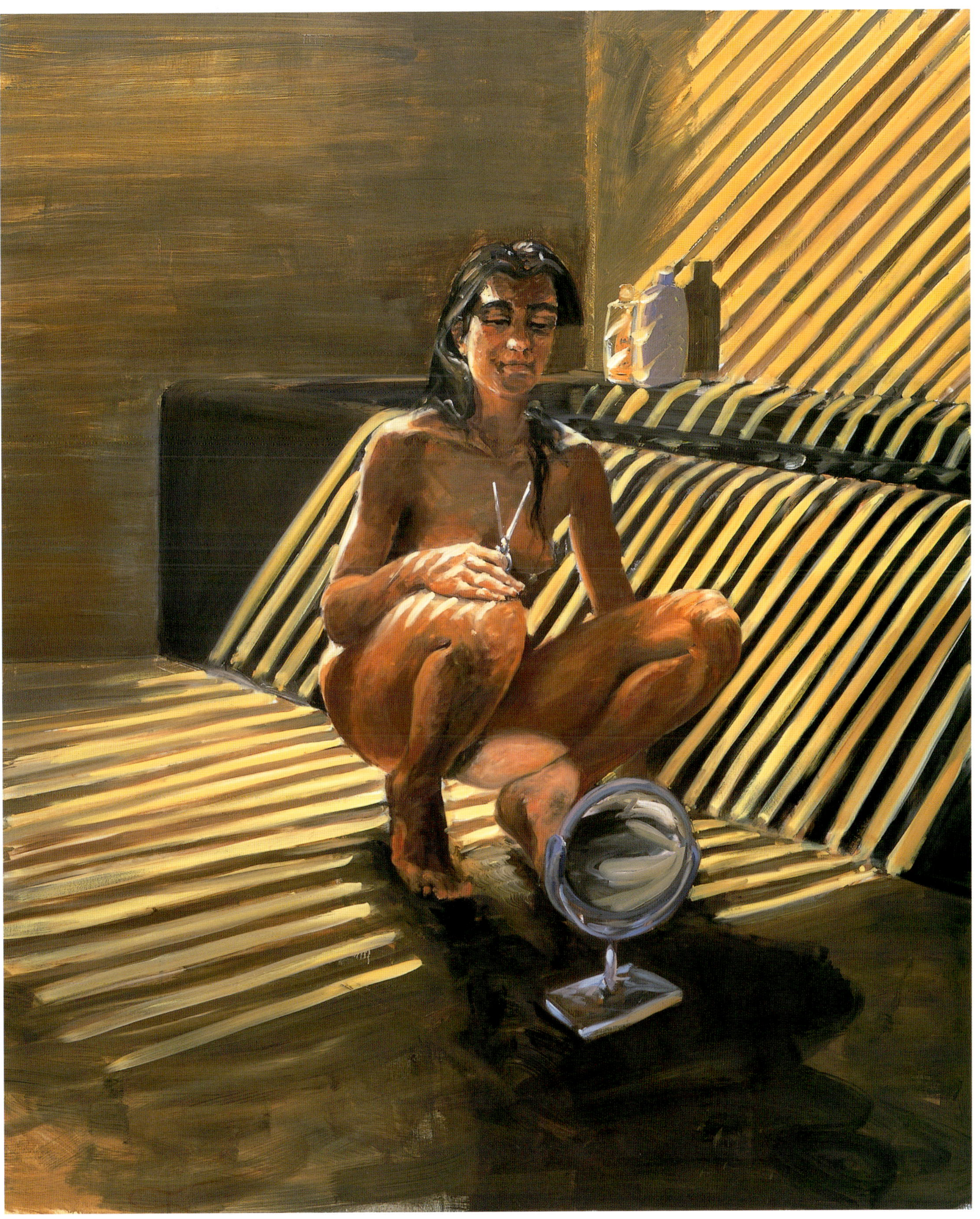

David Salle (b. 1952)
*Wild Locust Ride,* 1985
Acrylic and oil on canvas with fabric, 75 x 104 ½ inches
Collection of Harriet and Larry Weiss

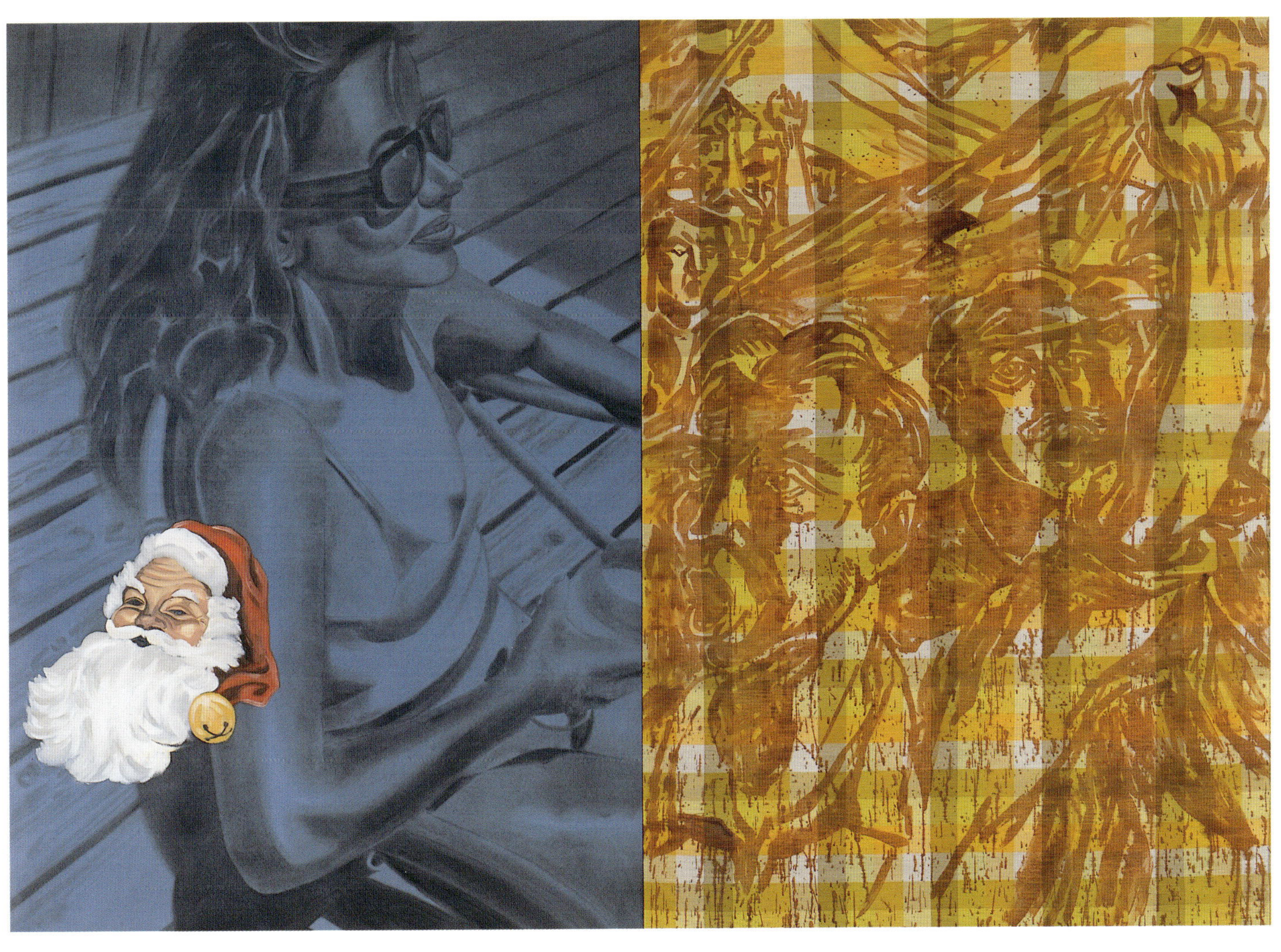

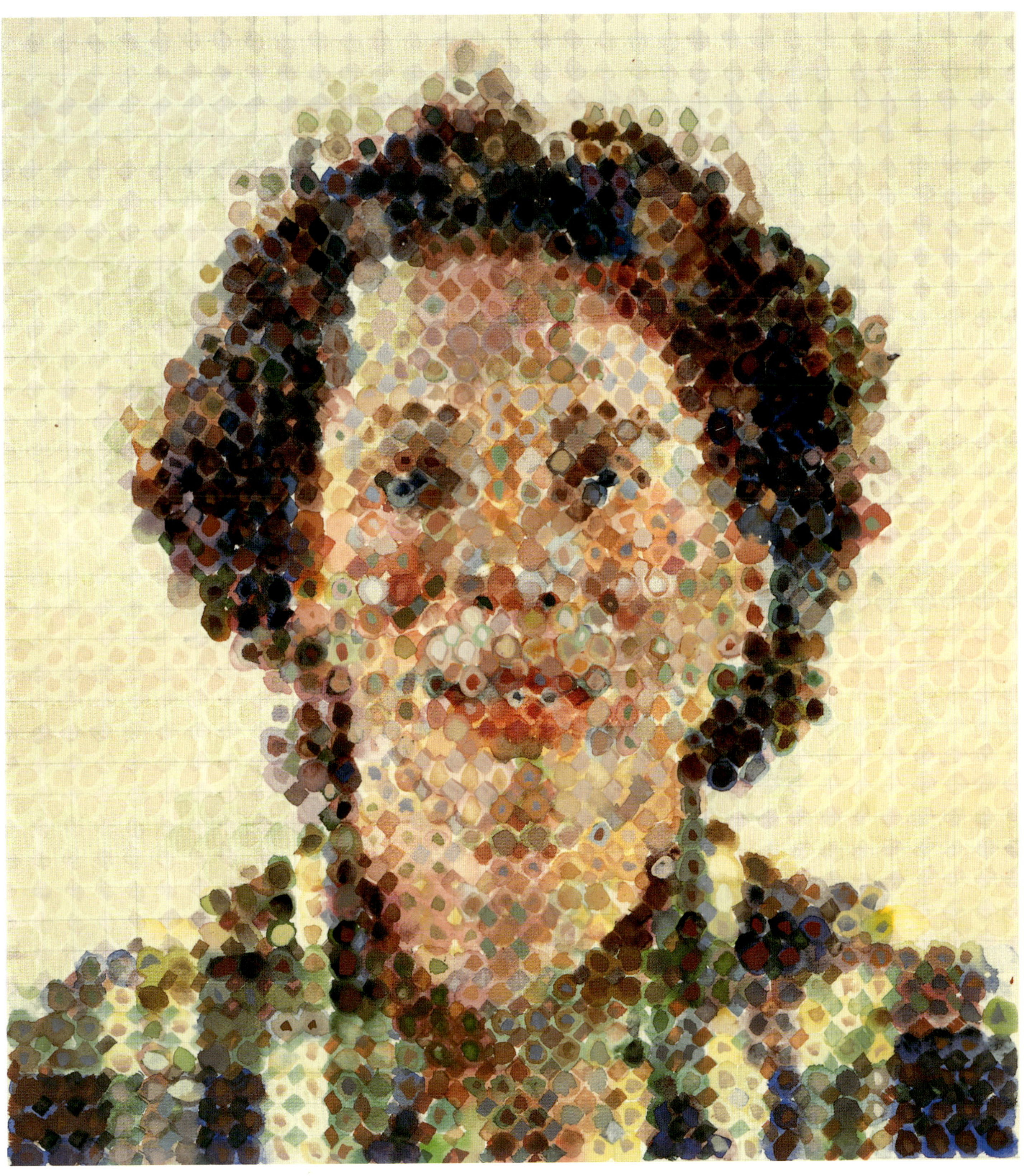

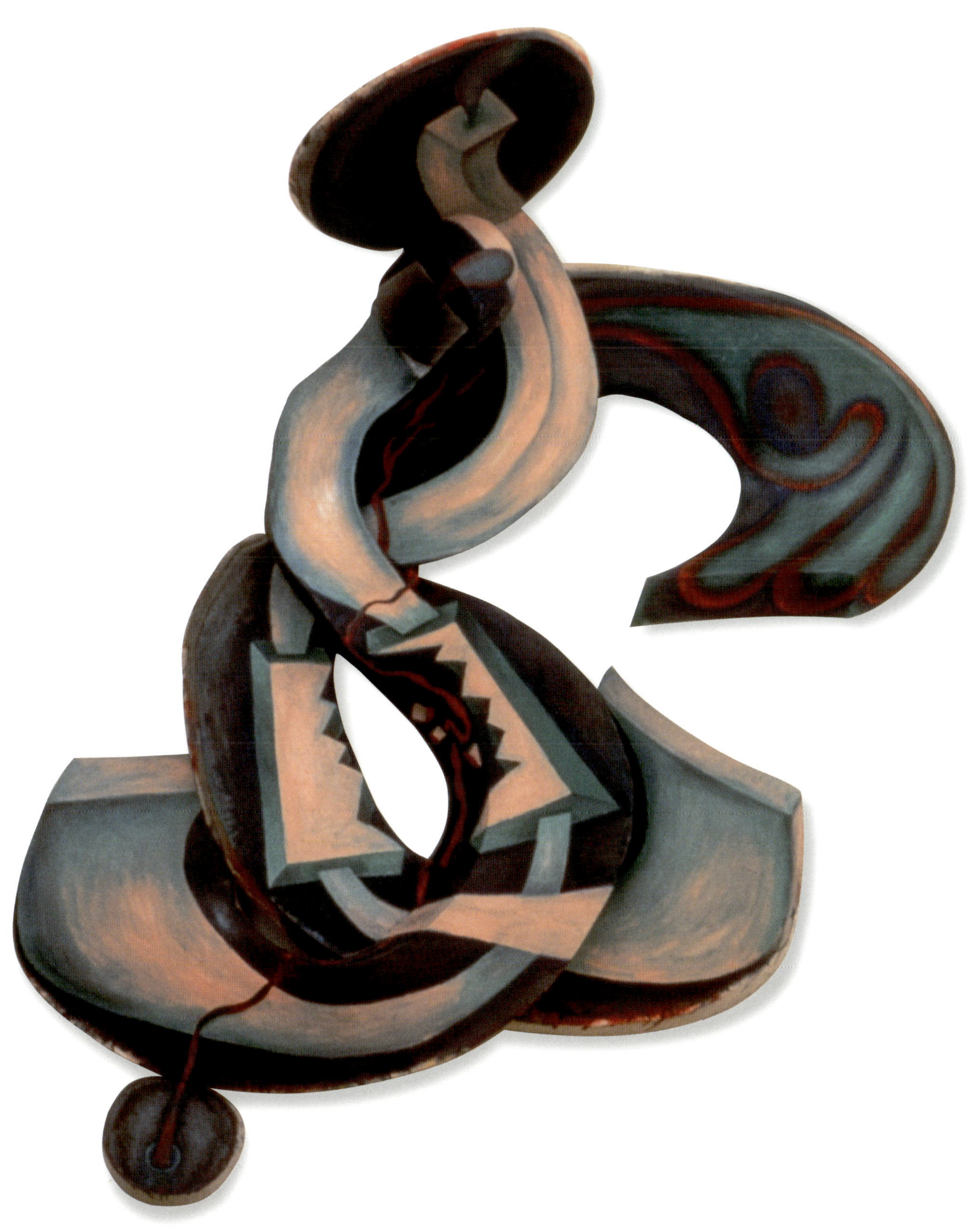



PLATES

PLATE 92
Sean Scully (b. 1945)
*Morning*, 1986
Oil on linen, 96 x 96 inches
Collection of Luther W. Brady

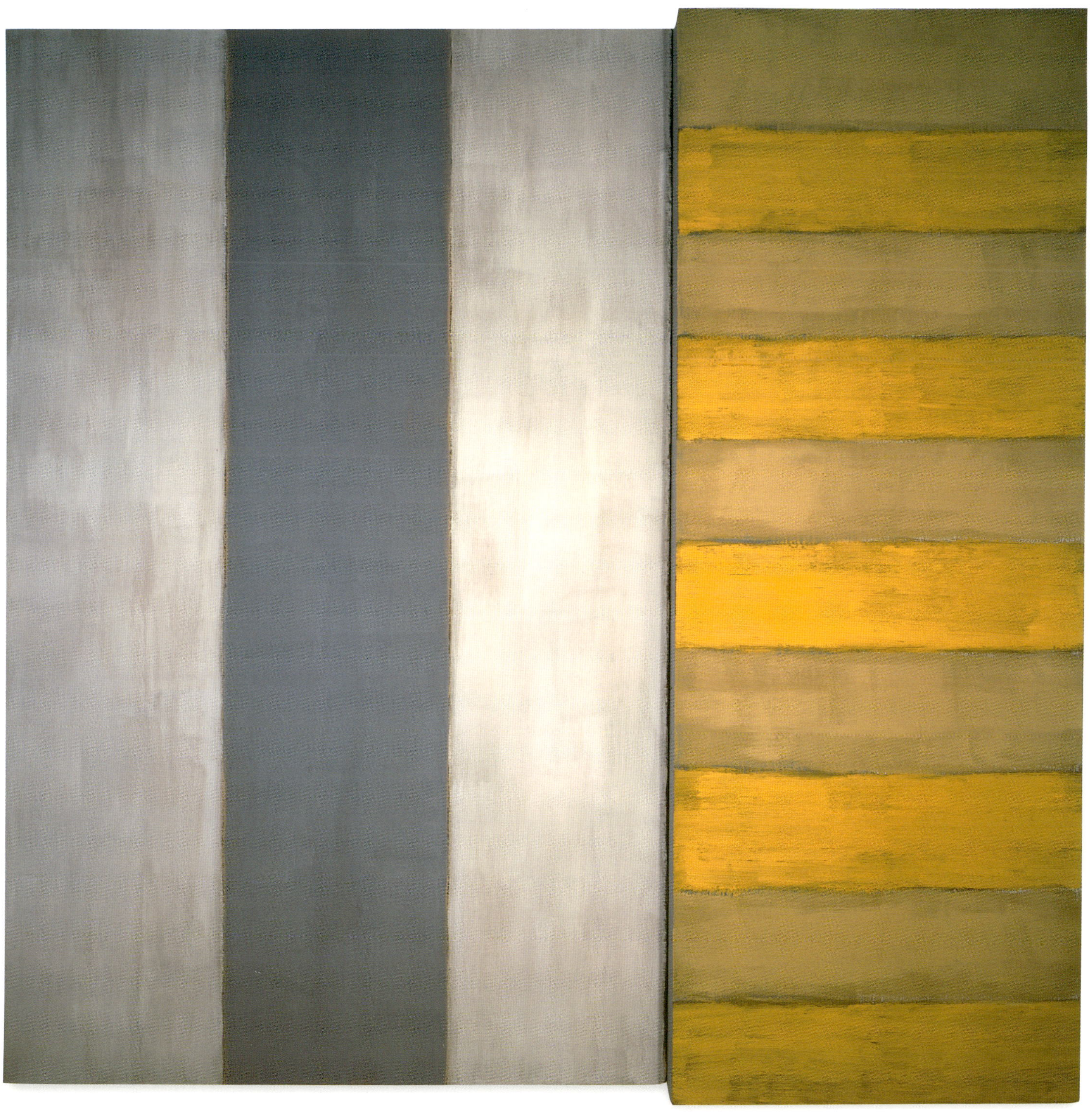

Tim Rollins (b. 1955) + K.O.S. (Kids of Survival)
*The Interior of a Heart,* 1987–88
Mixed media, 90 x 102 inches
Collection of Jane and Leonard Korman

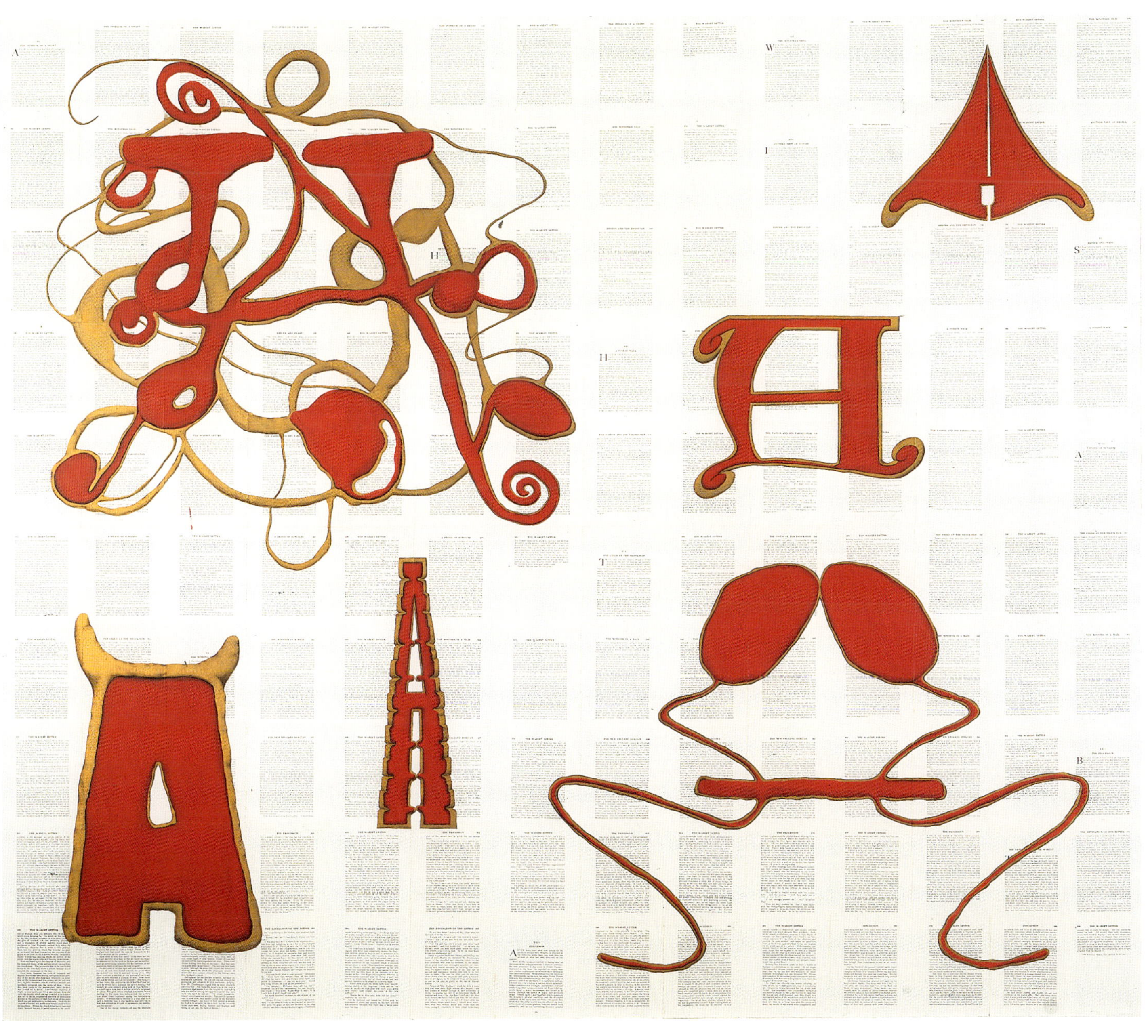

PLATE 94
Wayne Thiebaud (b. 1920)
*Meringues,* 1988
Oil on canvas, 30 x 30 inches
Private Collection, Washington, D.C.

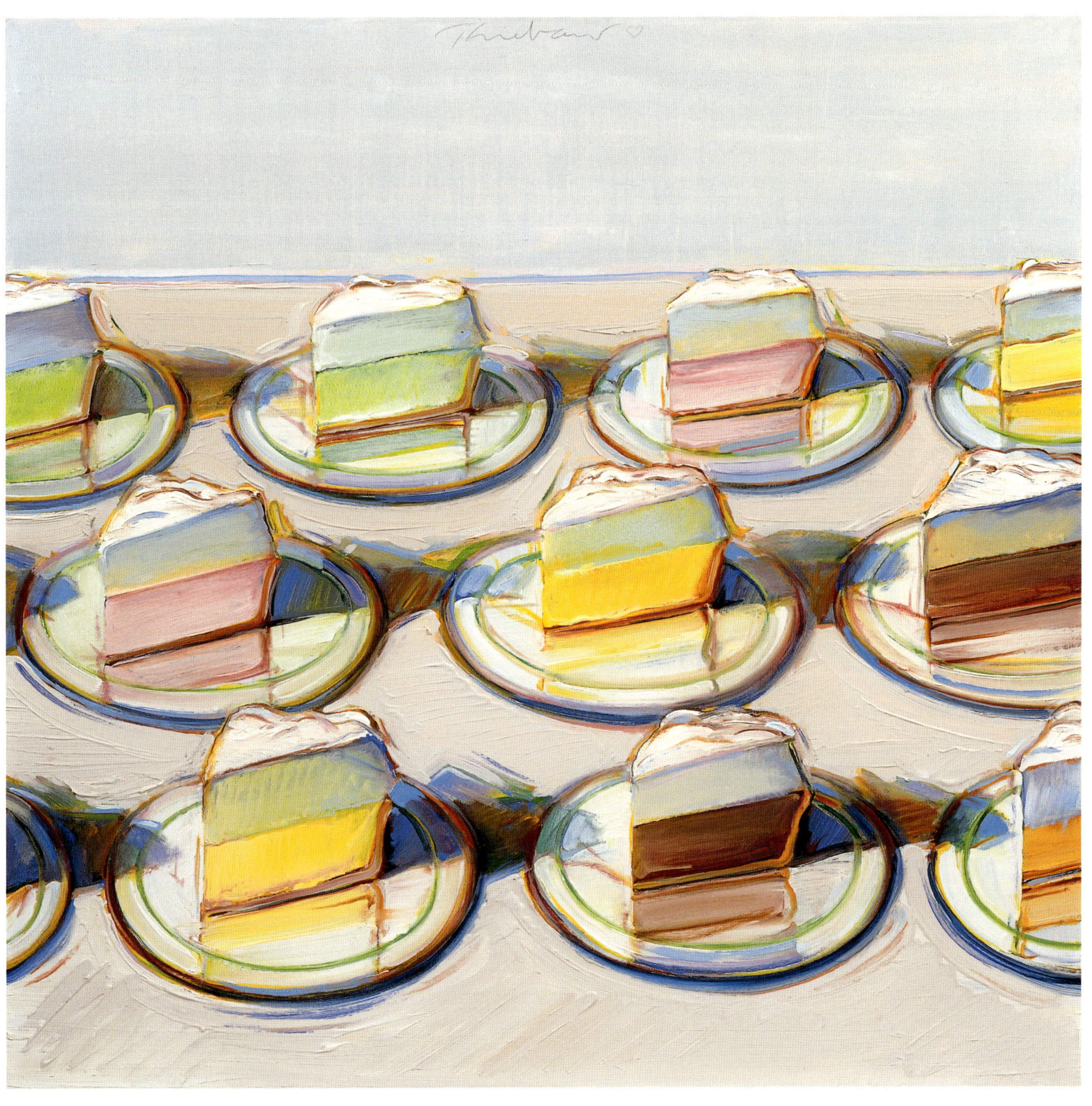

**PLATE 95**
Brice Marden (b. 1938)
*Bear,* 1996–1997
Oil on linen, 84 x 60 inches
Anonymous Loan

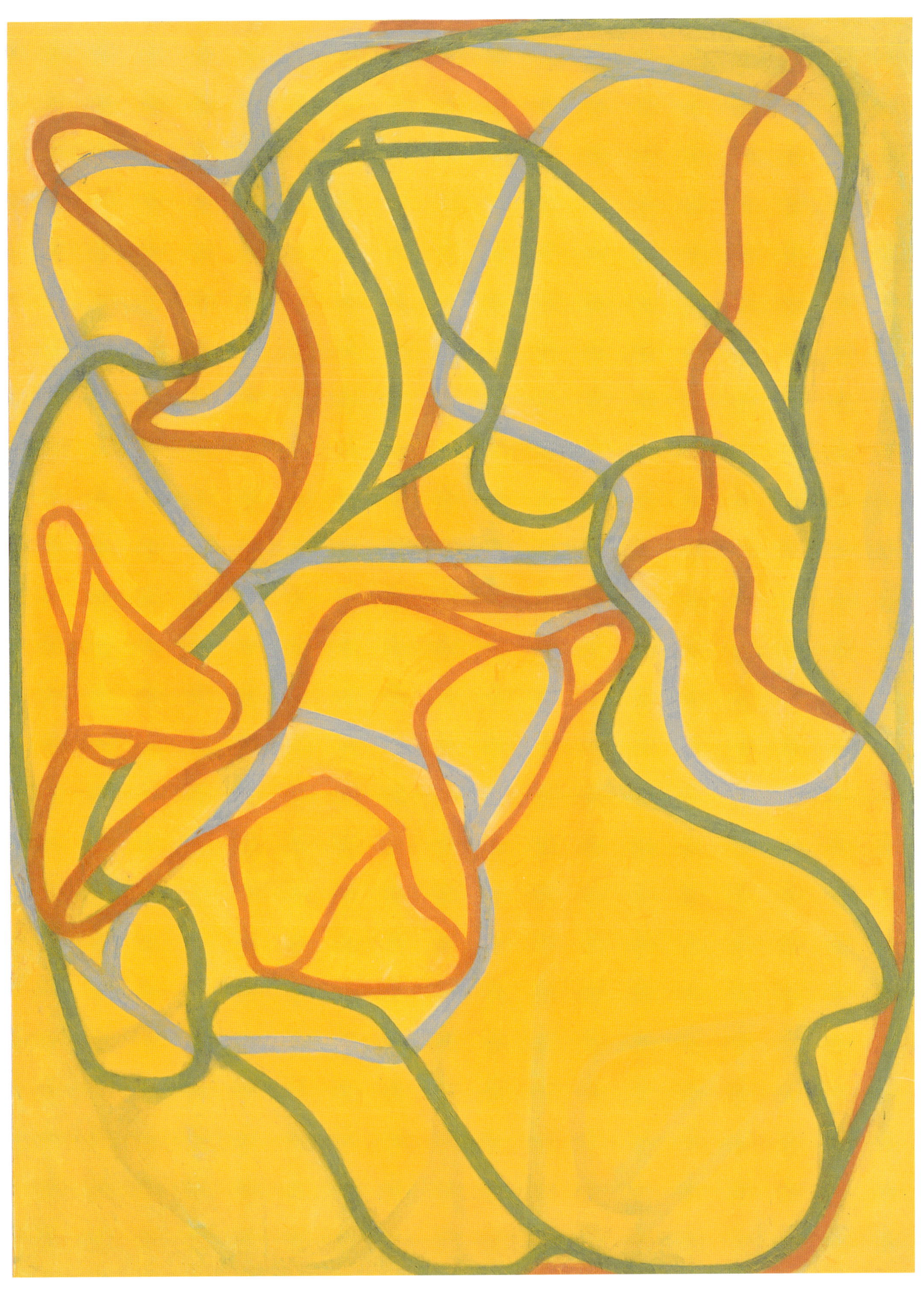

Robert Colescott (b. 1925)
*April in Paris,* 1998
Oil on canvas, 84 x 72 inches
Private Collection, New York

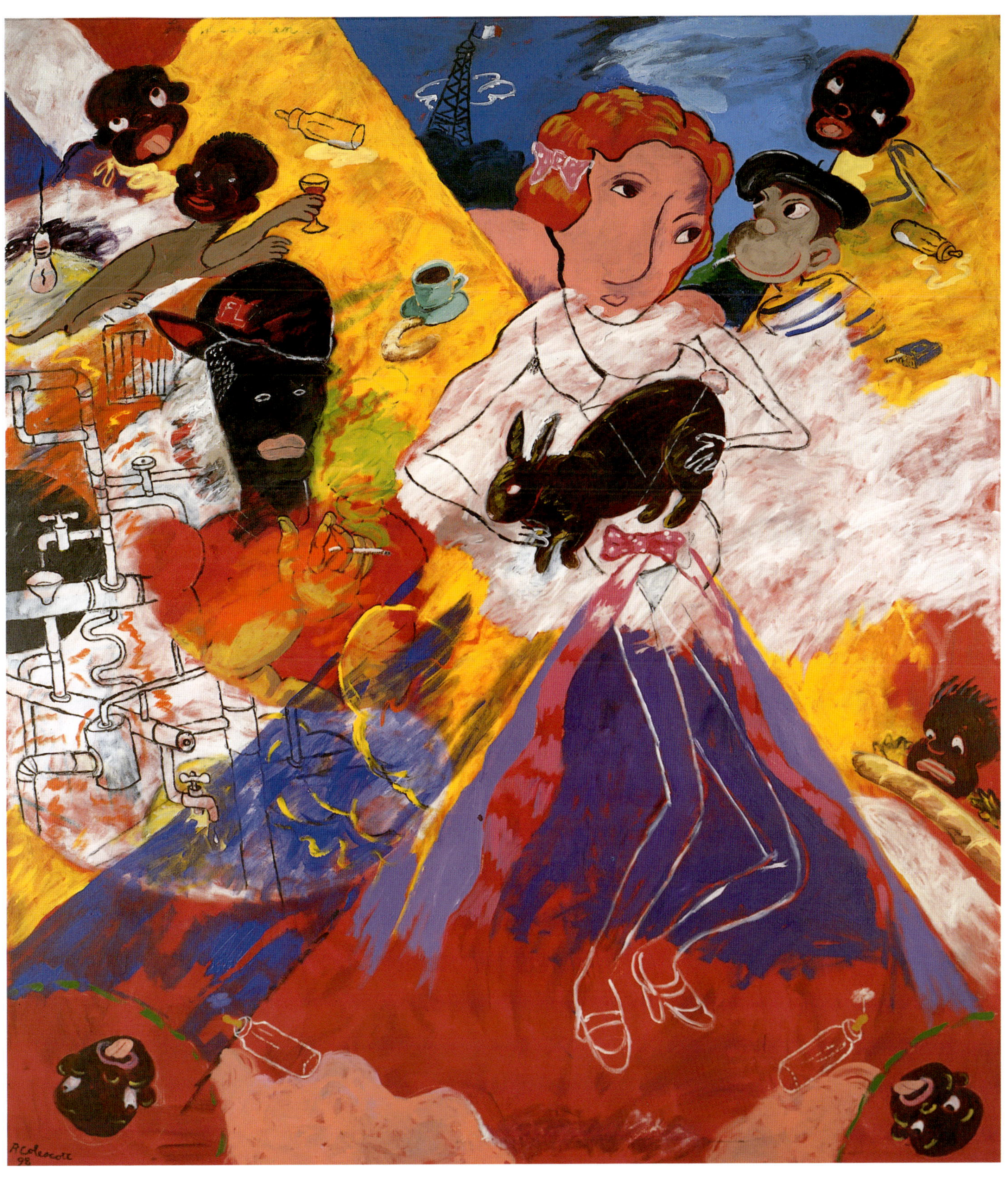

PLATE 97
Ellen Gallagher (b. 1965)
*Mobb Deep*, 1998
Acrylic and oil on canvas, 120 x 96 inches
Private Collection, New York

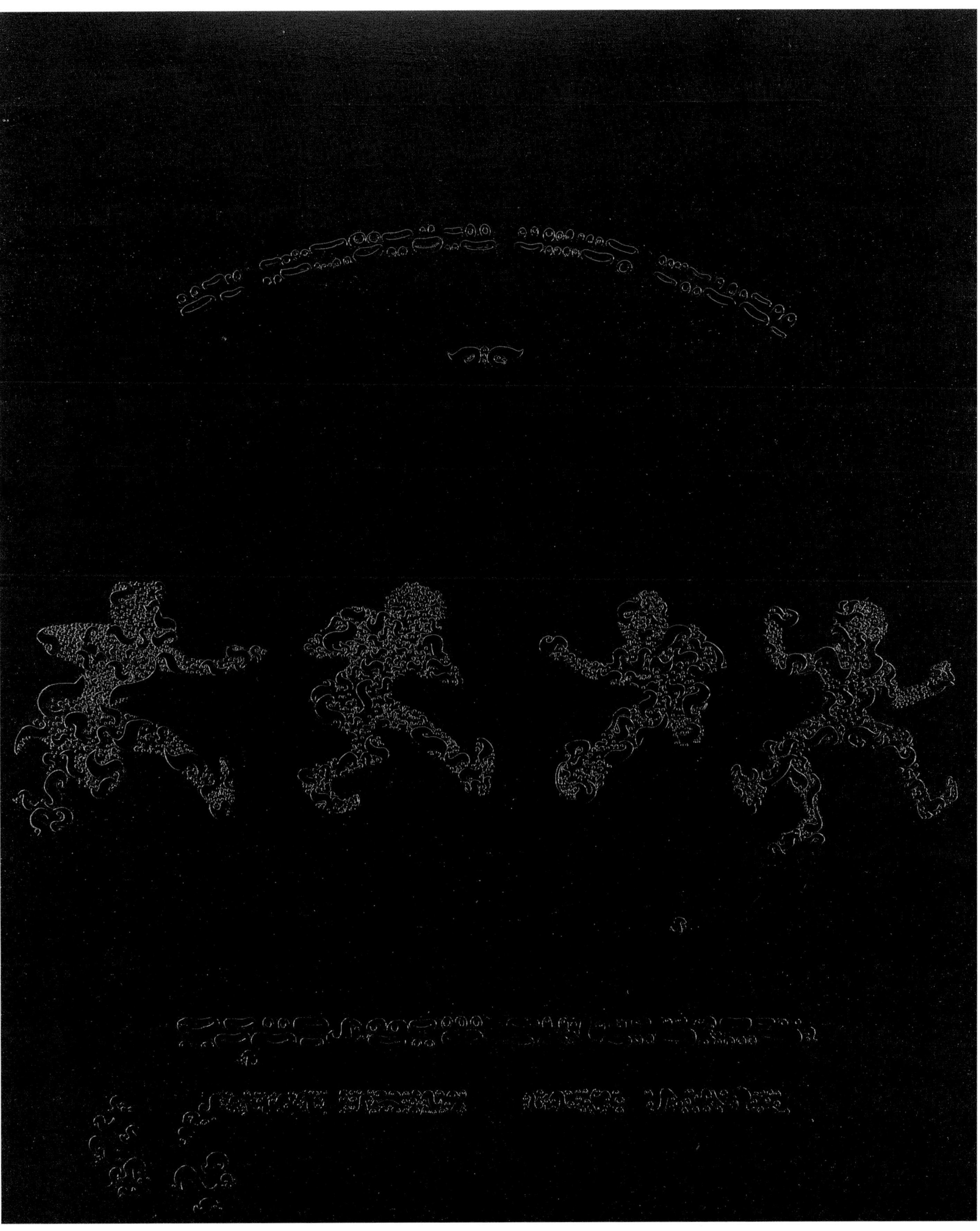

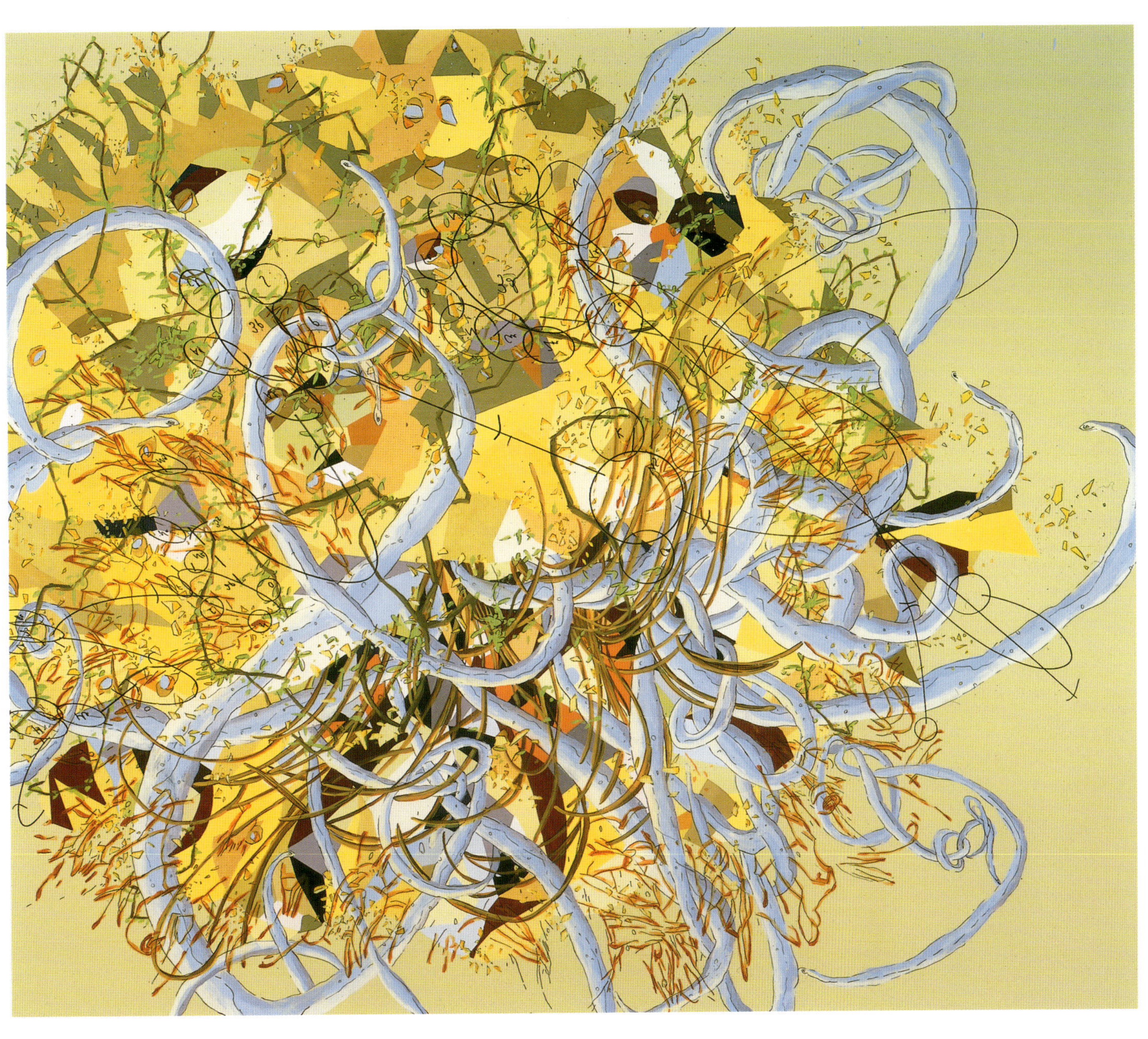



PLATES

PLATE 99
Carroll Dunham (b. 1949)
*Edge of His World (Four),* 2002–2003
Oil on canvas, 79 x 82 inches
Private Collection, New York

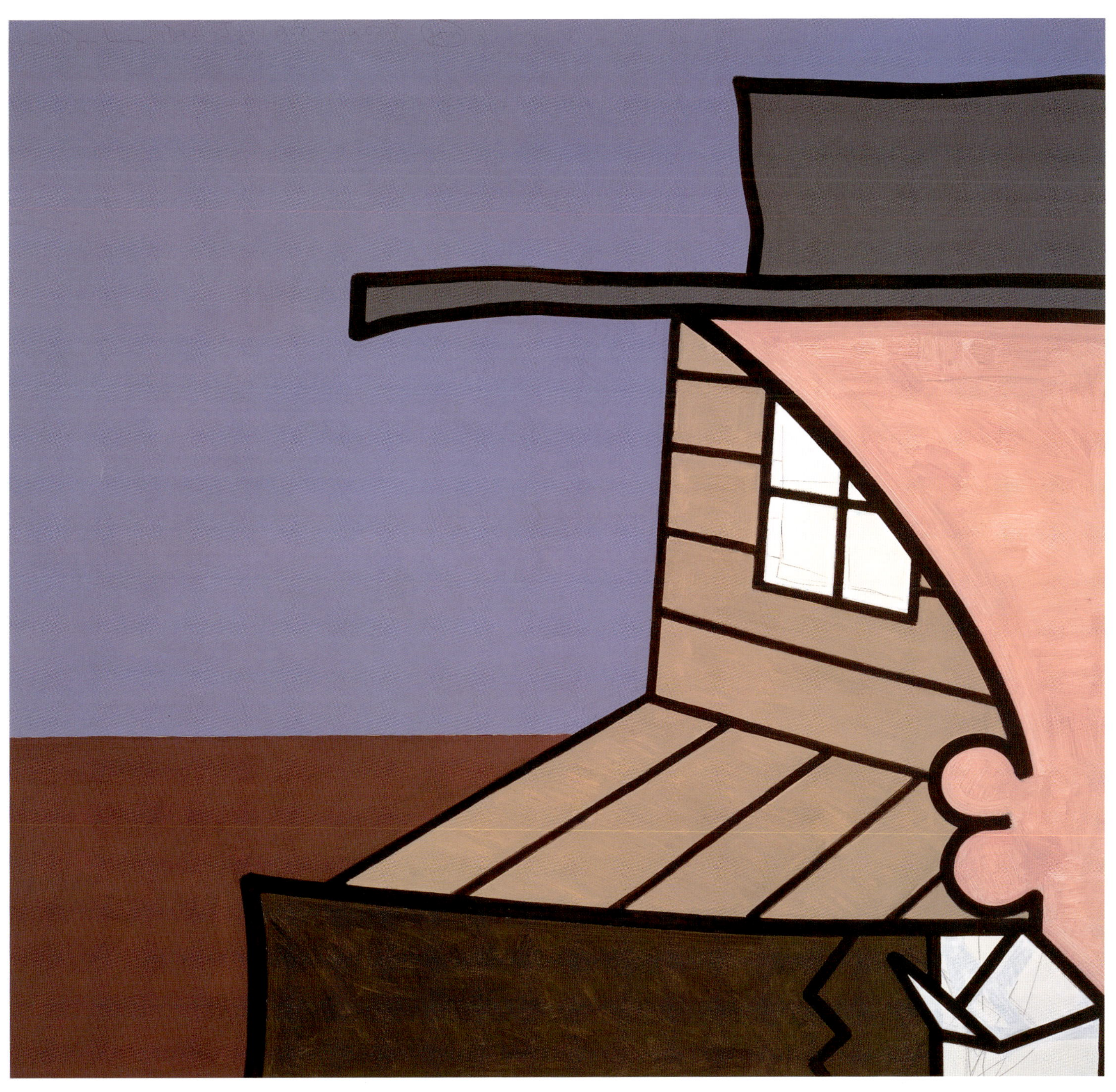

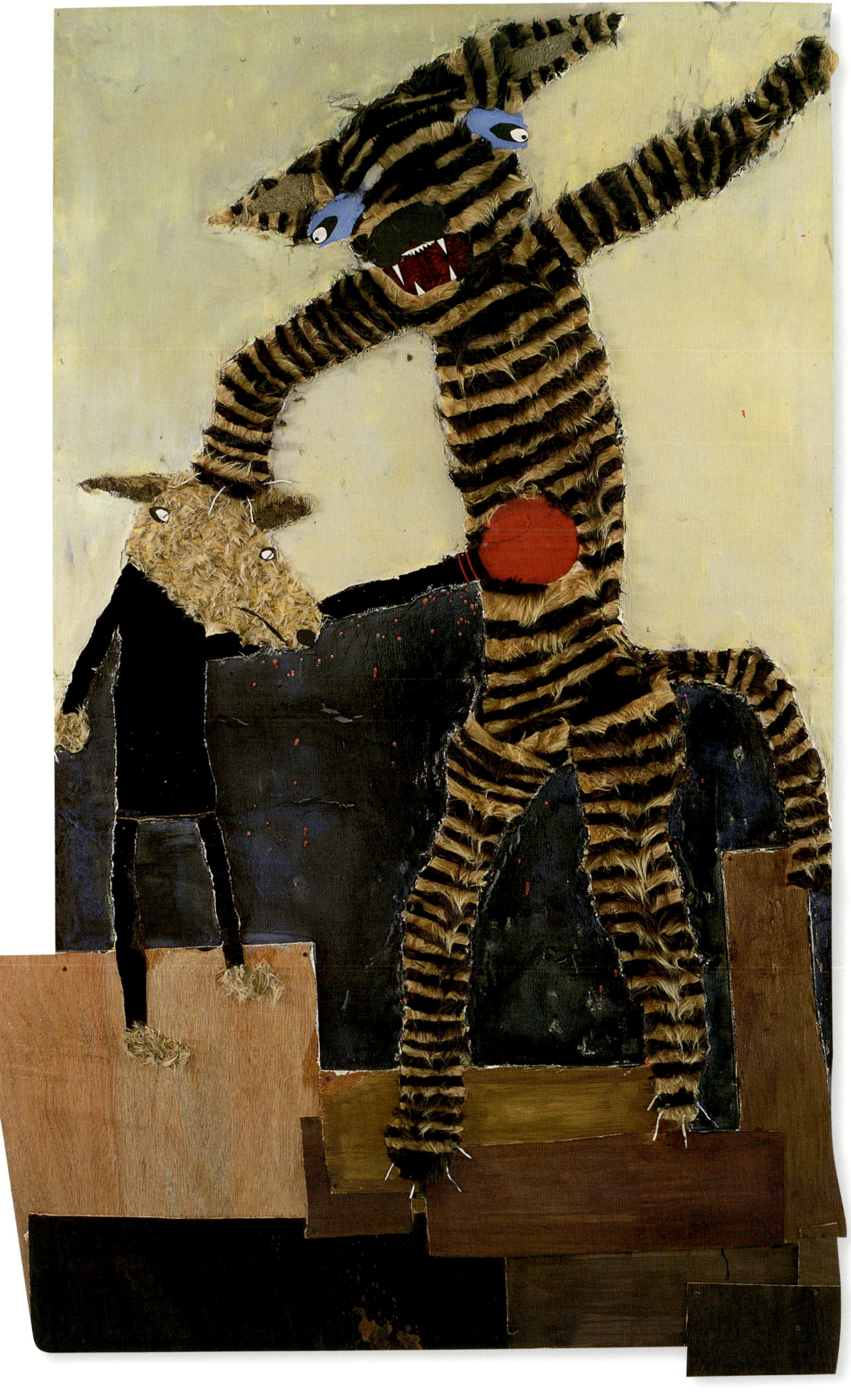

# Checklist of the Exhibition

Milton Avery (1885–1965)
*Birds over Sea*, 1957
Oil on canvas, 56 x 42 inches
Collection of Luther W. Brady

Jean-Michel Basquiat (1960–1988)
*Untitled*, 1981
Acrylic, oil paint stick and spray paint on
wood, 73 ¼ x 49 ¼ inches
Collection of Aimee and Robert Lehrman,
Washington, D.C.

Romare Bearden (1911–1988)
*Morning*, 1975
Collage on paper, 13 ½ x 17 ½ inches
Collection of David and Thelma Driskell

Cecilia Beaux (1855–1942)
*The Silver Box*, 1911
Oil on canvas, 32 x 22 inches
Collection of Jonathan L. Cohen

George Bellows (1882–1925)
*The Fisherman*, 1917
Oil on canvas, 30 x 44 inches
Private Collection

Thomas Hart Benton (1889–1975)
*Judgment of Paris,* or *The Golden Apple
of Discord*, 1949
Oil on canvas, 33 ½ x 43 ¼ inches
Anonymous Loan

Albert Bierstadt (1830–1902)
*Wind River Wyoming*, ca. 1870
Oil on canvas, 54 x 85 inches
Courtesy of The Anschutz Collection

Albert Bierstadt (1830–1902)
*The Shore of the Turquoise Sea*, 1878
Oil on canvas, 42 ½ x 64 ½ inches
Manoogian Collection

Charles Burchfield (1893–1967)
*Dandelion Seed Heads and the Moon*, ca. 1965
Watercolor on paper, 56 x 39 ⅝ inches
Collection of Karen A. and Kevin W.
Kennedy

Paul Cadmus (1904–1999)
*Hinky Dinky Parley Voo*, 1939
Oil and tempera on linen on panel,
36 x 36 inches
Collection of Linda Lichtenberg Kaplan

William Merritt Chase (1849–1916)
*The Ring Toss*, 1896
Oil on canvas, 40 ⅜ x 35 ⅛ inches
Collection of Marie and Hugh Halff

Chuck Close (b. 1940)
*Leslie/Watercolor II*, 1986
Watercolor on paper, 30 ½ x 22 ¼ inches
Collection of James and Barbara Palmer

Thomas Cole (1801–1848)
*The Falls of Kaaterskill*, 1826
Oil on canvas, 43 x 36 inches
Private Collection, Tuscaloosa, Alabama

Thomas Cole (1801–1848)
*Schroon Lake*, ca. 1835–38
Oil on canvas, 34 ⅛ x 46 ⅛ inches
Manoogian Collection

Robert Colescott (b. 1925)
*April in Paris*, 1998
Oil on canvas, 84 x 72 inches
Private Collection, New York

Jasper Francis Cropsey (1823–1900)
*On the Connecticut River: The Oxbow with
Sugarloaf Mountain in the Distance*, 1877
Oil on canvas, 16 x 30 inches
Private Collection, Washington, D.C.

Stuart Davis (1892–1964)
*Egg Beater*, 1923
Oil on canvas, 37 x 21 ¾ inches
A Virginia Collector

Stuart Davis (1892–1964)
*Eye Level*, 1951–54
Oil on canvas, 17 x 12 inches
William H. Lane Collection, courtesy of the
Museum of Fine Arts, Boston

Willem de Kooning (1904–1997)
*Woman*, 1966
Oil on canvas, 23 ¾ x 18 inches
Anonymous Loan

Charles Demuth (1883–1935)
*Jass*, 1921
Oil on canvas, 20 x 16 inches
Private Collection

Richard Diebenkorn (1922–1993)
*Untitled (Ocean Park Series)*, 1971
Oil on panel, 29 ¼ x 21 inches
Collection of Gisela and Dennis Alter

Arthur Dove (1880–1946)
*Hardware Store*, 1938
Oil and silver leaf on canvas, 25 x 35 inches
Collection of Robert J. Hurst

Carroll Dunham (b. 1949)
*Edge of His World (Four)*, 2002–03
Oil on canvas, 79 x 82 inches
Private Collection, New York

Herbert Ferber (1906–1991)
*Rutgers II*, 1962
Oil and Magna on canvas, 67 x 50 ½ inches
Collection of Luther W. Brady

Eric Fischl (b. 1948)
*Haircut*, 1985
Oil on linen, 104 x 84 inches
The Broad Art Foundation, Santa Monica,
California

Audrey Flack (b. 1931)
*World War II* (*Vanitas*), 1976–77
Oil over acrylic on canvas, 96 x 96 inches
Anonymous Loan

Helen Frankenthaler (b. 1928)
*Happiest New 1960*, ca. 1959
Mixed media on paper, 48 x 91 inches
Anonymous Loan

Ellen Gallagher (b. 1965)
*Mobb Deep*, 1998
Acrylic and oil on canvas, 120 x 96 inches
Private Collection, New York

Daniel Garber (1880–1958)
*Frog Hollow*, 1918
Oil on canvas, 30 ½ x 30 ¼ inches
Collection of Marguerite and Gerry Lenfest

Sanford Robinson Gifford (1823–1880)
*Mount Mansfield*, 1858
Oil on canvas, 30 ½ x 60 ½ inches
Manoogian Collection

William Glackens (1870–1938)
*Little May Day Procession*, ca. 1905
Oil on canvas, 25 x 30 inches
Manoogian Collection

Sidney Goodman (b. 1936)
*On and On*, 1962
Oil on canvas, 41 ½ x 50 ½ inches
Anonymous Loan

Arshile Gorky (1904–1948)
*Central Park at Dusk*, 1936–42
Oil on canvas, 24 ½ x 30 ½ inches
Private Collection, Minneapolis, Minnesota

Philip Guston (1913–1980)
*Studio Celebration*, 1978
Oil on canvas, 52 x 60 inches
Collection of Mrs. Robert S. Lee

John Haberle (1853–1933)
*The Changes of Time*, 1888
Oil on canvas, 24 ⅜ x 20 ¼ inches
Manoogian Collection

William Michael Harnett (1848–1892)
*Still Life with Tankard*, 1883
Oil on canvas, 5 x 7 inches
Private Collection

Marsden Hartley (1877–1943)
*Young Seadog with Friend Billy*, 1942
Oil on canvas, 40 x 30 inches
Private Collection, Minneapolis, Minnesota

Childe Hassam (1859–1935)
*Country Fair, New England*, 1890
Oil on canvas, 24 ¼ x 20 ⅛ inches
Private Collection

Childe Hassam (1859–1935)
*Poppies*, ca. 1890–94
Oil on canvas, 18 x 25 ¼ inches
Private Collection, Washington, D.C.

Martin Johnson Heade (1819–1904)
*Heliodore's Woodstar with Pink Orchid*,
1890–95
Oil on canvas, 15 x 20 inches
Anonymous Loan

Hans Hofmann (1880–1966)
*The Red Serpent*, 1949
Oil on canvas, 52 x 70 inches
Collection of Luther W. Brady

Winslow Homer (1836–1910)
*How Many Eggs?*, 1873
Watercolor and gouache on paper,
13 ⅛ x 19 ⅝ inches
Collection of Karen A. and Kevin W. Kennedy

Winslow Homer (1836–1910)
*Gloucester Sunset*, 1880
Watercolor on paper, 9 ½ x 13 ½ inches
Collection of Mrs. George M. Kaufman

Winslow Homer (1836–1910)
*Cape Trinity, Saguenay River Moonlight*, 1904
Oil on canvas, 28 ½ x 48 ½ inches
Private Collection, Minneapolis, Minnesota

George Inness (1825–1894)
*Delaware Water Gap*, ca. 1857
Oil on canvas, 32 x 52 inches
Private Collection, Washington, D.C.

George Inness (1825–1894)
*Approaching Storm*, 1869
Oil on canvas, 30 ¼ x 45 ¼ inches
Collection of Jan and Frederick Mayer

Jasper Johns (b. 1930)
*Flag*, 1965
Encaustic and newspaper collage with photo
collage, 8 x 11 ½ inches
Collection of Marsha and Jeffrey Perelman

Eastman Johnson (1824–1906)
*The Cranberry Pickers*, 1875
Oil on paperboard, 22 ½ x 26 ¾ inches
Private Collection

Ellsworth Kelly (b. 1923)
*Dark Blue Curve II*, 1982
Oil on canvas, 92 ⅝ x 105 inches
Collection of Mari and Peter Shaw

John Frederick Kensett (1816–1872)
*Coastal Scene at Newport*, 1864
Oil on canvas, 20 ½ x 32 inches
Private Collection, Washington, D.C.

Franz Kline (1910–1962)
*Untitled*, 1959
Oil on paper, 10 ¾ x 15 ⅝ inches
Anonymous Loan

John La Farge (1835–1910)
*The Last Waterlilies*, 1862
Oil on canvas, 9 ¼ x 7 ½ inches
Private Collection, courtesy of Thomas
Colville Fine Art

Fitz Hugh Lane (1804–1865)
*Boston Harbor at Sunset*, 1853
Oil on canvas, 24 x 39 inches
Anonymous Loan

Jacob Lawrence (1917–2000)
*Christmas in Harlem*, 1937
Tempera on paper, 25 x 27 ½ inches
Collection of Rachel Skolnick and Joshua
Skolnick

Roy Lichtenstein (1923–1997)
*Cape Cod Still Life II*, 1973
Oil and Magna on canvas, 60 x 74 inches
Private Collection

George Luks (1866–1933)
*Thompson and Bleecker Streets*, ca. 1905
Oil on canvas, 20 x 30 inches
Collection of James and Barbara Palmer

Brice Marden (b. 1938)
*Bear*, 1996–97
Oil on linen, 84 x 60 inches
Anonymous Loan

John Marin (1870–1953)
*Deer Isle, Islets, Maine*, 1922
Watercolor and charcoal on paper,
17 ⅛ x 20 ¼ inches
Private Collection, courtesy of Meredith
Ward Fine Art, New York

John Marin (1870–1953)
*Movement in Grays and Yellows*, 1946
Oil on canvas, 22 x 28 inches
Private Collection, courtesy of Meredith
Ward Fine Art, New York

Reginald Marsh (1898–1954)
*Gayety Burlesque*, 1932
Oil on canvas, 24 x 30 inches
Private Collection

Thomas Moran (1837–1926)
*Stranded Ship on East Hampton Beach*,
1894–95
Oil on canvas, 30 x 60 inches
The Hevrdejs Collection

Robert Motherwell (1915–1991)
*In Ochre with Gestural Black*, 1956
Oil and commercial paint on canvas,
74 x 89 inches
Anonymous Loan

Elizabeth Murray (b. 1940)
*Flesh Table*, 1986
Oil on four canvases, 102 x 86 inches
Private Collection

Alice Neel (1900–1984)
*Dennis Florio*, 1978
Oil on canvas, 48 x 38 inches
Private Collection, Washington, D.C.

Kenneth Noland (b. 1924)
*Grave Light*, 1965
Acrylic on canvas, 102 x 210 inches
The Gund Art Foundation

Georgia O'Keeffe (1887–1986)
*Black Spot No. 2*, 1919
Oil on canvas, 24 x 16 inches
Collection of Robert J. Hurst

Georgia O'Keeffe (1887–1986)
*Birch and Pine Trees–Pink*, 1925
Oil on canvas, 36 x 22 inches
Private Collection, courtesy of Thomas
Colville Fine Art

Jules Olitski (b. 1922)
*Zore*, 1966
Acrylic on canvas, 96 x 14 inches
Private Collection, New York

Horace Pippin (1888–1946)
*John Brown Reading His Bible*, 1942
Oil on canvas board, 16 x 20 inches
Private Collection, Minneapolis, Minnesota

Jackson Pollock (1912–1956)
*Number 23, 1949*, 1949
Oil and enamel on canvas mounted on
fiberboard, 26 ½ x 12 ⅛ inches
Collection of Eugene V. Thaw

Jackson Pollock (1912–1956)
*Search*, 1955
Oil and enamel on canvas, 57 ½ x 90 inches
Collection of Samuel and Ronnie Heyman,
New York

Jon Pylypchuk (b. 1972)
*Untitled*, 2004
Mixed media, 97 x 57 inches
Private Collection, New York

Robert Rauschenberg (b. 1925)
*Drawing III for 700th Birthday of Dante* (A)
and (B), 1965
Solvent transfer, collage, graphite and acrylic
on paper,
(A) 14 ¼ x 30 ¼ inches
(B) 13 ½ x 30 inches
Anonymous Loan

Frederic Remington (1861–1909)
*Return of a Blackfoot War Party*, 1887
Oil on canvas, 28 ½ x 50 inches
Courtesy of The Anschutz Collection

William Trost Richards (1833–1905)
*Autumn in the Adirondacks*, ca. 1857–58
Oil on canvas, 24 ⅛ x 36 ½ inches
Private Collection

William Trost Richards (1833–1905)
*Forest Interior in Autumn*, ca. 1861–65
Oil on canvas, 29 x 24 inches
Collection of Mr. and Mrs. Allan E. Bulley, Jr.

Matthew Ritchie (b. 1964)
*Big Top*, 2000
Oil and marker on canvas, 84 x 96 inches
Private Collection, New York

Theodore Robinson (1852–1896)
*Low Tide, Riverside Yacht Club*, 1894
Oil on canvas, 18 x 24 inches
The Margaret and Raymond Horowitz
Collection

Tim Rollins (b. 1955) + K.O.S.
(Kids of Survival)
*The Interior of a Heart*, 1987–88
Mixed media, 90 x 102 inches
Collection of Jane and Leonard Korman

Mark Rothko (1903–1970)
*No. 6*, 1947
Oil on canvas, 60 ¼ x 47 inches
Estate of Herbert Ferber

Ed Ruscha (b. 1937)
*Cut*, 1968
Oil on canvas, 36 x 40 inches
Collection of Marsha and Jeffrey Perelman

Robert Ryman (b. 1930)
*Catalyst II*, 1985
Impervo enamel and graphite on aluminum,
48 x 48 inches
Collection of Eileen Rosenau

David Salle (b. 1952)
*Wild Locust Ride*, 1985
Acrylic and oil on canvas with fabric,
75 x 104 ½ inches
Collection of Harriet and Larry Weiss

John Singer Sargent (1856–1925)
*Capri*, 1878
Oil on canvas, 20 x 25 inches
Private Collection, Tuscaloosa, Alabama

John Singer Sargent (1856–1925)
*San Vagilio: A Boat with Golden Sail*, 1913
Oil on canvas, 22 x 28 inches
Private Collection

Sean Scully (b. 1945)
*Morning*, 1986
Oil on linen, 96 x 96 inches
Collection of Luther W. Brady

Charles Sheeler (1883–1965)
*Industrial Forms*, 1947
Tempera on illustration board,
22 x 20 inches
William H. Lane Collection, courtesy of
the Museum of Fine Arts, Boston

Charles Sheeler (1883–1965)
*Lunenburg*, 1954
Oil on canvas, 25 x 34 inches
William H. Lane Collection, courtesy of
the Museum of Fine Arts, Boston

John Sloan (1871–1951)
*Gray and Brass*, 1907
Oil on canvas, 21 ½ x 26 ½ inches
Collection of Karen A. and Kevin W. Kennedy

Frank Stella (b. 1936)
*Saskatoon II*, 1968
Acrylic on canvas, 96 x 192 inches
The Gund Art Foundation

Joseph Stella (1877–1946)
*The Heron*, 1925
Oil on canvas, 48 x 29 inches
Private Collection, Washington, D.C.

Thomas Sully (1783–1872)
*Mrs. Nicholas Biddle ( Jane) (1793–1856)*,
1826–27
Oil on canvas, 25 x 30 inches
The Andalusia Foundation

Thomas Sully (1783–1872)
*Nicholas Biddle (1786–1844)*, 1836
Oil on canvas, 25 x 30 inches
The Andalusia Foundation

Wayne Thiebaud (b. 1920)
*Meringues*, 1988
Oil on canvas, 30 x 30 inches
Private Collection, Washington, D.C.

John Vanderlyn (1775–1852)
*Sleeping Ariadne–Torso Study*, ca. 1809–14
Oil on canvas, 15 ½ x 21 ¼ inches
Anonymous Loan

Andy Warhol (1928–1987)
*Sixteen Jackies*, 1964
Silkscreen on canvas, 80 x 64 inches
Anonymous Loan

Max Weber (1881–1961)
*New York*, 1913
Oil on canvas, 40 x 31 ⅝ inches
Collection of Marguerite and Gerry Lenfest

James Abbott McNeill Whistler (1834–1903)
*Study of Head of Miss Cecily Alexander*,
1872–73
Oil on canvas, 18 ¾ x 14 ½ inches
Private Collection, Tuscaloosa, Alabama

Andrew Wyeth (b. 1917)
*The Drifter*, 1964
Drybrush and watercolor on paper,
22 ½ x 28 ½ inches
Collection of Mr. and Mrs. Andrew Wyeth

Andrew Wyeth (b. 1917)
*Outpost*, 1968
Tempera on panel, 23 ¼ x 23 ¼ inches
Collection of Mr. and Mrs. Andrew Wyeth

# Index of Illustrated Works of Art

   INDEX OF ILLUSTRATED WORKS OF ART

# Photo Credits and Copyright Information